Manchester Art Gallery

Exhibition of the royal house of Tudor

Manchester Art Gallery

Exhibition of the royal house of Tudor

ISBN/EAN: 9783742843289

Manufactured in Europe, USA, Canada, Australia, Japa

Cover: Foto ©Andreas Hilbeck / pixelio.de

Manufactured and distributed by brebook publishing software (www.brebook.com)

Manchester Art Gallery

Exhibition of the royal house of Tudor

Exhibition

OF THE

ROYAL HOUSE OF TUDOR.

CORPORATION OF MANCHESTER
ART GALLERY.

1897.

Patron:
HER MAJESTY THE QUEEN.

The General Committee.

President:

THE RIGHT HON. JOHN FOULKES ROBERTS, LORD MAYOR OF MANCHESTER.

Vice-Presidents:

A. E. LLOYD, Esq., DEPUTY LORD MAYOR.
J. ERNEST PHYTHIAN, Esq., CHAIRMAN, ART GALLERY COMMITTEE.
C. J. POOLEY, Esq., DEPUTY-CHAIRMAN, ART GALLERY COMMITTEE.

Sir WILLIAM AGNEW, Bart.
The EARL OF ANCASTER.
The LORD BALCARRES, M.P.
Right Hon. ARTHUR J. BALFOUR, M.P., First Lord of the Treasury.
Sir HENRY BEDINGFELD, Bart.
CHARLES H. BRADDON, Esq., Councillor.
N. BRADLEY, Esq., Councillor.
The LORD BRAYE.
J. COMYNS CARR, Esq., Director of the New Gallery, London.
WILLIAM E. CARY, Esq., Councillor.
FREDERICK CAWLEY, Esq., M.P.
C. PURDON CLARKE, Esq., C.I.E., F.S.A., Director Art Division, South Kensington.
The EARL OF CRAWFORD, K.T., F.R.S., LL.D., F.S.A.
G. MILNER-GIBSON-CULLUM, Esq., F.S.A.
LIONEL CUST, Esq., F.S.A., Director, Keeper, and Secretary of the National Portrait Gallery.
Sir HUMPHREY DE TRAFFORD, Bart.
The DUKE OF DEVONSHIRE, K.G.
The VISCOUNT DILLON, F.S.A.
Major-General Sir J. F. DONNELLY, K.C.B., Secretary Science and Art Department.
The LORD EGERTON OF TATTON.
The EARL OF ELLESMERE.
The Right Hon. Sir JAMES FERGUSSON, Bart., K.C.M.G., G.C.S.I., M.P.
Sir A. WOLLASTON FRANKS, K.C.B., Litt.D., President Society of Antiquaries.

W. J. GALLOWAY, Esq., M.P.
T. WALTON GILLIBRAND, Esq.
H. J. GOLDSCHMIDT, Esq., Councillor.
EVERARD GREEN, Esq., F.S.A., Rouge Dragon, Poursuivant of Arms.
*J. HENRY GREENHOW, Esq., Councillor.
H. P. GREG, Esq.
*HERBERT A. GRUEBER, Esq., F.S.A., Assistant Keeper of Coins, British Museum.
*CHARLES E. HALLÉ, Esq., Director of the New Gallery, London.
ERNEST F. G. HATCH, Esq., M.P.
The MARQUESS OF HERTFORD.
The HIGH SHERIFF OF LANCASHIRE.
RICHARD R. HOLMES, Esq., F.S.A., Her Majesty's Librarian, Windsor Castle.
W. H. ST. JOHN HOPE, Esq., Assistant Secretary, Society of Antiquaries.
JOHN HOPKINSON, Esq., Alderman.
Sir WILLIAM HOULDSWORTH, Bart., M.P.
The LORD HOWARD OF GLOSSOP.
Sir HENRY H. HOWORTH, K.C.I.E., M.P.
JAMES HOY, Esq., Alderman.
JOHN HUTT, Esq., Councillor.
The LORD JAMES OF HEREFORD, Chancellor of the Duchy of Lancaster.
The Right Hon. Sir UGHTRED KAY-SHUTTLEWORTH, Bart.
LEES KNOWLES, Esq., M.P.
The EARL OF LATHOM, G.C.B., Lord Chamberlain of H.M. Household.

ERNEST LAW, Esq.
WILLIAM A. LINDSAY, Esq., F.S.A., Windsor Herald.
*LEONARD C. LINDSAY, Esq., F.S.A., Secretary New Gallery, London.
The LORD DE L'ISLE and DUDLEY.
The MARQUESS OF LORNE, K.T., G.C.M.G., M.P.
J. W. MACLURE, Esq., M.P.
JOHN MARK, Esq., Alderman.
The Right Rev. the BISHOP OF MANCHESTER.
H. C. MAXWELL-LYTE, Esq., C.B., F.S.A., Deputy Keeper of the Public Records.
J. D. MILNE, Esq.
FLETCHER MOSS, Esq., Councillor.
The LORD NEWTON.
The DUKE OF NORFOLK, K.G., Earl Marshal, H.M. Postmaster-General.
*F. M. O'DONOGHUE, Esq., F.S.A., Assistant Keeper of Prints and Drawings, British Museum.
The EARL OF PEMBROKE, Lord Steward of H.M. Household.
*J. E. PHYTHIAN, Esq., Councillor, Chairman Art Gallery Committee.
The Hon. Sir SPENCER PONSONBY-FANE, K.C.B.
*C. J. POOLEY, Esq., Deputy-Chairman Art Gallery Committee.
CHARLES H. READ, Esq., Keeper of British and Mediæval Antiquities, British Museum, Secretary of the Society of Antiquaries.

The DUKE OF RICHMOND AND GORDON, K.G.
Sir J. C. ROBINSON, Knt., H.M. Surveyor of Pictures.
The Right Rev. the BISHOP OF SALFORD.
*E. SALOMONS, Esq., F.R.I.B.A.
C. E. SCHWANN, Esq., M.P.
The EARL OF SEFTON, K.G., Lord Lieutenant of the County of Lancashire.
J. BEGG SHAW, Esq.
The EARL SPENCER, K.G.
ISIDORE SPIELMANN, Esq., F.S.A.
W. BARCLAY SQUIRE, Esq., F.S.A.
GEORGE T. STANLEY, Esq., Alderman.
*J. ARTHUR STRONG, Librarian of the House of Lords.
J. EDWARD TAYLOR, Esq.
His Eminence CARDINAL VAUGHAN, Archbishop of Westminster.
Sir PETER CARLAW WALKER, Bart.
The LORD WANTAGE, V.C.
Professor A. W. WARD, Litt.D., LL.D., Principal of Owens College.
T. HUMPHRY WARD, Esq.
The EARL OF WHARNCLIFFE.
*S. J. WHAWELL, Esq.
THOMAS WORTHINGTON, Esq., F.R.I.B.A.
The DUKE OF WESTMINSTER, K.G.
Professor A. S. WILKINS, Litt.D., LL.D.
His Grace the ARCHBISHOP OF YORK.

Managers:

CHARLES E. HALLÉ. | LEONARD C. LINDSAY.

* The names with an asterisk form the Executive Committee

Art Gallery Committee:

COUNCILLOR J. ERNEST PHYTHIAN, *Chairman.*

MR. CHARLES J. POOLEY, *Deputy-Chairman.*

THE RIGHT HONOURABLE JOHN FOULKES ROBERTS, LORD MAYOR.

ALDERMAN HOPKINSON.	COUNCILLOR HUTT.
,, HOY.	,, MOSS.
,, MARK.	MR. T. W. GILLIBRAND.
,, STANLEY.	,, H. P. GREG.
COUNCILLOR BRADDON.	,, J. D. MILNE.
,, N. BRADLEY.	,, E. SALOMONS.
,, CARY.	,, J. B. SHAW.
,, GOLDSCHMIDT.	,, T. WORTHINGTON.
,, GREENHOW.	

COUNCILLOR J. H. GREENHOW, *Chairman of the House Sub-Committee.*

Curator:
WILLIAM STANFIELD.

PREFATORY NOTE.

THE Lord Mayor and Corporation of the City of Manchester desire to recognise the generosity with which their appeal for loans for the present Exhibition has been met.

This ready response has made it possible to give the people of Manchester and the surrounding district the opportunity of seeing Works and Objects of the greatest interest, such as are not usually available except to those who are able to visit the Winter Exhibitions of the London Galleries.

In thus expressing their gratitude, the Lord Mayor and Corporation beg to assure those who have so kindly lent their treasures that no efforts will be spared to make the Exhibition as widely useful as possible.

The Committee of the Tudor Exhibition have to thank Mr. H. A. Grueber for the biographical notes, and the descriptions of the pictures and personal relics; and Mr. H. Jenner, Mr. Strong, and Mr. Churchill for the portions of the catalogue relating to books, manuscripts, coins, and medals. They have also to thank Mr. F. M. O'Donoghue for his notes on the pictures, and the assistance he has given in preparing the catalogue for press; and Mr. Whawell for the valuable collection of arms and armour he has obtained, described, and arranged for the Exhibition.

The very warmest recognition is due to Mr. Leonard C. Lindsay for the research and untiring energy he has displayed in securing and bringing to Manchester the present invaluable collection of portraits and other objects of interest connected with the House of Tudor. To him and to Mr. C. E. Hallé the thanks of the Lord Mayor and Corporation of Manchester are specially tendered for the organisation and general supervision of this Exhibition, which, it is hoped, is only the first of a series illustrating the history of England to be held in the City Art Gallery.

*The EXHIBITION will be open from 10 to 6, 1s.;
6 to 9, 6d.; and will close AUGUST 2nd, 1897.*

CHRONOLOGY OF THE TUDOR PERIOD.
1485-1603.

HENRY VII. (1485-1509).

1485. Battle of Bosworth Field, and Henry, Earl of Richmond, proclaimed King.
1486. Henry marries Elizabeth of York, January 18, and unites the claims of York and Lancaster.
1487. Lambert Simnel personates Edward, Earl of Warwick, and pretends to the throne.
1492. Perkin Warbeck appears in Ireland as Richard, Duke of York, younger son of Edward IV.
1497. Perkin makes a descent upon Cornwall, but is captured.
1499. Perkin and the Earl of Warwick executed.
1501. Marriage of Prince Arthur and Katherine of Aragon.
1502. Death of Prince Arthur.
1509. Death of Henry VII., and Margaret, Countess of Richmond.

HENRY VIII. (1509-1547).

1509. Henry succeeds to the throne, and marries Katherine of Aragon.
1513. Capture of Terouenne and Tournay; the Scots defeated at Flodden Field, and James IV. slain.
1515. Wolsey made Cardinal and Chancellor.
1516. Birth of Queen Mary.
1520. Interview between Henry and Francis I. of France at the Field of Cloth of Gold.
1521. The King receives the title of "Defender of the Faith" from Pope Leo X.
1523. Wolsey aspires to the Papal See.
1529. Trial of Henry's suit for a divorce from Katherine of Aragon.
1530. Death of Cardinal Wolsey.
1533. Henry marries Anne Boleyn. Cranmer pronounces the King's divorce from Katherine of Aragon. Birth of Queen Elizabeth.
1534. The Papal power abrogated in England.
1535. Execution of Cardinal Fisher and Sir Thomas More.
1536. Death of Katherine of Aragon. Execution of Anne Boleyn. Henry marries Jane Seymour. Dissolution of the smaller monasteries.
1537. The Pilgrimage of Grace. Birth of Edward VI. Death of Jane Seymour.
1538. The English Bible set up in every church.
1539. All the monasteries dissolved. Law of the Six Articles passed.
1540. Henry marries Anne of Cleves. Attainder and execution of Cromwell, Earl of Essex. Divorce of Anne of Cleves. Henry marries Catherine Howard.
1541. Execution of Margaret, Countess of Salisbury, last of the Plantagenets.
1542. Catherine Howard executed. Death of James V. of Scotland, and accession of Mary Queen of Scots.
1543. The King marries Katherine Parr. Death of Holbein.
1544. Henry besieges and captures Boulogne.
1547. Execution of Henry, Earl of Surrey. Death of the King, January 28.

EDWARD VI. (1547-1553).

1547. King crowned, February 20. Earl of Hertford (afterwards Duke of Somerset) "Protector." Defeat of the Scots at Pinkie.

1548. Lord Seymour intrigues against the "Protector." Proclamation for removal of images, &c.
1549. The Liturgy reformed. Lord Seymour beheaded. The "Protector" deposed.
1550. The Earl of Warwick (after, Duke of Northumberland) supreme in the Council.
1551. Warwick intrigues to alter the succession.
1552. Somerset beheaded.
1553. Death of Edward VI., July 6.

MARY (1553-1558).

1553. Lady Jane Grey proclaimed Queen. Queen Mary's title acknowledged. Northumberland executed. The Roman Catholic religion restored.
1554. Wyat's rebellion. Execution of Lady Jane Grey. Marriage of Mary with Philip of Spain. Cardinal Pole returns.
1556. Cranmer burnt. Cardinal Pole Archbishop of Canterbury.
1557. Battle of St. Quentin.
1558. Calais lost. Death of Mary and Cardinal Pole.

ELIZABETH (1558-1603).

1559. Coronation of Elizabeth. Restoration of the Protestant worship. Service-book of Edward VI. confirmed.
1560. The Geneva Bible published.
1561. Mary Queen of Scots returns to Scotland.
1562. Assistance to Protestants in France.
1565. Marriage of Mary Queen of Scots with Darnley.
1567. Murder of Darnley.
1568. Mary Queen of Scots escapes to England, and is detained a prisoner.
1569. Rising of the Catholics in the North under the Earls of Northumberland and Westmoreland.
1570. Pope Pius V. denounces Elizabeth as a heretic.
1572. The 4th Duke of Norfolk beheaded. Massacre of St. Bartholomew.
1577. Assistance given to the Netherlands.
1579. Negotiations for the marriage of the Queen and Francis, Duke of Anjou.
1584. The Virginian settlement in America founded.
1585. Elizabeth accepts the protection of the Netherlands. Drake's circumnavigation of the Globe. The Earl of Leicester sent to Holland.
1586. Battle of Zutphen, and death of Sir Philip Sidney. Babington's conspiracy. Mary Queen of Scots tried and condemned.
1587. Mary Queen of Scots beheaded February 8. Sir Francis Drake burns Spanish fleet at Cadiz.
1588. Defeat of the Spanish Armada.
1594. Capture of Brest.
1595. Expeditions of Drake and Hawkins to the West Indies.
1596. Expedition to Cadiz.
1598. The Earl of Cumberland's expedition to West Indies.
1599. The Earl of Essex appointed Lord Lieutenant of Ireland to put down Tyrone's rebellion. His disgrace.
1601. Rebellion and execution of Essex.
1602. Capture of Kinsale. Tyrone submits.
1603. Death of Elizabeth, March 24.

Arrangement of the Exhibition.

ROOM I.
PICTURES OF THE REIGN OF HENRY VII.
Armour, Embroideries, Sculpture.

ROOM II.
PICTURES OF THE REIGN OF HENRY VIII
Armour, Books, Furniture.

ROOM III.
PICTURES OF THE REIGN OF EDWARD VI.
Miniatures and Relics.

ROOM IV.
PICTURES OF THE REIGN OF MARY.
Autograph Letters.

ROOM V.
PICTURES OF THE REIGN OF ELIZABETH.
Furniture, Plate, Relics, Coins, and Seals.

ROOM VI.
Drawings, Engravings, Needlework, &c.
Books.

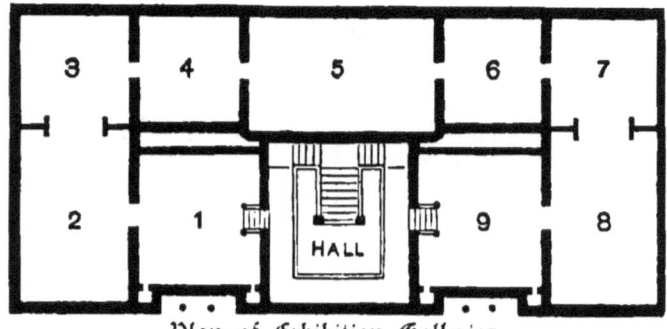

Plan of Exhibition Galleries.

CATALOGUE.

The Numbers commence in Room I., and continue from left to right.

⁂ Throughout the Catalogue, in describing the pictures and medals, the RIGHT and the LEFT mean those of the spectator facing the portrait. "His" or "her" apply strictly to the persons represented.

The works are catalogued under the names given to them by the Contributors.

The Committee can accept no responsibility as to their authenticity.

ROOM I.

Pictures, Sculpture, Arms, Armour, and Embroideries.

REIGN OF HENRY VII. (1485-1509.)

Henry VII., son of Edmund Tudor, Earl of Richmond (son of Owen Tudor and Katherine of France), and Margaret, dau. of John Beaufort, Duke of Somerset, and great grand-daughter of John of Gaunt, fourth son of Edward III., born at Pembroke Castle, July 26, 1455; proclaimed King by Sir William Stanley on the Field of Bosworth immediately after the Battle, August 22, 1485; crowned October 30, ensuing; died at Richmond, April 21, 1509, and was buried in his own chapel at Westminster. He married, January 18, 1486, Princess Elizabeth Plantagenet, eldest daughter and heiress of Edward IV., who died February 11, 1503.

Exhibition of the Royal House of Tudor.

1. MARGARET BEAUFORT, COUNTESS OF RICHMOND AND DERBY.

Hands as in prayer, book open on desk before her; on background s. of arms, and motto, "Sovvent me sovvient," and date of death, "3 calen Julii." Panel 29 × 24 in., engraved.

Lent by The EARL OF DERBY.

2. MARGARET BEAUFORT, COUNTESS OF RICHMOND AND DERBY (1441–1509).

Life-size, full length, kneeling to left, under gold cloth of state, bearing Tudor arms; black gown, white diamond-shaped hood with gorget, hands clasped in prayer; before her open book on prie-dieu, covered with cloth of gold; in background, stained glass window, on which the Tudor arms are repeated. Panel 71 × 45 in.

Margaret Beaufort, Countess of Richmond and Derby, known as "The Lady Margaret," the only dau. and heiress of John Beaufort, Duke of Somerset, great grandson of Edward III. and Margaret Beauchamp, was born at Bletsoe, in Bedfordshire, in 1441, and at the age of fourteen was married to Edmund Tudor, Earl of Richmond (son of Owen Tudor and Katherine of France, and half-brother of Henry VI.), by whom she had one son, afterwards Henry VII. On the death of her husband, November 3, 1456, she married Sir Henry Stafford, son of the Duke of Buckingham, by whom she had no issue. She next married Thomas, Lord Stanley, created Earl of Derby in 1485, who died before her in 1504. Margaret died June 21, 1509, just two months after Henry VII., and was buried in his chapel at Westminster. Lady Margaret was an accomplished woman, and translated *The Mirroure of Golde to a Sinfull Soul*, and also the fourth book of the *Imitatio Christi*; but she has perpetuated her name principally by her foundation of St. John's and Christ's Colleges, Cambridge, and of a divinity professorship richly endowed. After she had married her third husband, the Earl of Derby, she engaged herself in religious vows, which is the reason of her being painted in the habit of a nun.

Lent by ST. JOHN'S COLLEGE, CAMBRIDGE.

3. ISABEL NEVILL, DUCHESS OF CLARENCE.

Half-length, full face; diapered greyish dress, square-cut body with jewelled edge, open sleeves, miniver-lined; angular jewelled head-dress, and black fall behind. Panel 22 × 17½ in.

Eldest daughter of Richard, Earl of Warwick, the "King-maker"; married (1470) George Plantagenet, Duke of Clarence.

Lent by The TRUSTEES OF THE LATE LORD DONINGTON.

4. HUGH OLDHAM, BISHOP OF EXETER (d. 1519).

Three-quarter length, life-size, to right; white surplice, black stole, black cap; in right hand, staff; left rests on book, lying on cushion, placed on table: shield of arms surmounted by mitre. Panel 44 × 34 in.

Hugh Oldham, Bishop of Exeter, born at Manchester, was educated at Oxford and Cambridge, appointed chaplain to Margaret Beaufort, Countess of Richmond, and received successively the livings of Swineshead in Lincolnshire, and Cheshunt. In 1494 he became Prebendary of Lincoln,

ROOM I.]   *Portraits.*

in 1499 Prebendary of York, and in 1504 was advanced to the See of Exeter, where he died June 15, 1519. He was not only a man of profound learning but also an encourager of it. He contributed to the foundation of Corpus Christi College, Oxford, and founded the Grammar School at Manchester.

Lent by CORPUS CHRISTI COLLEGE, OXFORD.

5. THE THREE CHILDREN OF HENRY VII., *circ.* 1496.

Three children, in small half-length, at a table. The one in the middle wears black over-coat, doublet, and white shirt embroidered round the neck, a black cap with broad brim, and around his neck a double chain; the child on his right, who is younger, is without hat, and wears a square-cut dress with ermine sleeves, shirt with lace frill, and a chain of large pearls round his neck; the one on his left, who is younger still, wears black dress with ermine sleeves, chemise plaited round the neck and white hood with black falling veil. They all have their arms on the table, which is strewn with apples; the youngest holding one in her left hand. Panel 13 × 18 in.

This picture was purchased by J. C. Dent, Esq., at the Strawberry Hill sale, in 1842. Horace Walpole, who obtained it from Mr. Richard Cosway, thus records it in his description of Strawberry Hill: "Prince Arthur, Prince Henry, and Princess Margaret, children of Henry VII., by Mabuse, from Cosway's Collection." Of this picture there are several repetitions, viz., at Hampton Court, at Wilton House (the Earl of Pembroke, see No. 10), and others belonging to Lord Radnor and Lord Methuen. The example at Hampton Court, the one engraved by Vertue, is described by him in his catalogue made for Queen Caroline in 1743, as "The pictures of Prince Arthur and his two sisters, children of Henry VII., by *Holbein*." In King Charles I.'s catalogue it is mentioned, and though no names are given it is clearly to be identified in the following entry: "Item, a Whitehall piece curiously painted by Mabusius, wherein were two children and one woman child playing with some oranges (*sic*) in their hands by a green table; little half-figures upon a board in a wooden frame." There is no mention in James II.'s catalogue; but in the old catalogue of Henry VIII. is the following entry: "Item, a table with the pictures of the three children of the Kynge of Denmarke with a curtayne of white and yellow sarcanett panel together." This entry Mr. Scharf thinks must refer to the picture in question, and in an interesting paper published in the *Archæologia* (vol. xxxix., p. 245), he identifies the figures with those of the three children of Christian II. of Denmark—John, the eldest, born in 1518, Dorothy, born in 1520, and Christina, afterwards Duchess of Milan, born in 1521 (see No. 10). In June, 1523, Christian II., banished from his kingdom, landed at Dover, accompanied by his Queen, Elizabeth, niece of Katherine of Aragon, and their three children. After a visit of about three weeks they proceeded into Flanders. It was at this time, then, that Mr. Scharf thinks this picture was painted. The grounds for this belief are that the costumes are rather those of the reign of Henry VIII. than of Henry VII., and apparently not earlier than 1525; that the features are quite unlike those which we are accustomed to find in portraits of English royal children of that period, and that the eyes of the children are brown, while Henry VIII.'s are blue. The opinion that these were portraits of children of Henry VII. does not, however, rest solely with Vertue, as on the back of the Hampton Court picture is the following inscription, written roughly in black ink: *Henry huitieme Roy de la Grande Bretagne avec ses deux soeures Marie espouse Louis XII., Roy de France en Suitte Brandon. Marguerita espouse Jaques IIII., Roy d'Escose. Mabuge*"; an inscription certainly dating before 1743. On the frame also of the

Wilton Picture is inscribed:

"K. Henry VII. Three of his children, Arthur, Henry, Margaret. { Häns Holbein / ye Father. } p. 1495." Mr. Scharf accounts for the many repetitions of this picture in the close relationship of the royal families of England and Denmark; but Mrs. Dent *(Annals of Winchcombe and Sudeley)* says, "The fact of there being four replicas in England and not one abroad favours the opinion that the figures are those of the children of Henry VII."

By JAN DE MABUSE. Lent by MRS. DENT of Sudeley.

6. HENRY VII. (1485–1509).

Small half-length, to right; cloth of gold vest, crimson surcoat trimmed with fur, black cap with jewel; rose in right hand. Panel 14½ × 10½ in.

Lent by CHRIST CHURCH, OXFORD.

7. ELIZABETH OF YORK, QUEEN OF HENRY VII. (1465–1509).

Small bust, to left, showing left hand; red velvet dress trimmed with jewels and ermine, black diamond-shaped head-dress trimmed with gold and jewels; pearl necklace, jewel pendant. Panel 15 × 11 in.

Elizabeth Plantagenet, Queen of Henry VII., called the "White Rose of York," the eldest child of Edward IV. and Elizabeth Woodville, born at Westminster Palace, February 11, 1465, was betrothed to Henry VII., then Earl of Richmond, in 1483, but the marriage was not solemnized till January 18, 1486, and her coronation was deferred till November 25, 1488, to the disgust of the adherents of her family. She died in the Tower of London on her birthday, February 11, 1503, and nine days after the birth of her child, Catherine. She bore the character of being gentle and good, and her effigy in Westminster bears testimony to her beauty. Bacon tells us that "the King all his lifetime showed himself no indulgent husband towards her; but that his aversion towards the house of York was so predominant in him, as it found place not only in his wars and councils, but also in his chamber and bed."

Lent by CHRIST CHURCH, OXFORD.

8. HENRY VII. (1485–1509).

Half-length, life-size, to right; black cap, with jewelled *enseigne*, red fur-trimmed gown over dress of cloth of gold, rose in right hand. Panel 21 × 18 in.

Lent by The DUKE OF DEVONSHIRE, K.G.

9. MARRIAGE OF HENRY VII. AND ELIZABETH OF YORK, JANUARY 18, 1486.

View of the interior of a church; on the right, under the arch of a screen, stands Henry VII. in royal robes, crowned, and holding sceptre in right hand; on his right is a figure in ecclesiastical dress holding a cross, supposed to be Cardinal Bourchier, Archbishop of Canterbury, who officiated at both his coronation and marriage; on the left of the picture, also under a screen, stands

Elizabeth of York, wearing a white dress, ornamented with roses, and cap; near her is St. Thomas (?), holding a spear. Through the arches on either side are seen landscapes. Panel 54⅔ × 42⅔ in.

This picture was in the Strawberry Hill Collection, and was bought at the sale, in 1842, by J. C. Dent, Esq. Walpole (*Anecdotes*), in describing the picture, says: "The only work besides that (the portrait of the Three Children of Henry VII., No. 5) I know of this master in England is a celebrated picture in my possession. It was bought for £200 by Henrietta Louisa, Countess of Pomfret, and hung for some years at their seat at Easton Neston in Northamptonshire, whence it was sold after the late Earl's death. The Earl of Oxford once offered £500 for it. It is painted on board, and is four feet six inches and three-quarters wide, by three feet six inches and three-quarters high. It represents the inside of a church, an imaginary one, not at all resembling the abbey where those princes were married. The perspective and the landscape of the country on each side are good. On one hand, on the foreground, stand the King and the Bishop of Mola, who pronounced the nuptial benediction. His Majesty is a trist, lean, ungracious figure, with a downcast look, very expressive of his mean temper, and of the little satisfaction he had in the match. Opposite to the Bishop is the Queen, a buxom well-looking damsel, with golden hair. By her is a figure, above all proportion with the rest, unless intended, as I imagine, for an emblematic personage, and designed from its lofty stature to give an idea of something above human. It is an elderly man, dressed like a monk, except that his habit is green, his feet bare, and a spear in his hand. As the frock of no religious order ever was green, this cannot be meant for a friar. Probably it is St. Thomas, represented, as in the martyrologies, with the instrument of his death. The Queen might have some devotion to that peculiar saint, or might be born or married on his festival. Be that as it may, the picture, though in a hard manner, has its merit, independent of the curiosity."

By JAN DE MABUSE.   Lent by MRS. DENT of Sudeley.

10. THREE CHILDREN OF HENRY VII.

(See No. 5.)
By J. MABUSE.   Lent by The EARL OF PEMBROKE.

11. HENRY VII. (1485-1509).

Bust, to right; plain black cap, furred gown over dress of cloth of gold, red rose in right hand. Panel 14 × 10 in.

Lent by The DUKE OF DEVONSHIRE, K.G.

12. CHARLES BRANDON, DUKE OF SUFFOLK, K.G. (1485-1545).

Small half-length, to left; low-necked doublet, body and sleeves slashed, shewing an under-garment of red, fur-lined surcoat, white shirt with gold inscribed border, black cap with brooch; around his neck black cord; he holds with both hands a dagger. Panel 12½ × 8 in.

Lent by SIR HENRY BEDINGFELD, BART.

13. CHARLES BRANDON, DUKE OF SUFFOLK, K.G. (1485-1545).

Three-quarter length, life-size, seated, full face; crimson doublet, black surcoat lined with fur, black cap; collar of the Garter with George; right hand gloved and holding glove; in left, flowers. Panel 34 × 27 in.

Charles Brandon, Duke of Suffolk, was the son of Sir William Brandon, standard-bearer to Henry VII., who was slain at Bosworth Field by Richard III. Brandon was the chosen companion of Henry VIII., and on his accession was appointed one of his esquires, Chamberlain of the Principality of North Wales, and in 1511 Marshal of the Royal Household. On May 15, 1513, he was elevated to the peerage as Viscount Lisle, and attended the King at the sieges of Terouenne and Tournay, and also at the Battle of the Spurs. For his distinguished services in this campaign he was created Duke of Suffolk, February 1, 1514, and in the following year secretly married Mary, Dowager Queen of France, sister of Henry VIII.; she was his third wife. In 1520 Suffolk accompanied Henry VIII. to the Field of the Cloth of Gold, and in 1523 commanded the army which invaded France. In 1536 he suppressed the rebellion in the North known as *The Pilgrimage of Grace*, was one of the judges at the trial of Catherine Howard, and commanded at the siege of Boulogne, at which the King also was present. Suffolk died August 24, 1545, at Guildford, and was buried at Windsor.

By HANS HOLBEIN.   Lent by The TRUSTEES OF THE LATE LORD DONINGTON.

14. THOMAS HOWARD, 2ND DUKE OF NORFOLK (1444-1524).

Half-length, life-size, profile to right, robes and collar of the Garter; in right hand white staff; left hand raised, index finger extended. Inscribed: THOMAS HOWARD *Dux Norff. Obiit aº. dni.* 1524. Panel 30 × 24 in.

Thomas Howard, Earl of Surrey, 2nd Duke of Norfolk, son of John, 1st Duke, born in 1444, was on the death of his father also attainted and deprived of his Earldom. After suffering an imprisonment of three years in the Tower, he was restored to his title of Earl of Surrey and to a portion of his estates, and elected a K.G. In 1508 he was made Lord Treasurer, in 1509 Earl Marshal, and for his services in commanding the English forces at Flodden Field, in which battle James IV. of Scotland was slain, he was restored to the title held by his father of Duke of Norfolk. He continued to take an active part in the affairs of the country till 1522, when he resigned the office of Lord Treasurer, which the King at once bestowed upon his son Thomas, Earl of Surrey. The Duke died May 21, 1524, at Framlingham, and was buried at Thetford. He was twice married—first, to Elizabeth, dau. and heir of Sir Frederick Tilney, Knt., of Boston, by whom he had, with other issue, Henry, 3rd Duke, and Edmund, father of Catherine, 5th wife of Henry VIII.; and secondly, Agnes, dau. of Hugh Tilney, by whom he had two sons, William, the elder, being the ancestor of the Earls of Effingham, and four daughters.

Lent by The DUKE OF NORFOLK, E.M., K.G.

15. SHIELD GIVEN TO HENRY HOWARD, EARL OF SURREY, by the Duke of Tuscany in 1536, as a prize gained at a tournament at Florence. It represents a Roman battle scene on the outside, and in the inside Mucius Scævola is figured.

Ascribed to STRADANUS.   Lent by The DUKE OF NORFOLK, E.M., K.G.

Room I.]   *Portraits.*   7

16. Henry VII. (1485–1509).

Bust, life-size, to right; black cap, with jewelled *enseigne*; red dress with fur-trimmed surcoat, large collar of jewels on shoulders. Panel 22 × 17 in.

Lent by The Society of Antiquaries.

17. Richard Foxe, Bishop of Winchester (1448 ?–1528).

Life-size, half-length, to right; in white surplice with fur stole, black cap; both hands grasping a staff; shield of arms in each corner, at the base an inscription relating to the foundation of the College. On the original frame was the name of Joannes Corvus (see *Archæologia*, vol. xxxix. p. 39). Panel 30 × 23¼ in.

Richard Foxe, Bishop of Winchester, born about 1448, at Ropesley, Lincolnshire, is said to have been educated at Magdalen Hall, Oxford, and went to Paris, where he became the friend of Dr. Morton, Bishop of Ely, who recommended him to the Earl of Richmond, afterwards Henry VII. On the accession of that monarch he was made a Privy Councillor, and successively Bishop of Exeter in 1487, of Bath and Wells in 1492, of Durham in 1494, and of Winchester in 1501, where he died, October 5, 1528. He was sent on several embassies; was Lord Privy Seal to Henry VII. and Henry VIII.; founded Corpus Christi College, Oxford, in 1516, and the Grammar Schools at Taunton and Grantham in 1522; and embellished Winchester Cathedral.

This picture is a copy of one by Joannes Corvus in the Hall of Corpus Christi College.

Lent by Corpus Christi College, Oxford.

18. Cartoon of Henry VII. and Henry VIII. (1537).

Full-length figure, life-size, standing to right of Henry VIII. in the foreground, and behind him his father, Henry VII., standing on a raised step; architectural background. 103 × 54 in.

This cartoon was made by Holbein for the fresco painting in the Privy Chamber at Whitehall, which perished in the fire in January, 1698. Happily Charles II. had ordered a small copy to be taken of it thirty years before, which is still preserved in Hampton Court, by the Flemish artist, Remigius van Leemput, for which work the artist received the handsome sum of £150.

This copy has been engraved by Vertue. It represents life-size portraits of Henry VII., Henry VIII., Elizabeth of York, and Queen Jane Seymour standing in a highly-ornamented room or corridor. In the centre is a large tablet with an inscription setting forth the royal "nobless" of his ancestors and family, then joined with the Seymours, and perpetuating the era or date when the Reformation of religion was settled in England. On the left of the tablet stands Henry VIII., and a little behind him on a step his father, Henry VII., his left arm resting on the tablet. On the right is Queen Jane Seymour, her hands joined, a dog lying at her feet, and behind her Elizabeth of York leaning against the tablet.

The date on the engraving shows that the picture was painted in 1537. It is, therefore, to Charles II.'s anxiety to possess a smaller picture of this composition that we owe the preservation of one of Holbein's most important and interesting designs. The cartoon before us is done with the brush in Indian ink on white paper. The outline has been pricked for transferring the design on the wall.

The attitude in which Henry is represented is very characteristic, and appears to have been rather a favourite one with him: the arms a-kimbo and the legs apart. He was proud of his proportions, more especially of his legs; and Piero Pasqualigo, the Venetian Ambassador, who visited England in April, 1515, when the King was in his twenty-fourth year, tells the following anecdote in a letter dated May 3, 1515, to Sebastian Giustinian: "His Majesty came into our arbour, and addressing me in French, said, 'Talk with me awhile. The King of France, is he as tall as I am?' I told him there was little difference. He continued, 'Is he as stout?' I said he was not; and he then enquired, 'What sort of legs has he?' I replied, 'Spare.' Whereupon he turned aside the front of his doublet, and slapping his thigh with his hand, said, 'Look here! I have also a good calf to show.'" (See Wornum, *Life and Works of Holbein*.)

By HANS HOLBEIN.   Lent by The DUKE OF DEVONSHIRE, K.G.

19. MARY TUDOR, DOWAGER QUEEN OF FRANCE, afterwards Duchess of Suffolk (1497–1534).

Half-length, life-size, towards right; square-cut grey gown edged with pearls, undersleeves embroidered with the Tudor rose, diamond-shaped jewelled cloth of gold hood with black veil; necklace of pearls and diamonds; jewel on breast with pendent pearl; hands rest on ledge; in right, apple. Panel 22¼ × 18 in.

Mary Tudor, dau. of Henry VII. and Elizabeth of York, born in 1497, was noted for her beauty, gentleness of disposition, and vivacity of manner. At an early age she was affianced to Prince Charles of Castile, but the engagement was broken off in 1513, and in the following year she was married to Louis XII. of France, who was as near as possible three times her age. Louis having survived his marriage but a few months, she privately espoused Charles Brandon, Duke of Suffolk, with whom it is said she fell in love for his bravery at the tourney in honour of her coronation. In April, 1515, they were publicly married at Greenwich in the presence of Henry VIII., who at the first intelligence of the secret union had affected great displeasure. We know little of the subsequent history of Mary, who died January 23, 1534, at the age of 37. She had by her second marriage one son and one daughter, Henry, Earl of Lincoln, and Frances, mother of Lady Jane Grey.

By JOHANNES CORVUS.   Lent by MRS. DENT of Sudeley.

20. THE WHEEL OF FORTUNE.

Tempera painting, touched with gold; on canvas. 27¼ × 18 in.

On the left, Fortune stands on a globe turning her wheel, on the top of which is seated a king. Behind him, clinging to the spokes of the wheel, is a young man wearing a coroneted cap; and in front of him, in the act of falling, is an old man, whose crown has dropped from his head and broken. On the ground, at the feet of Fortune, is a man who has not yet started on his course. Above, in the clouds, is the Deity, and two figures bearing scrolls, on which are German inscriptions. The picture is marked with Holbein's monogram—the double H; and the date, 1533.

By HANS HOLBEIN.   Lent by The DUKE OF DEVONSHIRE, K.G.

Room I.]   *Portraits.*   9

21. Bronze Medallion

Of a man, surrounded with the Garter.   Size, 17 in. circular.

Lent by Sir J. C. Robinson.

22. Frame of Wood Carving.

Taken from the house formerly occupied by John Winchcombe, *alias* "Jack of Newbury," who died in 1520. Portions of the house are still standing.

Lent by Mrs. Dent of Sudeley.

23. Wood Carving.

Group of St. Anne, holding on her lap the Virgin, who is nursing the infant Saviour; above is a crenellated canopy. Formerly in the chapel of Bude Castle, Cornwall. *English.* Late 15th century.

Lent by The Science and Art Department.

24. The Marriage of Henry VIII. with Katherine of Aragon.

Memorial picture of the union of Henry and Katherine, who are surrounded by members of their respective families. Panel 11 × 29 in.

Lent by The Earl of Ancaster.

25. Thomas Stanley, 2nd Earl of Derby, K.G. (d. 1521).

Bust, showing right hand holding white stick; black jewelled cap and red plume; small frill and close white doublet, dark furred cloak, collar K.G. Panel 19 × 14 in.

Eldest son of George, Baron Strange, K.G.; succeeded his grandfather as Earl of Derby, 1504; appointed by Henry VII.'s Commission to hold a Chapter of the Garter, May 7th, 1502; attended Henry VIII. in his expedition to France, 1513; on occasion of the visit of the Emperor Charles V. to Henry VIII., at Dover, Lord Stanley bore the sword of state on the royal progress to Canterbury.

Lent by The Earl of Derby.

26. Thomas Stanley, 1st Earl of Derby, K.G. (d. 1504).

Bust, to right, life-size; black doublet with jewelled buttons, white ruff, black cap; collar of the Garter with George; right hand holding white staff. Panel 19 × 14 in.

Thomas Stanley, 1st Earl of Derby, eldest son of Thomas, 1st Lord Stanley, was first summoned to Parliament among the Barons, May 24, 1461, about which time he married Eleanor, dau. of Richard Neville, Earl of Salisbury. In 1482 he went with the Duke of Gloucester to Scotland, and, having command of the right wing of his army, took Berwick by assault. The next year he was constituted Constable of England for life, and elected a K.G. Having married

B

Exhibition of the Royal House of Tudor.

as his second wife Margaret of Lancaster, widow of Edmund Tudor, Earl of Richmond, and mother of Henry VII., he joined the latter on his landing in England, was present at the battle of Bosworth Field, and placed on his head the crown, presenting him as Henry VII. For these services Stanley was advanced to the dignity of Earl of Derby, October 14, 1485, and appointed one of the Commissioners for executing the office of Lord High Steward on the day of the coronation. He died in 1504, and was succeeded by his grandson, Thomas Stanley.

Lent by The EARL OF DERBY.

27. GEORGE STANLEY, LORD STRANGE, K.G. (d. 1497.)

Bust; cap and collar of K.G., with pendant; close frill, dark doublet, miniver-lined mantle. Panel 19 × 13 in.

The son of the 1st Earl of Derby and Eleanor Nevill, sister to the "King-maker," Earl of Warwick. He was detained by Richard III. as a hostage for the fidelity of his father, 1485. Married Jane, daughter to John, Lord Strange, of Knockyn. Elected Knight of the Garter 1487. Died 5th December, under suspicion of poison, 1497. The figure is very Elizabethan both in costume and character.

Lent by The EARL OF DERBY.

27a. SIDEBOARD of Oak.

Lent by CHETHAM COLLEGE.

27b. ARM CHAIR.

Panel carved with shields of arms, and dated 1603.

Lent by The EARL OF DERBY.

27c. PANEL of Old Oak, richly carved with the arms of Henry VII.
From the Strawberry Hill Collection. *Lent by The EARL OF DERBY.*

ROOM II.

Pictures, Sculpture, Arms, Books, Relics, and Furniture.

REIGN OF HENRY VIII. (1509-1547.)

Henry VIII., son of Henry VII. and Elizabeth of York, born at Greenwich, June 28th, 1491, became Prince of Wales on the death of his brother Arthur, April 20, 1502; succeeded April 21, 1509; crowned June 24, 1509; died at Whitehall, January 28, 1547, and was buried at Windsor. He married first, June 3, 1509, by Papal dispensation, Katherine of Aragon, widow of his brother Arthur, Prince of Wales, divorced May 23, 1533; secondly, November 14, 1532, Anne Boleyn, dau. of Sir Thomas Boleyn, created Earl of Wiltshire and Ormonde, beheaded May 19, 1536; thirdly, May 20, 1536, Jane Seymour, dau. of Sir John Seymour, died October 14, 1537; fourthly, January 6, 1539, Anne, dau. of John, Duke of Cleves, divorced in July of same year; fifthly, August 8, 1540, Catherine, dau. of Lord Edmund Howard, and niece of Thomas, 2nd Duke of Norfolk, beheaded February 13, 1542; sixthly, July 12, 1543, Katherine, dau. of Sir Thomas Parr, of Kendal, and relict of the Hon. Edward Borough, and of John Nevill, Lord Latimer, who survived him.

28. HENRY VIII. (1509-1547).

Small bust, full face; jewelled surcoat, black jewelled hat, collar of rubies, left hand holding staff. Panel 16 × 12 in.

By HANS HOLBEIN.   Lent by The DUKE OF DEVONSHIRE, K.G.

29. CARDINAL WOLSEY (1471-1530).

Small half-length; profile to left, in ecclesiastical vestments and biretta. Panel 15½ × 12¼ in.

Lent by HER MAJESTY THE QUEEN.
(Hampton Court.)

30. THOMAS WRIOTHESLEY, 1ST EARL OF SOUTHAMPTON, LORD CHANCELLOR, K.G. (d. 1550).

Half-length, under life-size, to left; black doublet, fur-lined surcoat, black cap; right hand resting on parapet, gloves in left; inscribed ANO ÆTATIS SVÆ 51 . 1545. Panel 24 × 18 in.

Thomas Wriothesley, 1st Earl of Southampton, Lord Chancellor, son of William Wriothesley, York Herald, was educated at St. John's College or Trinity Hall, Cambridge. In 1537 he was appointed coroner and attorney in the Court of Common Pleas, and in 1538 one of the King's secretaries, and was knighted. Though attached to the principles of the old religion, Wriothesley became a favourite with Henry VIII., and was employed on several missions. In 1540 he was made Constable of Southampton Castle, Chamberlain of the Exchequer, and in 1544 created Baron Wriothesley, of Titchfield, Hants. The same year he succeeded Lord Audley as Lord Chancellor, and shortly afterwards was elected K.G. By the will of Henry VIII., Wriothesley became one of his executors and a member of the Council of Edward VI., three days after whose coronation he was elevated to the Earldom of Southampton. Having placed the Great Seal into commission without the consent of the King he was accused of an illegal act, and in spite of his able defence was deprived of his office, March 6, 1547, and heavily fined. He died July 30, 1550.

By HANS HOLBEIN.   Lent by MAJOR-GENERAL F. E. SOTHEBY.

31. QUEEN KATHERINE OF ARAGON (1485-1536).

Bust, to left; red dress, with white chemisette; black diamond-shaped hood, with gold border; pearl necklace. Size 14 × 10¼ in.

Katherine of Aragon, 1st wife of Henry VIII., and fourth dau. of Ferdinand of Aragon and Isabella of Castile, born at Alcara de Henares in 1485, was married in 1501 to Arthur, Prince of Wales, and in 1509, by Papal dispensation, to his brother, Henry VIII., who divorced her in 1533. She then took up her residence first at Ampthill, in Bedfordshire, and afterwards at Kimbolton Castle, in Huntingdonshire, where she led an austere religious life until her decease, January 7, 1536. She had several children by Henry VIII., but only one daughter survived, who afterwards became Queen Mary.

Lent by The DUKE OF DEVONSHIRE, K.G.

32. QUEEN ANNE BOLEYN (1507-1536).

Small half-length, to left; square cut, low, dark dress; black hood, edged with pearls; pearl necklace, with pendent letter B. Canvas 15 × 12 in.

Anne Boleyn, second Queen of Henry VIII. and mother of Queen Elizabeth, born at Blickling, in Norfolk, about 1507, was sent at an early age by her father, Sir Thomas Boleyn, to France, where she was attached to the suite of Mary, sister of Henry VIII. and Queen of Louis XII. She became in 1527 maid of honour to Queen Katherine, and speedily attracted the King's favour. On November 14, 1532, she was privately married to Henry, though his marriage with Katherine was not annulled till some months later, and on the Whit-Sunday of the following year she was publicly crowned at Westminster Abbey. On September 7, 1533, her daughter Elizabeth was born. Naturally light and gay of heart, and educated at the French Court, where these qualities were likely to be developed, she conducted herself with an easy familiarity towards the courtiers, and in consequence was accused of infidelity with Norris, Brereton, Weston, and Smeton, gentlemen about the Court, and with her own brother, Viscount Rochfort, found guilty, and beheaded on Tower Hill, May 19, 1536. She was beheaded, according to Holinshed, by the hangman of Calais with a sword, but a Spaniard who was present at the execution states that it was a headsman from St. Omer, whom Henry sent for a week before.

Attributed to JANET.   Lent by The LORD ZOUCHE.

Room II.]   *Portraits.*   13

33. Henry VIII., Anne Boleyn, and Others.   "The Dancing Picture."

Six small whole-length figures of Henry VIII., Thomas Howard, Duke of Norfolk, Charles Brandon, Duke of Suffolk, Anne Boleyn, Mary Tudor, Dowager Queen of France, and Margaret, Dowager Queen of Scotland : the three pair dancing in a meadow with Greenwich Palace in the background.   Panel 52 × 42 in.

According to Sir Peter Lely, the male figures in the picture were painted by Holbein, the female by François Clouet, *dit Janet*. It was probably done for Holbein's patron (the Duke of Norfolk), in whose family it descended till sold in 1701, when it was purchased by the ancestor of the present owner.   John Evelyn, in his *Diary*, under date August 23, 1675, mentions having seen it at the Duke's house.   "Upon Sir Robert Reading's importunity, I went to visit the Duke of Norfolk at his new Palace at Weybridge, where he has laid out in building near £10,000. The rooms are wainscoted and some of them richly pargated with cedar, yew, cypress, &c. There are some good pictures, especially that incomparable painting of Holbein, where the Duke of Norfolk, Charles Brandon, and Henry VIII. are dancing with three ladies, with most amorous countenances, and sprightly motion exquisitely expressed.   It is a thousand pities (as I told my Lord of Arundel his son) that that jewel should be given away."   Walpole also refers to the picture as follows :   "There is a very curious picture in the collection of Col. Sothby, said to be begun in France by Janet (François Clouet), and which Vertue thinks might be retouched by Holbein, as it was probably painted for his patron, the Duke of Norfolk, from whom it descended immediately to the Earl of Arundel, out of whose collection the father of the present possessor purchased it.   It represents three royal pair dancing in a meadow, with a magnificent building at a distance; they are Henry VIII. and Anne Boleyn, and his sisters, Margaret, Queen of Scots, and Mary, Queen of France, with their second husbands, Archibald Douglas and Charles Brandon.   The circumstances of these matches so unequal assembled together, induced Vertue, with much probability, to conclude that it was a tacit satire, and painted for the Duke of Norfolk, who, however related to Anne Boleyn, was certainly not partial to her, as protectress of the reformed."   To this Walpole adds the following note : "This was Vertue's opinion. The account in the family calls the man in the middle the Duke of Norfolk, and him on the right hand the Duke of Suffolk.   If the tradition that this picture represents only English personages were not so well grounded, I should take it for a French composition.   The person in the middle is a black swarthy man with a sharp beard, like Francis I., and resembling neither of the Dukes of Norfolk and Suffolk, the former of whom is never drawn with a beard, the latter always with a short square one: add to this that the figure called Henry VIII., and which certainly has much of his countenance, is in the obscure corner of the picture, and exhibits little more than the face."

Lent by Major-General F. E. Sotheby.

34. Queen Jane Seymour (1509-1537).

Small bust, to left ; cloth of gold square-cut dress with black sleeves, and diamond-shaped hood with black veil ; hands joined ; pearl necklace.   Panel 16½ × 14 in.

Jane Seymour, 3rd wife of Henry VIII., and eldest dau. of Sir John Seymour, of Wolfhall, Wiltshire, and of Margaret Wentworth, dau. of Sir John Wentworth, of Nettlestead, in Suffolk, born in 1509, was Maid of Honour to Anne Boleyn, and succeeded her in the favour of the King, as Anne had succeeded Katherine of Aragon.   She was married to Henry, May 20, 1536, the day after the execution of Anne.   She died at Hampton Court, October 24, 1537, twelve days after the birth of Edward VI.

Lent by The Society of Antiquaries.

35. QUEEN KATHERINE PARR (1513-1548).

Small three-quarter length, seated at a table, holding book in right hand; red velvet dress, white and red hood with black veil; double chain with pendent cross round the neck; on table gold chalice. Panel 17½ × 13 in.

Katherine Parr, 6th Queen of Henry VIII., born in 1513, was the dau. of Sir Thomas Parr, of Kendal, Master of the Wards and Comptroller of the King's Household, and Mary, dau. of Sir Thomas Green, of Boughton. At an early age she married, first, Edward Borough, afterwards Lord Borough, who died in 1529; and secondly, John Neville, Lord Latimer, who died at the close of 1542. Soon after his death Katherine became a Protestant, of which creed she remained an earnest friend and defender. On the death of her second husband, she was immediately sought in marriage by Sir Thomas Seymour, brother of the deceased Queen Jane, and had already consented when she received the alarming and unwelcome news that she had been selected for the sixth wife of the King. It was impossible to resist the royal will, and she became Henry's wife, July 12, 1543. On account of her strong attachment to the reformed religion, Gardiner sought to lay snares for her destruction, but by her tact and prudent management she escaped the fate designed for her even when it was resolved to send her to the Tower. She was an accomplished woman, and devoted much of her time to study, composition, and scholarly pursuits, and took great interest in the education of her step-children, even persuading Henry to restore the right of succession to his daughters. After the death of Henry, she married her old lover, Sir Thomas Seymour, then Lord Admiral of England, but her married life was rendered unhappy by his neglect and by his familiarity with the young Princess Elizabeth. She died in child-bed at Sudeley Castle, in Gloucestershire, September 5, 1548, and was buried in the chapel there, where her remains were found in 1782.

Lent by The MARQUESS OF HERTFORD.

36. EDWARD STAFFORD, DUKE OF BUCKINGHAM, K.G. (1478-1521).

Small half-length, to right; green doublet showing white shirt, brown fur-lined surcoat, black cap with gold badge, black ribbon round neck; staff in right hand and glove in left; background inscribed *Stafford, Duke of Buckingham*. Panel 19½ × 13½ in.

Edward Stafford, 3rd Duke of Buckingham, born in 1478, son of Henry, 2nd Duke, who was attainted and beheaded by Richard III. in 1483, and Katherine Woodville, sister to the Queen of Edward IV., was on his father's side descended from Thomas of Woodstock, son of Edward III., and quartered the royal arms. He was restored to the dukedom in 1486, commanded the royal forces during the rebellion of Perkin Warbeck, elected K.G. in 1505, and Lord High Constable of England. Having incurred the enmity of Wolsey, that ambitious prelate planned and quickly succeeded in accomplishing his ruin. He was charged on the evidence of a former steward (Knevet) of aspiring to the Crown, and of plotting against the lives of the King, Wolsey, and others. Buckingham pleaded his own cause, but was found guilty, sentenced to death, and beheaded on Tower Hill, May 17, 1521. When Charles V. heard of the Duke's death, he exclaimed, "The butcher's dog hath pulled down the finest buck in Europe." He was the founder of Magdalene College, Cambridge.

By HANS HOLBEIN. Lent by SIR HENRY BEDINGFELD, BART.

Room II.]   *Portraits.*   15

---

37.   Sir Anthony Denny, Knt. (1501–1549).

Bust, life-size, full face; black doublet, small white frills and black embroidered cape, inscribed *Sir Anth· Denny*.   Panel 15½ × 11½ in.

Sir Anthony Denny, favourite of Henry VIII., second son of Sir Edmund Denny, Chief Baron of the Exchequer, born January 16, 1501, was educated at St. Paul's School, and St. John's College, Cambridge, where he became an excellent scholar. His merits having attracted the notice of Henry VIII., he was summoned to Court, appointed King's Remembrancer and Groom of the Stole, and succeeded in raising a considerable fortune from grants of the dissolved monasteries. He was knighted at Boulogne, September 30, 1544, and appointed by the King one of the executors of his will, and a member of the Council of Edward VI. He was the only one about the King who in his last illness had the courage to inform him of the near approach of death. He died at Christchurch, September 10, 1549. Roger Ascham says that "Denny's whole time and cares were occupied with religion, learning, and affairs of State."

Lent by Sir Henry Bedingfeld, Bart.

38.   Portrait of a Man.

Small half-length, nearly full face, beard; black cap and dress; holds a pink in right hand. Panel 14 × 9 in.

"A picture of great delicacy of feeling and remarkably beautiful colouring; the reddish glow of the tone of the second period of the master being combined with the more transparent painting of the third epoch. The picture may be of the date 1530." (Waagen, vol. ii. p. 93.)

By Hans Holbein.   Lent by The Duke of Devonshire, K.G.

39.   Hugo Price, LL.D., Founder of Jesus College, Oxford (d. 1574).

Bust to right, less than life-size; black dress, black cap.   Panel 18¼ × 13 in.

Hugh Price, born in the county of Brecon, was the first Prebendary of the Church of Rochester, and Treasurer of the Church of St. David's. In 1571 he procured the Charter of Foundation of Jesus College, Oxford, from Queen Elizabeth, and gave large benefactions in money.   Died 1574.

By Hans Holbein.   Lent by Jesus College, Oxford.

40.   John Calvin.

Small bust, to left; black gown and cap.   Panel 5¼ in. circular.

John Calvin, the celebrated reformer; born near Paris, 1509; settled at Geneva, where he established his ecclesiastical discipline; died 1564.

By Hans Holbein.   Lent by The Duke of Devonshire, K.G.

41.   Erasmus (1467–1536).

Half-length, life-size, to left; black fur-lined dress, black cap, hands resting on book; on background on left, view of church and other buildings.   Panel 25½ × 21½ in.

Desiderius Erasmus, born at Rotterdam, October 28, 1467, was educated at Deventer, and at the monastery of Emäus, near Gouda. At a very early age his talents began to display themselves in so brilliant a manner that it was even then predicted that he would one day be the most learned man of his time. From Gouda he went to Paris, and in 1497 he came to England, and was well received by Henry VII. Returning to Paris, he next visited Italy, where the most flattering offers of promotion were made to him, not only by Cardinal Grimani, but also by Pope Julius II. These he declined, and returning to England resided with Sir Thomas More, in whose house he wrote his *Encomium Moriæ*, or *Praise of Folly*. For a short time he filled the office of Professor of Greek at Cambridge, but, disappointed with his very scanty supplies of subsistence, he returned in 1514 to the Low Countries, and thence took up his residence in Basel, where in 1516 he published his celebrated edition of the Greek Testament. He removed in 1529 to Freiburg, but a few years later returned to Basel, where he died July 12, 1536. Though a kind-hearted and generous man, Erasmus had little of the hero or martyr in his composition, and in one of his letters he states: "Even if Luther had spoken everything in the most unobjectionable manner, I had no inclination to die for the truth. Every man has not the courage to make a martyr; and I am afraid, if I were put to the trial, I should imitate St. Peter."

Lent by CHARLES BUTLER, ESQ.

42. MARGARET PLANTAGENET, COUNTESS OF SALISBURY (1471-1541).

Half-length, life-size, towards left; low black dress with ermine on sleeves, white scarf, diamond-shaped ermine hood; in right hand W shaped jewel, in left honeysuckle; on background shield of arms and inscription, *Margareta Comitissa Sarum Georgij Ducis Clarentiæ Filia*. Canvas 26 x 20 in.

Margaret Plantagenet, dau. of George, Duke of Clarence, and Lady Elizabeth Nevill, dau. and heir of Richard, Earl of Warwick and Salisbury, born in 1474, became the last of the Plantagenets upon the execution of her brother Edward, Earl of Warwick, in 1499. She married in 1494 Sir Richard Pole, K.G., and in 1513 had restoration of the honours and estates of her maternal family, being created Countess of Salisbury. She was selected to preside over the household of Princess Mary, at the same time acknowledging with regard the kindness of Henry VIII. to her own children. Her younger son, Reginald Pole, having published a treatise denouncing the King's supremacy, his divorce and second marriage, the Countess and all the members of her family were seized and attainted of treason. The aged Countess was imprisoned in the Tower in 1539, and two years later, May 27, 1541, her grey head fell upon the fatal scaffold. Lord Herbert says: "That when commanded to lay her head on the block, she refused, saying, 'So should traitors do; I am none,' and turning her head every way, she told the executioner if he would have it, he must get it as he could." By Sir Richard Pole she had three sons, Henry, Lord Montagu, executed in 1538, Reginald, the Cardinal, and Geoffrey. By a decree of Pope Leo XIII., December, 1886, she was declared to be a Martyr.

Lent by The TRUSTEES OF THE LATE LORD DONINGTON.

43. JOHN JEWELL, BISHOP OF SALISBURY (1522-1571).

Half-length, to right, in episcopal robes, black cap. Panel 18 x 14½ in.

John Jewell, Bishop of Salisbury, born at Buden, in the parish of Berry Narber, Devonshire, May 24, 1522, was educated at Barnstaple and Merton, and Corpus Christi College, Oxford.

ROOM II.] *Portraits.* 17

In the reign of Edward VI. he made a public profession of the reformed religion, and contracted a friendship with Peter Martyr. In 1551 he obtained the rectory of Sunningwell, Berks, but at the accession of Mary retired to Frankfort, and thence to Strasburg, where he renewed his acquaintance with Martyr. At the accession of Elizabeth he returned home, and in 1559 was made Bishop of Salisbury. Died at Monkton Farley, Wilts, September 21, 1571.

Lent by MERTON COLLEGE, OXFORD.

44. HENRY VIII. (1509-1547).

Half-length, life-size, full face, hands resting on bench; cloth of gold slashed doublet with jewel clasp, red fur-lined surcoat, black jewelled cap with feather; collar of rubies; in right hand glove, left grasps hilt of dagger. Panel 33 × 25 in.

By HANS HOLBEIN. *Lent by* MISS SUMNER.

45. SIR THOMAS MORE.

Half-length, life-size, to right; in black cap and gown, with collar of SS. Panel 23 × 19¾ in.

Sir Thomas More, Lord Chancellor, son of Sir John More, Justice of the King's Bench, born in Milk Street in 1478, was educated at St. Anthony's School, Threadneedle Street, and at Oxford, where he made the acquaintance of Erasmus. He was sent on several missions for the King, was made a Privy Councillor in 1516, knighted in 1522, elected Speaker of the House of Commons in the following year, and in 1529 succeeded Cardinal Wolsey, with whom he had been at issue, as Lord Chancellor. When he was seated in the Court of Chancery, his father, Sir John More, who was nearly ninety, was the oldest Judge of the King's Bench, and it was "a beautiful spectacle to see the son ask the blessing of the father every day upon his knees before he sat upon his own seat." More steadily opposed the divorce of Queen Katherine of Aragon, and refused to be present at the coronation of Anne Boleyn. Having declined to subscribe to the Act of Supremacy, he was committed to the Tower, accused of high treason, and beheaded on Tower Hill, May 6, 1535. His sweet temper and affectionate disposition, his blameless life, his learning and probity, will for ever endear the memory of More to his country. He preserved to his last moments the serenity and cheerfulness which had ever distinguished him, and as he placed his foot upon the ladder to mount the scaffold, which shook, he said to Sir William Kingston, the Lieutenant of the Tower, "See me safe up; for my coming down I can shift for myself;" and as he put aside his beard so that it might not be injured by the headsman, he murmured, "Pity that should be cut, that has not committed treason." His famous work, entitled *Utopia*, a kind of political romance, which gained him the highest reputation as an author, is an idea of a perfect republic in an island supposed to be newly discovered in America. By a decree of Pope Leo XIII., December, 1886, he was declared to be a Martyr.

Lent by THE RIGHT HON. THE SPEAKER.

46. WILLIAM WARHAM, ARCHBISHOP OF CANTERBURY (1456?-1532).

Half-length, life-size, to left; red cassock, rochet, chimere, fur tippet, black cap, hands resting on cushion, beside which lies an open service book; in background, mitre and cross; cartel inscribed, ANNO DNI MDXXVII. ÆTATIS SUÆ LXX. Panel 32¼ × 26 in.

William Warham, Archbishop of Canterbury, born at Oakley, in Hampshire, about 1456, was educated at Winchester School, and afterwards at New College, Oxford. In 1488 he practised in the Arches, and attracted the notice of Henry VII., who in 1493 sent him with Sir Edward Poynings on an embassy to the Duke of Burgundy respecting Perkin Warbeck. In the following year he was made Master of the Rolls ; Keeper of the Great Seal, August 11, 1502 ; Bishop of London, October 1 ; and Lord Chancellor, January 1, following. In the latter part of 1504 he was translated to the See of Canterbury, being selected for that high office by Henry VII. on account of his "profound cunning, virtuous conversation, and approved great wisdom." In 1515, Warham resigned the Great Seal, and was succeeded by Wolsey ; but before and after this time there were many contests as to jurisdiction between the Archbishop and the Cardinal ; Wolsey constantly encroaching, Warham as often resisting with dignity. Whilst others signed their letters in gross flattery to Wolsey, Warham had but one finishing sentence for him : he uniformly wrote, "At your grace's commandment." Warham lived to see Wolsey's fall, and the Seals were again offered to him but were declined on account of advanced years. He died at Canterbury, August 23, 1532. Warham has been highly commended by his contemporaries for his humility, piety, and learning.

By HANS HOLBEIN.   Lent by The ARCHBISHOP OF CANTERBURY.

47. CHRISTINA, DUCHESS OF MILAN (1521–1590).

Full length, life-size, full face ; black satin gown, lined with fur, and small white frills, edged with black at neck and wrists, black hood ; she holds a long, light glove in her two hands ; on background, cartel inscribed, *Christine, daughter to Christierne, K. of Denmark, Duches of Lotragne and hered. Dutches of Milan.* (See No. 5.) Panel 70 × 32 in.

This picture was in the possession of Henry VIII. at his death, and is thus described in the King's Catalogue : "Item, a greate table with the picture of the Duchyes of Myllayne being her whole stature." It is, no doubt, the finished work of Holbein, done from the small panel with the head and hands of the Duchess now at Windsor, which he painted at Brussels by command of Henry, and which, as Hatton wrote to Cromwell, was done in three hours (*Archaeologia*, vol. xxxix., p. 7). Zucchero, when in England in 1574, saw this picture, and said he had never seen so fine a portrait in Rome. Wornum (*Life and Works of Holbein*, p. 321) writes of it, "Though the portrait is strictly an iconic figure, it is a stupendous picture, and may be compared with 'Mr. Morett' in the Dresden Gallery. We have few young ladies painted by Holbein, and but for this picture could scarcely form a sound opinion on his capability of portraying female beauty in its prime ; but this picture shows that he could do anything. There is no portrait that can be compared with it for simplicity and grandeur combined ; both paint and painter are forgotten in looking at a work like this ; you see only the incarnate spirit, and feel its very sphere. Well might Zucchero say that he had never seen anything like it in Rome. There is no portrait whatever that has the sphere of vitality so positively expressed ; and there, though the woman is not really beautiful, the expression is fascinating in the highest degree. The beauty of this exquisite portrait is indeed beyond ordinary powers of description."

Christina, Duchess of Milan, the younger dau. of Christian II. of Denmark and Elizabeth of Austria, born in 1521, married, first, Francis Sforza, 2nd Duke of Milan, in 1534, who died in 1535 ; and secondly, Francis, 1st Duke of Lorraine, in 1541, who died in 1545, and by whom she had one son, Charles, afterwards Charles II. of Lorraine, and two daughters. She died in 1590. In 1538, after the death of Jane Seymour, it was proposed to Henry VIII. that he should marry Christina, and negotiations were opened through Sir Thomas Wriothesley, Ambassador at

Brussels; but when Christina heard of the proposal, she remarked, "that she had but one head; if she had two, one should be at his Highness's service." John Hatton, English Minister at Brussels, in a letter to Cromwell, Earl of Essex, dated December 9, 1537, thus describes Christina: "I am informed she is of the age of sixteen years, very high of stature for that age. She is higher than the Regent, a goodly personage of body, and competent of beauty, of favour excellent, soft of speech, and very gentle in countenance. She weareth mourning apparel after the manner of Italy."

By HANS HOLBEIN. Lent by The DUKE OF NORFOLK, E.M., K.G.

48. SIR NICHOLAS POYNTZ, KNT. (1510–1567).

Half-length, profile, life-size, to left; black doublet and cap with feather, gold chain round neck. Panel 24 × 17 in.

Sir Nicholas Poyntz was eldest son of Anthony Poyntz, of Iron Acton, Gloucestershire, and Elizabeth, dau. and heir of William Hudson, of Devonshire. Poyntz does not appear to have held any high office, as we do not find any record of him in the memorials of his time. He died in 1557. He married Joan, dau. of Thomas, Lord Berkeley, by whom he had five sons and two daughters.

By HANS HOLBEIN. Lent by The RIGHT HON. EVELYN ASHLEY.

49. THOMAS HOWARD, 3RD DUKE OF NORFOLK, K.G. (1473–1554).

Half-length, nearly full face, slightly turned to left; red doublet, black ermine-lined surcoat, collar and badge of the Garter, and black cap; he holds the gold stick as Earl Marshal in right hand, and the white staff as Treasurer in left. Inscribed: "THOMAS DUKE OF NORFOLK MARSHALL AND TREASURER OFF INGLONDE THE LXVI YERE OF HIS AGE." Panel 30 × 23 in.

Thomas Howard, Earl of Surrey, 3rd Duke of Norfolk, son of Thomas, 2nd Duke, born in 1474, was bred to arms. In 1510 he was elected a K.G. He succeeded in 1513 his brother, Sir Edmund Howard, as High Admiral of England, and in the same year aided his father in gaining the battle of Flodden Field, for which service he was created Earl of Surrey. He went to Ireland in 1520 as Lord Lieutenant, and whilst there suppressed the dangerous rebellion under O'Neil. On the death of his father in 1524 he became Duke of Norfolk, and was one of the lords who subscribed to the articles against Cardinal Wolsey, and also to the declaration to the Pope for the divorce of Henry VIII. from Katherine of Aragon. Notwithstanding his eminent services, Norfolk, with his accomplished son Henry, Earl of Surrey, was accused in 1546 on frivolous charges of attempting to deprive the King of his crown and dignity, was attainted and condemned to be beheaded, but the King dying before the date fixed for his execution a respite was granted, and he was kept a prisoner in the Tower throughout the reign of Edward VI. On the accession of Mary in 1553 he was restored to his rank and property, contributed to the suppression of Wyat's rebellion, and died in 1554. He was twice married—first, to Princess Anne, 3rd dau. of Edward IV., by whom he had no issue; and secondly, to Elizabeth, dau. of Edward Stafford, Duke of Buckingham, by whom he had one son, Henry, the Poet, and three daughters.

By HANS HOLBEIN. Lent by The DUKE OF NORFOLK, E.M., K.G.

50. AN OLD MAN.

Half-length, life-size, turned and looking to left, clean shaven; black cap, black furred gown, and white frilled shirt; landscape background. Panel 18 × 12 in.

Lent by MARTIN COLNAGHI, ESQ.

51. HENRY VIII. (1509-1547).

Half-length, life-size, full face; crimson gold-embroidered and jewelled surcoat, lined with ermine, buttoned to throat, jewelled black cap; collar of rubies and pearls; in right hand a glove, in left a staff. Panel 33½ × 27 in.

Lent by The GOVERNORS OF BRIDEWELL HOSPITAL.

52. AN ABBESS OF GODSTOW.

Three-quarter length, seated in armchair, to left; black dress, white cap and collar, red jewelled girdle, from which a coral rosary hangs over her folded hands. Panel 25½ × 19½ in.

Lent by ST. JOHN'S COLLEGE, OXFORD.

53. EDWARD STAFFORD, 3RD DUKE OF BUCKINGHAM, K.G. (1478-1521).

Half-length, life-size, to left; cloth of gold doublet, black surcoat lined with fur, cap with badge, collar and George of the Garter; right hand resting on dagger-hilt, left on edge of picture. Panel 22½ × 18 in. (See No. 36.)

By HANS HOLBEIN. Lent by The TRUSTEES OF THE LATE LORD DONINGTON.

54. HENRY VIII.

Half-length, to right; jewelled hat with ostrich feather, puffed and jewelled dress with fur-trimmed surcoat; both hands only partially seen, glove in right; blue background. Panel 10¼ × 7½ in.

By HANS HOLBEIN. Lent by EARL SPENCER, K.G.

55. CHARLES BRANDON, DUKE OF SUFFOLK, K.G. (1485-1545).

Half-length, life-size, full face; black fur-lined doublet, showing crimson sleeves, white collar, black hat and feather, collar of the Garter with George; he holds a bunch of flowers in left hand. Panel 34 × 27 in. (See No. 13.)

Lent by The EARL OF ANCASTER.

56. CATHERINE POLE, COUNTESS OF HUNTINGDON.

Three-quarter length, life-size, to left; black dress with white muslin sleeves, black and gold hood, small close-fitting ruff, gold chain round waist, held by her right hand. Panel, 34 × 25 in.

Catherine Pole, Countess of Huntingdon, eldest daughter and co-heir of Lord Montagu, eldest son of Sir Richard Pole, K.G., and Margaret, Countess of Salisbury, and great-granddaughter of George, Duke of Clarence; married Francis Hastings, 2nd Earl of Huntingdon, K.G.

By HANS HOLBEIN. Lent by The TRUSTEES OF THE LATE LORD DONINGTON.

57. Queen Jane Seymour (1509–1537).

Small half-length, to left; crimson square-cut dress with brown and gold-braided sleeves, black diamond-shaped hood, turned up with white and gold, pearl necklace with pendant, brooch with pendent pearls; chain hanging from girdle; hands joined. Panel 24 × 18 in.

Lent by The Lord Sackville.

58. Embarkation of Henry VIII. from Dover, 31st May, 1520, to meet Francis I. at the Field of the Cloth of Gold.

View of Dover Harbour, with the Castle on the left. The ship, the *Henri Grace-de-Dieu*, or *Great Harry*, is represented as just sailing out of the harbour, having her sails set. Her sails and pennants are of cloth of gold, damasked, and the royal standard is flying on each of the four quarters of the forecastle; the quarters, sides, and stern are also decorated with shields and royal badges. On the main deck stands the King, richly attired in crimson, with a coat of cloth of gold. Following this, and to the right, are other ships, filled with yeomen of the guard, men beating drums, holding flags, &c. In the offing are a number of ships, and between them small boats, filled with spectators. In the foreground, to right and left, are two circular forts, on which are spectators, billmen, and officers, and from which a salute is being fired. Canvas 121 × 63½ in.

The number of those who embarked with Henry VIII. on this occasion included, besides the great nobles and their followers, 4,334 men, with 1,637 horses. Cardinal Wolsey's train alone consisted of.. twelve chaplains, fifty gentlemen, 238 servants, and 150 horses. The *Henri Grace-de-Dieu* was built expressly for the King, and on the day of its christening, June 19, 1514, he received the Queen and all the Court, the Pope's Legate, and the Emperor's Ambassadors on board, and himself conducted them through the ship. It had no equal in bulk, and was mounted "by an incredible number of guns." The bills for its decorations are still extant in the Record Office; and the cost of every flag, streamer, and badge can be ascertained. One Vincent Volpe, an Italian, painted the streamers; and John Brown, the King's painter, did the badges, flags, &c. (See *Archæologia*, vol. vi., pp. 179-200.) This picture has been attributed to the above-mentioned Vincent Volpe, who painted for the King "plats," or "descriptions," that is, bird's-eye views, such as this picture.

By Vincent Volpe.   Lent by Her Majesty the Queen.
(Hampton Court.)

59. Sir Thomas More, Knt. (1478?–1535).

Half-length, to right; black cloak lined with fur, black hat; hands joined, resting on book, and holding a scroll upon which is written "*Henricus Rex* 1532 *pinx* 1532." Gold collar of SS.; inscribed on the background *Sr Thomas Moore*. Panel 21 × 17 in. (See No. 45.)

By Hans Holbein.   Lent by Miss Sumner.

60. Cardinal Wolsey (1471–1530).

Bust, in profile, to left; wearing Cardinal's scarlet robes and biretta; shield of arms surmounted by the Cardinal's hat on the background. Panel 21 × 17 in.

Exhibition of the Royal House of Tudor.

Thomas Wolsey, Cardinal and statesman, born at Ipswich in 1471, his father (Robert) being perhaps, as is commonly asserted, a butcher, but evidently wealthy, was educated at Magdalen College, Oxford, and took his degree at the age of fifteen. Having been recommended by Sir John Nanfan, the treasurer of Calais, to Henry VII., he was employed in embassies to Germany and Scotland, acquitting himself so dexterously that the King rewarded him with the Deanery of Lincoln. On the accession of Henry VIII. Wolsey became at once a favourite with him, and so rapidly did he rise in the King's estimation that he was made Bishop of Lincoln and Archbishop of York in 1514, and in 1515 succeeded Archbishop Warham as Chancellor. In the latter year he was also promoted by the Pope to the dignity of Cardinal. He held at various times the Sees of Bath and Wells, Durham, and Winchester. From this time till his fall Wolsey was one of the most important men in Europe; at home his power was almost without limit, and he enjoyed from Henry the most unbounded favour and confidence. He lived in great magnificence, his retinue surpassing even that of royalty; he built Hampton Court Palace, which he afterwards presented to the King, and founded Christ Church, Oxford, which was first known as "Cardinal's College." Having incurred the displeasure of Henry by his opposition to his divorce from Queen Katherine and his marriage with Anne Boleyn, an indictment was perferred against him in 1529, he was stripped of all his honours, and driven with ignominy from the Court. The Archbishopric of York was, however, restored to him along with other of his minor preferments, and he retired there in order that he might devote himself to the duties of a Christian bishop; but he was soon arrested on the charge of treason, and ordered to be conveyed to London for trial. On his journey he was attacked with dysentery, and died at the monastery of Leicester, November 29, 1530.

By HANS HOLBEIN.   Lent by MISS SUMNER.

61. HENRY VIII. (1509-1547).

Three-quarter length, life-size, to right, head towards spectator; in rich gold doublet and fur-lined surcoat; gold collar with jewels, jewelled cap with feather; left hand holding gloves, in right a dagger. Size, 47 × 35 in. Panel.

Lent by MARTIN COLNAGHI, ESQ.

62. MEETING OF HENRY VIII. AND FRANCIS I. AT THE FIELD OF THE CLOTH OF GOLD IN 1520.

This famous meeting between Henry VIII. and Francis I. took place in the fields situate between the towns of Guisnes and Ardres, on May 20, 1520. The various incidents of this celebrated interview are depicted on this picture in very minute and elaborate historical accuracy. The two monarchs, after saluting each other in the most cordial manner, retired for secret conference into a tent. This conference was succeeded by a series of tournaments and entertainments unparalleled in the history of the two countries, and the magnificence then displayed by the nobility of England and France procured for the place of interview the name of *The Field of the Cloth of Gold*. The painter of this picture is unknown. It was probably executed by some artist who accompanied Henry VIII. for the purpose, and who made it up from sketches taken on the spot. Mr. Wornum suggests that it is very possibly the work of John Crust, a painter living in the earlier years of Henry VIII., concerning whom there exist Exchequer records.

On the left side of the picture is shown the arrival of the English cavalcade at the town of Guisnes, of which we see the church, the gabled houses, and the castle, from which salutes are being fired. In the foreground is the chief part of the procession, prominent in which is King Henry himself, riding on a white charger, "apparelled in red gown and surcoat of cloth of gold;" his horse covered with "gold trappings." By the side of the King rides Wolsey on a mule. In front of the King rides the Marquess of Dorset, with the sword of state; while behind ride many other officers of state, prominent among whom is Charles Brandon, Duke of Suffolk. These are followed by halberdiers and pikemen. The advanced part of the procession is composed of the King's billmen and various officers on horseback, also Wolsey's chaplains, &c., who are all passing into the castle.

On the right side of the picture is seen in the middle background the plain of Ardres studded with trees, amidst which is the pavilion of Henry VIII., all in cloth of gold with two flags. Beyond is the gilt tent, lined with fleurs-de-lis on blue ground, of Francis I.; above which rises the figure of St. Michael. Inside this tent we see the meeting of the two monarchs, affectionately embracing one another, their squires hold their horses without, and their retinues are grouped around. More in the foreground is the famous palace, outside which stand the two gold fountains "running with red, white, and claret wine," with which the English and French toasted each other "et disoient ces paroles: *Bons amys, Francoys et Angloys*, en les repetant plusieurs foys en beuvant lung a lnultre de bon couraige." In other parts are shown other incidents of the meeting: thus to the right are seen the lists half-way between Guisnes and Ardres, with the galleries of the Kings and Queens, and the great *perron* or tree of nobility. Lower down are the kitchens, and a tent with a banquet. In the upper left corner is the English pale under water, and above a dragon, which is stated to have suddenly appeared in the sky, while the Cardinal, attended by bishops as deacons, was singing the great High Mass. On the right is the old town of Ardres. Canvas 66 x by 159 in.

Lent by HER MAJESTY THE QUEEN.
(Hampton Court.)

63. HENRY FITZALAN, 23RD EARL OF ARUNDEL (1511–1580).

Three-quarter length, life-size, to right; gold-brocaded doublet and trunks, black ermine-lined cloak, white ruff, black cap with white feather; right hand on hip, glove in left. Panel 36 x 28 in.

Henry Fitzalan, the last Earl of Arundel of his family, born in 1511, was the only son of William, 22nd Earl, and Anne, dau. of Henry, 4th Earl of Northumberland. He was appointed Deputy of Calais in 1540, elected a K.G. in 1544, in the same year was present at the siege of Boulogne, and succeeded in 1554 to the title and great estates of his ancestors. For his bravery in the assault on that city Henry VIII. made him Governor of Calais, Comptroller of the Royal Household, and afterwards Lord Chamberlain. He was a member of the Council of Edward VI., but having excited the envy of the Earl of Warwick was deprived on a frivolous charge of all his employments, committed to the Tower, and fined £12,000. He strongly supported Mary at her accession, and received the offices of President of the Council and Steward of the Queen's Household. These appointments were confirmed by Elizabeth, who added those of High Constable and High Steward of England. In 1569 he was one of the Commissioners to inquire into the murder of Darnley, and, having favoured Mary, became an object of suspicion, for which he suffered a short imprisonment in the Tower in 1572. From that time till his death in 1580 he lived in retirement. He married, first, Catherine, dau. of Thomas Grey, second Marquess of Dorset; and secondly, Mary, dau. of Sir John Arundel, of Lanherne, Cornwall, but having no surviving issue, his titles and estates devolved on Philip, eldest son of Thomas, fourth Duke of Norfolk.

By CORNELIUS KETEL. Lent by The DUKE OF NORFOLK, E.M., K.G.

64. SIR THOMAS MORE, LORD CHANCELLOR (1478?–1535).

Half-length, nearly life-size, to right; dark green fur-trimmed gown over crimson robe, black cap, collar of SS. with Tudor rose pendant, right arm on table; hands touching, right holding folded paper. Panel 29 × 23½ in. (See No. 45.)

Lent by MARTIN COLNAGHI, ESQ.

65. QUEEN KATHERINE OF ARAGON (1485–1536).

Bust, life-size, to left; black square-cut dress edged with jewels, white chemisette edged with black, red-brown, and gold, diamond-shaped hood trimmed with jewels. Inscribed CATHERINA PRIMA VXOR HENRICI OCTAVI. Panel 23 × 17 in.

Lent by MERTON COLLEGE, OXFORD.

66. THOMAS, LORD SEYMOUR OF SUDELEY, LORD HIGH ADMIRAL, K.G. (d. 1549).

Bust, life-size, to left; black dress, lace collar, and black cap. Panel, circular, 19 in.
From the Northwick Collection.   Lent by MRS. DENT of Sudeley.

67. QUEEN JANE SEYMOUR (1509–1537).

Small three-quarter length figure, to left, hands folded; red square-cut dress, long hanging sleeves lined with ermine, yellow undersleeves slashed; diamond-shaped hood with pearls; necklace of pearls, with "Tau" cross; on breast, jewel with three pendent pearls; background inscribed, QVEENE IANE SEYMER. Panel 21 × 13¼ in.

Lent by The MARQUESS OF HERTFORD.

68. FAMILY GROUP OF THE MORE FAMILY IN TWO GENERATIONS.

From the picture in the possession of Mrs. Strickland, of Cokethorpe. (See Walpole, *Anecdotes*, vol. i., p. 92.) (See No. 71.)
By PETER OLIVER.   Lent by MAJOR-GENERAL F. E. SOTHEBY.

69. QUEEN ANNE BOLEYN.

Half-length, life-size, to left; in low black fur-lined dress, right hand holding a carnation pearl necklace, from which is suspended a jewel with letter "B." Panel 22½ × 17¾ in.
By HANS HOLBEIN.   Lent by C. J. RADCLIFFE, ESQ.

70. SIR THOMAS MORE, LORD CHANCELLOR (1478?–1535).

Half-length, to right; dark green fur-trimmed gown over crimson robe, black cap, collar of SS. with Tudor rose pendant, right arm on table; hands touching, right holding paper; green curtain background. Panel 16 × 11 in.

Lent by JOHN EYSTON, ESQ.

71. SIR THOMAS MORE AND FAMILY.

Whole-length figures, life-size. Sir Thomas, aged 50, and his father, Sir John, aged 76, are seated in the centre; Margaret Roper, the eldest daughter, aged 22, and Cecilia Heron, the third daughter, aged 20, sit together on the right, the former holding open on her knee Seneca's tragedy of Œdipus; on the left stand Elizabeth Dancey, Sir Thomas's second daughter, aged 21, and Margaret Gigs, wife of Dr. Clements; on Sir Thomas's left hand sits his son John, aged 19, whose wife, Anne Crisacre, is seen between Sir Thomas and Sir John; behind, on the right, are Henry Pattison, the family jester, and John Harris, Sir Thomas's secretary. The figure of Sir Thomas's wife, Alice, which originally occupied the extreme right of the picture, has been cut away. Canvas 91 × 118 in. (See No. 68.)

Attributed to HOLBEIN.   Lent by JOHN EYSTON, ESQ.

72. CARDINAL WOLSEY (1471–1530).

Bust, life-size, in profile, to right; in Cardinal's robes, red biretta; scroll in right hand; on background, in left corner, church and other buildings seen through a window; on right, mirror with ornamental frame. Panel 18 × 10 in.

Lent by The HON. SIR SPENCER PONSONBY-FANE, K.C.B.

73. THOMAS CRANMER, ARCHBISHOP OF CANTERBURY (1489-1556).

Small bust, to left; in black cassock, rochet, chimere, and black biretta, holding book in both hands; ring on first finger of left hand. Cartel inscribed, *Anno dom* MDXLVII. *Ætatis uæ x Julii*, 50. Panel 17¼ × 12 in.

Thomas Cranmer, Archbishop of Canterbury, born in 1489, was educated at Jesus College, Cambridge, and in 1526 constituted Archdeacon of Taunton. Henry VIII., being pleased with the views which he propounded respecting the divorce of Queen Katherine, took him into favour, bestowed upon him Church preferments, and employed him abroad in various missions. In 1532 Cranmer succeeded Warham as Archbishop of Canterbury, and in the following year pronounced the King's marriage with Katherine of Aragon to have been null and void. By aid of Cromwell, Earl of Essex, Cranmer procured the King's authority that a copy of the new translation of the Bible, known by his name, should be placed for public reading in every parish church throughout the realm. To Cromwell he wrote in gratitude for his success, adding, "And this deed you shall hear of at the Great Day, when all things are made manifest." He favoured the divorce of Anne of Cleves, and disclosed to Henry the infidelities of Catherine Howard. He attended Henry VIII. in his last moments, and crowned Edward VI., being one of his council and an executor of his father's will. On the accession of Mary, Cranmer was sent a prisoner to the Tower; thence in 1554 he was removed, together with Ridley and Latimer, to Oxford, and having been tried on the charge of heresy was condemned, but to save his life recanted. Finding, however, that it was determined to put him to death he retracted his recantation, and was burnt at the stake March 21, 1556. Cranmer was twice married, and had several children.

By HANS HOLBEIN.   Lent by JESUS COLLEGE, CAMBRIDGE.

73*. A Surgical Operation.
    By Lucas v. Leyden.　　　　　Lent by John Harley, Esq., M.D.

74. Recumbent Effigy of Henry VII.
    Plaster cast. The original of cast copper, gilt, is on the monument in Henry the Seventh's Chapel, Westminster Abbey; executed by Pietro Torrigiano between the years 1512 and 1518.
    Lent by The Science and Art Department.

75. Court-Cupboard.
    Carved oak; the lower part contains two drawers, and is surmounted by a cupboard with receding sides, which supports the flat top, also partly resting on two spiral columns. On the cupboard door is carved the portrait of a lady wearing a ruff and lace collar. The front of the top, the sides of the cupboard, and the front of the lower part are carved with panels of floral scrollwork, symmetrically arranged. The cabinet is further decorated with narrow bands inlaid with small squares of wood, alternately light and dark. Between the drawers is an inlaid tulip. The whole is supported on four short baluster legs with cross-bars of the same design. Stated to be from Derby Old Hall. *English.* Dated "A.D. 1603."
    Lent by The Science and Art Department.

76. Mirror.
    Glass, in oak frame with carved scroll outline and narrow bands inlaid with small squares of wood, alternately light and dark. The uprights and feet of the stand are baluster-shaped. *English.* The frame dated 1603, but the glass 19th century. Stated to be from Derby Old Hall.
    Lent by The Science and Art Department.

76*. Tile, with Device of Queen Elizabeth.
    Lent by Sir John Evans, K.C.B.

77. Butter-Cupboard.
    Oak; in two parts. The upper part has two doors divided by a framed panel. At the side there are perforations to admit air. *Circa* 1620.
    Lent by The Hon. Sir Spencer Ponsonby Fane, K.C.B.

ROOM III.

Pictures, Miniatures, Books, and Relics.

REIGN OF EDWARD VI. (1547-1553.)

EDWARD VI., son of Henry VIII. and Jane Seymour, born at Hampton Court, October 12, 1537; succeeded January 28, 1547; crowned February 25th, 1547; died at Greenwich, July 6, 1553, and was buried at Westminster.

78. EDWARD VI. (1537-1553).

Bust, to left; jewelled cap with feather, gold-embroidered dark dress, trimmed with ermine. Panel 16 × 14 in.

Lent by The DUKE OF DEVONSHIRE, K.G.

79. EDWARD STANLEY, 3RD EARL OF DERBY, K.G. (1506-1574).

Head; open ruff, furred dress. Panel 13 × 10 in.

Son of Thomas, 2nd Earl; born 1506; placed under the charge of Cardinal Wolsey; succeeded his father 1521; attended Henry VIII. in France; suppressed the north-western insurrection in 1536; K.G. by Edward VI.; Lord High Steward by Queen Mary; noted for his charity to the poor, of whom it is stated that for thirty-five years 2,700 received on Good Friday meat, drink, and money; died 24th October, 1574. Camden says that with his death "the glory of hospitality seemed to fall asleep;" and his great descendant, the 7th Earl, writes that he "left so excellent a name behind him, that no fault or vice is of him at all remembered."

Lent by The EARL OF DERBY.

80. HENRY VIII. AND HIS FAMILY.

In the centre of a large room, supported on either side by pillars, is seated facing on a throne beneath a cloth of state Henry VIII., holding sceptre in right hand, and with left presenting sword of state to Edward VI., who kneels beside him. On the left stands Mary, his daughter,

Exhibition of the Royal House of Tudor.

holding a branch of roses, and Philip II. of Spain, behind whom is an allegorical figure of War. On the right is Elizabeth, introducing allegorical figures of Peace and Plenty. Through the pillars on either side are seen distant buildings. At the foot of the picture is inscribed in gold letters—

"THE QUENE TO WALSINGHAM THIS TABLET SENTE
MARKE OF HER PEOPLES AND HER OWNE CONTENTE."

and on the frame also in gold letters—

"A Face of muche nobelitye loe in a litle roome,
Fowr states with theyr conditions heare shadowed in a showe,
A father more then valyant, a rare and vertuous soon,
A zealaus daughter her kynd what els the world doth knowe,
And last of all a vyrgin queen to England's joy to see,
Successyvely to hold the right and vertues of the three."

Panel 51 × 71 in.

This very curious and interesting picture was no doubt, as the inscription at the bottom tells us, painted by order of Queen Elizabeth for presentation to Sir Francis Walsingham. From Scadbury, the seat of the Walsinghams, it was brought to Chislehurst, the residence of Mr. James West, and thence to Strawberry Hill, where it was purchased by J. C. Dent, Esq., at the sale in 1842. The picture tells its own tale. From Henry VIII. the crown passed in quiet succession to his son Edward. The accession of Mary and her marriage to Philip of Spain brought much trouble to England, and the nation was involved in strife both at home and abroad. A happier and more peaceful time is now to be looked for under the rule of the "Virgin Queen," who is therefore represented as introducing to her family the two divinities who are to be emblematic of her future rule. The great prominence given to the figure of the Queen, who is too large in proportion to the other figures, shows that she is intended to be the principal person in the picture. The features of Peace and Plenty have been said to be those of the Countesses of Shrewsbury and Salisbury ; but if the picture was painted early in the reign of Elizabeth that could not well be, as there was no Countess of Salisbury at that time. This picture was engraved by William Rogers.

By SIR ANTONIO MORE. Lent by MRS. DENT of Sudeley.

81. HENRY HOWARD, EARL OF SURREY, K.G. (1516-1547).

Under an archway, with figures on either side, each holding shield of arms, one with arms of Brotherton, the other France and England, quarterly, full-length figure, life-size, to left ; brown doublet and trunks embroidered with silver, and white stockings, brown fur-lined mantle, black cap with white feather ; right arm resting on broken column, glove in hand ; left placed on his hip ; collar of the Garter with George ; rich sword and dagger ; Garter on left leg ; pedestal of column inscribed SAT SVPER EST ; arch inscribed ANNO DNI 1546 ÆTATIS SVE 29 ; above two *putini* hold golden H ; through the archway is seen a landscape. Canvas 87 × 86 in.

This picture was purchased in 1720 at the sale of the Arundel Collection at Stafford House for Sir Robert Walpole, who made a present of it to the late Edward, Duke of Norfolk.

Henry Howard, Earl of Surrey, eldest son of Thomas, 3rd Duke of Norfolk, and Elizabeth, dau. of Edward Stafford, Duke of Buckingham, born in 1516, was one of the leaders in the poetic movement under Henry VIII. that heralded the great outburst of the Elizabethan period. Of his personal life outside his poetry only the barest outline is known. When his father in 1524 received the title of Duke of Norfolk his son was styled by courtesy Earl of Surrey. He probably received his education at Cambridge. In 1532 he went to Paris and Germany, and is said to have also made the tour of Europe as a knight-errant, upholding against all comers the superiority of his Mistress "Geraldine," who is commonly supposed to have been Elizabeth Fitzgerald, a daughter of the Earl of Kildare. He was elected a K.G. in 1541; the following year he served under his father in Scotland, and held a command in the expedition to Boulogne in 1544. When the King's death was known to be near, Surrey and his father were suspected of aiming at the throne, were arrested, and lodged in the Tower. Surrey was brought to trial for high treason, the main charge against him being that he had "falsely, maliciously, and treacherously set up and borne the arms of Edward the Confessor;" was found guilty, and executed on Tower Hill on January 19, 1547. Besides his well-known love verses, Surrey translated two books of Virgil's *Æneid*, which is the earliest specimen of blank verse in the English language. He married Frances Vere, dau. of John, 15th Earl of Oxford, by whom he had two sons, Thomas, 4th Duke of Norfolk, and Henry, created Earl of Northampton, and three daughters.

By GWILLIM STRETES.   Lent by The DUKE OF NORFOLK, E.M., K.G.

82. HENRY VIII. AND PRINCESS MARY, WITH WILL SOMERS.

Half-length figures, the King on the left, the Princess on the right, their hands resting on a carpet-covered table, on which lies a bunch of grapes; Somers standing behind, a lap-dog on his right hand. Canvas 50½ × 63½ in.

Lent by EARL SPENCER, K.G.

83. THOMAS, LORD SEYMOUR OF SUDELEY, LORD HIGH ADMIRAL, K.G. (d. 1549).

Small three-quarter length, to left; crimson doublet embroidered with gold, black slashed surcoat, black cap with red feather; glove in right hand, left on hip; background inscribed *Ano. Domine* 1533 *Ætatis suæ* 34. Panel 17½ × 12½ in.

Thomas Seymour, Lord Seymour of Sudeley, brother of the Protector Somerset, and of Jane Seymour, held high command during Henry VIII.'s invasion of France, and was nominated by him one of the twelve assistants to the executors of his will. At the accession of Edward VI. he was created Baron Seymour of Sudeley, appointed Lord High Admiral and a Privy Councillor, and elected a K.G. He aspired to the hand of the Princess Elizabeth, then fifteen years old, but finding no prospect of success he married the Queen Dowager, Katherine Parr, who died in childbed in 1548. After her death Seymour renewed his addresses to Princess Elizabeth, and conspired against the power of his brother, the "Protector." His designs having been intimated to the Council, he was committed to the Tower, condemned without any form of trial, and beheaded on Tower Hill, March 10, 1549.

Lent by The MARQUESS OF HERTFORD.

84. RICHARD COX, BISHOP OF ELY (1499–1581).

Half-length, small life-size, to right; grey beard, episcopal habit; left hand resting on red book, right holding stick. Panel 22½ × 18 in.

Educated at Eton and King's College, Cambridge; invited by Wolsey to Oxford, where he was imprisoned for adopting tenets of Reformers; on his release became Master of Eton; tutor to Prince Edward; Chancellor of Oxford, 1547; Dean of Westminster, 1549; deprived in Queen Mary's reign, and retired to Frankfort; but returned on the accession of Elizabeth, and made Bishop of Ely, 1559; one of the compilers of Liturgy, and engaged in translation of *Bishops' Bible*.

Lent by TRINITY HALL, CAMBRIDGE.

85. RICHARD BERTIE (1517-1582).

Half-length, life-size, to right; black doublet and surcoat, white lace collar, black hat with jewels; inscribed, RIC. BERTIE, ÆT. 30. A°. D. 1548, &c. Canvas 29 × 24 in.

Richard Bertie, son and heir of Thomas Bertie, of Bersted, Kent, born in 1517, was educated at Corpus Christi College, Oxford, and joined the household of Sir Thomas Wriothesley, Lord Chancellor, being reputed to be a very accomplished gentleman, well versed in Latin, French, and Italian, bold and shrewd in discourse, and quick at repartee. In 1552 he married Catherine, Baroness Willoughby de Eresby, widow of the Duke of Suffolk. His life and that of his wife being in danger owing to the persecutions of Bishop Gardiner, they fled to the Continent, and after suffering great hardships and dangers finally settled in Poland, where they were befriended by Sigismund II., who placed him in the Earldom of Krose, in Samogitia. At the accession of Elizabeth, Bertie with his wife returned to England, and sat in Parliament for the county of Lincoln. He died at Bourne, in Lincolnshire, April 9, 1582. His son, Peregrine, succeeded to the barony of Willoughby.

Lent by The EARL OF ANCASTER.

86. JOHN WINCHCOMBE, SON OF "JACK OF NEWBURY" (dated 1550).

Three-quarter length, life-size, full face; dated 1550; black satin doublet and fur-lined surcoat, white collar and black cap; in right hand a carnation, in left glove; above on the right tablet inscribed ANNO DOMINI 1550 ÆTATIS SVE 61; on left, shield of arms; the frame is inscribed—

> above IN RESPECT OF THINGS ETERNALL
> THIS IS VEARI VAYNE AND MORTALL
> and below SPENDE WELL THI MORTALL LIEF THERFORE
> THAT THOW MAIST LEVE FOR EVERMORE.

Panel 44 × 36 in.

John Winchcombe, whose real name was Smallwode, was the eldest son of John Winchcombe, of Newbury, *alias* "Jack of Newbury," whom Fuller describes as "the most considerable clothier England ever beheld." The father was a strong adherent of Henry VII.; he marched to Flodden Field with a troop of one hundred men, which he clothed and armed at his own expense. He also entertained Henry VIII. and Katherine of Aragon at his own house at Newbury. He died in 1520. John, the eldest son, the subject of the above picture, was also a man of position, and received in 1549 a grant of arms, being accounted "from henceforth to be, at all places of honour and worshippe amonges other noble parsons, accepted and reputed into the number of and company of auncient gentell and nobell men."

Lent by MRS. DENT of Sudeley.

87. Henry Fitzalan, Lord Maltravers (1538–1557).

Half-length, life-size, to right; black dress, white ruff, black cap. Inscription, with date of death, "1556 BEING OF AGE NOT FULLY XIX IEARES." Panel 23 × 18½ in.

Henry Fitzalan, styled Lord Maltravers, was the eldest son of Henry, 23rd Earl of Arundel, the last Earl of that family, and Lady Catherine Grey, dau. of Thomas, Marquess of Dorset. He was sent as Ambassador to the King of Bohemia, but having caught a fever, died at Brussels in 1557, aged 19. He married Anne, dau. and heir of Sir John Wentworth, of Gosfield, Essex, but had no issue.

Lent by The Lord Zouche.

88. Edward VI. Presenting the Charter to Bridewell (1553).

The King is seated under a rich cloth of state in his royal robes, his crown upon his head, his sceptre in his right hand, his left delivering to the citizens of London the royal charter, with the Great Seal attached, which contains the grant of his palace and manor of Bridewell to the mayor, aldermen, and commonalty of the City of London for a hospital and workhouse for the thriftless poor, vagrants, &c. The Lord Mayor, Sir George Barnes, William Gerrard and John Maynard, aldermen and then sheriffs of London, are represented as kneeling and receiving the royal donation, and near them stands William Blackwell, the town clerk, whose office it was to take and deposit the charter among the City archives. On the left also stands Dr. Thomas Goodrich, the Lord Chancellor, robed in his episcopal habit and holding the purse containing the Great Seal of England. On the right stands Sir Robert Bowes, Knt., Master of the Rolls, in his robes of office, and near him William, Earl of Pembroke, K.G., Master of the Horse and a member of the King's Council. The other figures are unknown. Canvas 115 × 108 in.

On April 10, 1547, Edward VI. sent for the Lord Mayor and aldermen to attend at Whitehall, where the royal charter for the foundation of Bridewell Hospital was delivered to them, and this painting was made in remembrance of the benefaction, which was afterwards confirmed by his charter 26th June following. The King had before given Christ's Hospital to the City for the use of the impotent poor, and also St. Thomas the Apostle for the poor by casualty; both which, together with Bridewell, were afterwards united and incorporated under the government of the Lord Mayor, commonalty, and citizens of the City of London.

Not only Vertue but also Walpole considered this picture to be the work of Holbein. Walpole says, "Holbein has placed his own head in one corner of the picture. It is believed it was not completed by Holbein, both he and the King dying immediately after the donation." It is now certain that it cannot be the work of that artist, as he died in 1543. It is by some considered rather the work of Gwillim Stretes, who sometimes signed himself "William Strote," an artist who obviously formed himself in manner and conception from Holbein, with whose later portraits he shows much affinity.

By Gwillim Stretes? *Lent by* The Governors of Bridewell Hospital.

89. Edward Seymour, Duke of Somerset, "The Protector" (d. 1552).

Three-quarter length, life-size, to left; black doublet slashed at the shoulder, white ruffs at neck and wrists, black cap; thumb of right hand in girdle; glove in left, which rests on table; inscribed Aº. 1535 &. svæ. ætatis · 28. Panel 35 × 26½ in.

Edward Seymour, Duke of Somerset, eldest son of Sir John Seymour, of Wolf Hall, Wiltshire, and Elizabeth, dau. of Sir Henry Wentworth, brother to Jane Seymour, and thus uncle to Edward VI., accompanied, in 1533, the Duke of Suffolk to France, and was knighted the same year. When his sister became Queen of Henry VIII., in 1536, he was created Viscount Beauchamp and Earl of Hertford, K.G. in 1540, and Lord Chamberlain of England in 1542. In 1544 he was appointed Lieut.-General of the North, commanded an expedition against the Scots, and in the same year was at the siege of Boulogne. By Henry VIII.'s will he was nominated one of his executors, and governor of his son; but was soon afterwards declared Protector of the Kingdom. In 1548 he was appointed Lord Treasurer, created Duke of Somerset, and made Earl Marshal of England. The same year he marched into Scotland and gained the victory of Musselburgh; yet though he raised his reputation, he could not counteract the plotting of his greatest enemy, the Earl of Warwick, and on his return was accused of high treason, and executed on Tower Hill, January 22, 1552. He married, first, Catherine, dau. and co-heir of Sir William Fillol, by whom he had two sons, the elder, Edward, being restored to the estates in 1553; and secondly, Anne, dau. of Sir Edward Stanhope, by whom he had two sons and three daughters, the eldest son, Edward, being afterwards created Earl of Hertford in 1558.

Lent by MRS. DENT of Sudeley.

90. WILLIAM SOMERSET, 3RD EARL OF WORCESTER, K.G. ? (d. 1589).

Half-length, life-size, to left; in buff doublet and fur-lined coat, looking towards spectator, jewel suspended from neck; inscribed ANNO DNI 1568 ÆTATIS 51. Panel 23 × 16¼ in.

Lent by The LORD ZOUCHE.

91. CATHERINE, BARONESS WILLOUGHBY DE ERESBY, DUCHESS OF SUFFOLK (d. 1580).

Half-length, life-size, full face; black gown, fur tippet, white frill and cuffs, black hood; in right hand, book; in left, gloves. Inscribed D. KATH. DUCISSA SUFFOLCIÆ VIDUA ÆT. 28. A°. D. 1548 DEINCEPS UXOR RICARDI BERTIE. Canvas 29 × 24 in.

Catherine, Baroness Willoughby de Eresby, dau. and heir of William, 9th Lord Willoughby, was under age at the time of her father's decease in 1525, and was placed under the guardianship of Charles Brandon, Duke of Suffolk, whom she afterwards married, and by whom she had issue two sons, Henry and Charles, who both died on the same day, 1551, of the sweating sickness. On the death of the Duke of Suffolk in 1545, she married Richard Bertie, and from this union sprang the Dukes of Ancaster, and Earls of Lindsey and Abingdon. During the reign of Mary, the Duchess of Suffolk, being a zealous supporter of the Reformation, was obliged to retire from England, accompanied by her husband. The Duchess and her husband returned to England on the death of Mary. She died September 19, 1580, and he April 9, 1582.

Lent by The EARL OF ANCASTER.

92. GEORGE CAVENDISH? (d. 1562).

Half-length, life-size, to left; in fur-lined coat with hands uplifted, wearing close-fitting cap. Arms of Cavendish, Sendamore, Brecknock, and Smith. Size, panel, 22 × 17 in.

George Cavendish, eldest son of Thomas Cavendish, of Cavendish, Overhall, and Alice, daughter and co-heir of John Smith, of Podbrook, co. Suffolk; the faithful attendant of Cardinal Wolsey through all fortunes, and retained by Henry VIII. after the death of Wolsey. He died about 1562.

Lent by The DUKE OF DEVONSHIRE, K.G.

93. HENRY GREY, DUKE OF SUFFOLK, K.G. (d. 1554).

Three-quarter length, to right; white and gold doublet and trunks, black fur-lined surcoat, white ruffs at neck and wrist, black hat with jewels and feathers; collar of the Garter with George; right hand on hip; left holds hilt of sword. Panel 14 × 10 in.

Lent by JOHN HARLEY, ESQ., M.D.

94. THOMAS, 1ST BARON WENTWORTH, KNT. (d. 1551).

Three-quarter length, life-size, to left; black doublet, black surcoat lined with fur; in right hand, gloves; in left baton; on background shield of arms, date ANNO DNI 1547; white tablet with inscription, &c. Panel 39 × 28 in.

Sir Thomas Wentworth, Knt., 1st Baron Wentworth. son of Sir Richard Wentworth, Knt., of Nettlested, Suffolk, and Anne, dau. of Sir James Tyrell, of Gipping, Suffolk, was knighted for his bravery in the taking of Bray and Montdidier in the expedition to France in 1523, was summoned to Parliament as a baron under the title of Lord Wentworth of Nettlested, December 2, 1529, and was one of the lords who subscribed the declaration to Pope Clement VII. for the divorce of Katherine of Aragon. In 1532 he attended Henry in his interview with the French King at Boulogne; and in 1545 was commissioned to array all men able to bear arms in Suffolk; appointed Lord Chamberlain to Edward VI., and a Privy Councillor; and accompanied the Marquess of Northampton in 1549 to suppress the rebellion of Ket the Tanner. He died 3 March, 1551, and was buried in Westminster Abbey. By Theodore Bernard.

Lent by The RIGHT HON. SIR C. W. DILKE, BART., M.P.

95. SIR WILLIAM LYGON, HIS WIFE ELIZABETH, AND THEIR FOUR CHILDREN.

Life-size group of six figures, seen to the waist. Sir William and his wife in the background, the eldest child to right holds a book; the two in the centre of the canvas hold each a flower. Panel 30 × 36 in.

Sir William Lygon, Knt., son of Richard Lygon, of Madresfield, and Mary, dau. of Sir Thomas Russell, Knt., of Streatham, Worcester, born 1567, died 1629. He was High Sheriff of Worcestershire in 1593, and Collins says of him that he sold many manors. He married Elizabeth, dau. of Sir Edmund Harewell, and by her had issue two sons, William and Henry, and two daughters, Elizabeth and Katherine. Lady Lygon died in March, 1631, and was buried at Malvern.

Lent by G. E. MARTIN, ESQ.

96. Henry Stanley, 4th Earl of Derby, K.G. (1531-1593).

To waist; black cap and plume, black dress; collar of K.G. Panel 32 × 25 in.

Eldest son of Edward, 3rd Earl (No. 153), by Dorothy, daughter of Thomas, Duke of Norfolk; born 1531; was in favour (when Lord Strange) at the Court of Edward VI., K.G. in 1575, employed by Queen Elizabeth in many important offices; died at Lathom, 25th September, 1593.

Lent by The Earl of Derby.

97. Sir Nicholas Throckmorton, Kt. (1513-1570).

Half-length; black cap, sable tippet. Canvas 26 × 20 in.

Soldier, statesman, and diplomatist; 4th son of Sir George Throckmorton; born 1513; commanded at the victory of Musselburgh, 1547; Ambassador from Queen Elizabeth in France and in Scotland; died suddenly at the Earl of Leicester's, 12 Feb., 1570, with the suspicion, then usual, of poison.

Lent by Sir William Throckmorton, Bart.

98. Sir Rowland Hill, Lord Mayor (d. 1561).

Half-length, under life-size, to right; black fur-lined doublet, brown fur-lined surcoat, black cap; his hands rest on a parapet, and hold large chain that passes round his neck. Inscribed above, ADIEV MONDE PVISQVE TV DESCOIS TOVT INFAMIS TOVT CHASTES TOVT A LA FIN OBLIVES TOVT; below, on tablet, Latin inscription setting forth his munificent acts, &c. Canvas 26½ × 20 in.

Sir Rowland Hill, son of Richard Hill, born at Hodnet, in Shropshire, was bred a mercer in London, Sheriff in 1541, and Lord Mayor in 1549, being knighted in that year. Died 1561. Being possessed of great wealth, he devoted much of it to useful and charitable purposes; he mended the causeways, built bridges, and founded schools.

Lent by The Lord Egerton of Tatton.

99. Edward VI. (1547-1553).

Three-quarter length, life-size, to left; cloth of gold doublet slashed with white, fur-lined crimson surcoat, black cap with white feather; right hand holding dagger; left in girdle; Hampton Court is seen through an open window. Panel 46 × 34 in.

By Hans Holbein. *Lent by* The Earl of Denbigh.

100. William Cecil, Lord Burghley, K.G. (1520-1598).

Bust, life-size, to left; white slashed doublet, fur-trimmed cloak, white ruff, black hat with jewel; collar of the Garter and George. (See No. 182.) Panel 19¼ × 12 in.

By Marc Gheeraedts. *Lent by* The Hon. Mrs. Trollope.

101. Sir A. Palmer.

Full-length, life-size, to left; in dark dress with gold braid. Size 82 × 51 in.

By Marc Gheeraedts. *Lent by* The Hon. Mrs. Trollope.

ROOM IV.

Pictures and Autographs.

REIGN OF MARY. (1553-1558.)

Mary, dau. of Henry VIII. and Katherine of Aragon, born at Greenwich, February 8, 1516; succeeded July 6, 1553; crowned November 30, 1553; died at St. James's, November 17, 1558, and was buried in Henry VII.'s Chapel in Westminster. She married, July 25, 1554, Philip II., King of Spain, son of Charles V. the Emperor, but had no issue.

102. LADY JANE GREY (1537-1554).

Small size, half-length, seated in a room near a window; rich crimson dress, with square-cut low body; right hand turning leaves of a missal, open on a desk beside her; tall, gilt-covered cup on table to her left. Panel 21 × 15 in.

Lady Jane Grey, celebrated for her talents, her virtues, and her misfortunes, was the eldest dau. of Henry Grey, Marquess of Dorset, and Frances Brandon (dau. of Charles Brandon, Duke of Suffolk, and Mary, sister of Henry VIII., and widow of Louis XII. of France). Lady Jane was born at Broadgate Hall, Leicestershire, in 1537, and having discovered at an early age surprising talents, received as tutor Aylmer, afterwards Bishop of London, under whose care she made rapid progress in the arts and sciences, and particularly in languages, being able to speak and write Latin and Greek, as well as French and Italian, adding to these some knowledge of Hebrew, Chaldee, and Arabic. She imbibed from her tutor the principles of the Reformation, to which she always remained firmly attached. When Dudley, Duke of Northumberland, perceived the declining health of Edward VI., he induced that monarch to pass over his sisters, Mary and Elizabeth, and to nominate Lady Jane his successor. His next move was to marry her to his son, Lord Guildford Dudley, thus hoping to secure the crown to his own family. On the death of Edward VI., Northumberland proclaimed Lady Jane Grey Queen, but her elevation to the throne, to which she herself was strongly opposed, only lasted a few days, and as it was during the Epiphany she was called the "twelfth-day Queen." The populace, resenting the unscrupulous conduct of Northumberland and of the Duke of Suffolk, rallied round Mary, and Lady Jane and her husband were confined in the Tower, accused of high treason, and being condemned, were both executed on the same day, February 12, 1554.

By LUCAS DE HEERE.   Lent by The EARL SPENCER, K.G.

103. LADY JANE GREY (1537-1554).

Three-quarter length, life-size, full face; jewelled cap; small, close-fitting, gold-edged ruff and cuffs; ermine-trimmed black surcoat over dark dress, with jewelled and embroidered sleeves; red rose in right hand, book in left. Panel 34 × by 25 in.

By LUCAS DE HEERE.   Lent by JOHN J. JACKSON, ESQ.

104. SIR EDMOND TRAFFORD, KNT. (1526-1590).

Born June 3rd, 1526. Three-quarter length, life-size; black hat, white doublet, dark, short cloak and trunk hose; shield of arms to his right; dated 1572, aged 45. Panel 45 × 35 in.

Lent by SIR HUMPHREY DE TRAFFORD, BART.

105. FRANCES BRANDON, DUCHESS OF SUFFOLK, AND HER SECOND HUSBAND, ADRIAN STOKES (dated 1559).

Small half-lengths of the Duchess of Suffolk on the left, and Adrian Stokes on the right. She wears black dress with tags and jewels, gold-edged ruffs at neck and wrists, black jewelled hood; two necklaces of pearls, one with pendant; right hand resting on cushion and holding glove, left holding ring. He wears light-coloured embroidered doublet, black fur-lined surcoat slashed and with tags, ruffs at neck and wrists edged with pink, chain round neck; right hand on hip, left holding gloves; sword at his side. Above her head, ÆTATIS XXXVI.; above his, ÆTATIS XXI. Dated MDLIX. Panel 19¼ × 27 in.

From the Strawberry Hill Collection. Vertue says of this picture:—"It is painted in oil colours in a very skilful and lively manner by a most curious hand. The date on it is 1559, and the mark HE shows it to have been painted by Lucas de Heere. The whole picture, well preserved, is now in the curious cabinet of pictures of the Honourable Horace Walpole, Esq., from whence the engraving is taken. It not only represents Frances, Duchess of Suffolk, relict of Henry Grey, Duke of Suffolk, in her 36th year; but also with her portrait is joined that of her second husband, Adrian Stokes, or Stock, Esq., æt. xxi., who erected a famous monument for her in St. Edmund's Chapel, in Westminster Abbey, soon after her death, an. dom. 1561." Walpole (*Anecdotes of Painting*) describes the picture as being "in perfect preservation, the colouring of the hands clear and with great nature, and the draperies, which are black, with furs and jewels highly finished and sound, though the manner of the whole is stiff. This picture was in the collection of Lord Oxford." Adrian Stokes, who married the Duchess of Suffolk, March 1, 1555, is said to have acted as her master of the horse. In spite of this disparity of social position, the marriage appears to have been a happy one, as at her death in December, 1559, she left him in possession of large estates in Warwickshire and Leicestershire. In 1571 Stokes was returned to Parliament for Leicestershire, having under his charge Lady Mary Grey, his step-daughter, and about that period married secondly, Anne, widow of Sir Nicholas Throgmorton. He died November 30, 1586, without issue, and his estates devolved upon his brother William.

By LUCAS DE HEERE.   Lent by COLONEL WYNNE-FINCH.

Room IV.] *Portraits.* 37

106. Sir William Cordell, Knt. (d. 1581).

Three-quarter length, seated in armchair, behind which is a dog, turned to right; black cap and dress, with fur-trimmed gown and small frill ruff; small book in left hand. AN. 1565, ÆTATIS 75. Panel 44¼ × 32 in.

Born at Edmonton, Middlesex; educated at Cambridge; entered Parliament, and was appointed Solicitor-General to Queen Mary in 1553. Constituted Master of the Rolls in 1557, and a member of the Privy Council; was continued in office by Queen Elizabeth, and sat in Parliament till his death. He took much interest in Merchant Taylors' School, and rendered material assistance in the foundation of St. John's College, Oxford.

By Cornelius de Zeen.   Lent by St. John's College, Oxford.

107. Portrait of a Lady.

Bust, life-size, to left; black gown and head-dress, with high open white ruff. Panel 17 × 14½ in.
By Sir Antonio More.   Lent by The Duke of Devonshire, K.G.

108. Cardinal Pole (1500–1558).

Nearly full-length, life-size, seated, to right, in Cardinal's robes and biretta; his right arm on chair, his left placed on left leg. Inscribed, REGINALDVS POLE CARDINALIS LEGATVS 1555. Canvas 40 × 39 in.

Reginald Pole, Cardinal and Archbishop of Canterbury, born in 1500, was a younger son of Sir Richard Pole, and Margaret, Countess of Salisbury, dau. of the Duke of Clarence, the brother of Edward IV. He was educated at Sheen and Magdalen College, Oxford, and in 1520 proceeded to Italy to prosecute his studies. Returning in 1525, he incurred the displeasure of Henry VIII. for opposing his divorce and the Reformation, and was attainted; but as the King could not seize his person, owing to his having withdrawn from England, his mother and several members of his family were put to death for corresponding with him. In 1537 Pole was sent as Legate by the Pope to France and the Low Countries, from both which states Henry in vain demanded his extradition. On the accession of Mary his attainder was reversed, and he was welcomed back to England as Papal Legate, and succeeded Cranmer as Archbishop of Canterbury in 1555. He died at Lambeth, November 18, 1558, on the same day as Mary, and was buried at Canterbury, leaving behind him the character of a strictly conscientious man, and of a mild, generous, and tolerant spirit. The cruelties of Mary's reign do not seem in any way imputable to Pole, although as Papal Legate the proceedings were often taken in his name; in fact, for his mildness, his conduct was displeasing at Rome, and he would have been removed from his office but for the personal favour of the Queen.

By Annibale Carracci.   Lent by The Trustees of the late Lord Donington.

109. Philip II. of Spain (1556–1598).

Head to right; black doublet, white ruff. Panel 17 × 12 in.
Lent by W. S. Ogden, Esq.

110. QUEEN MARY (1553-1558).

Three-quarter length, life-size, to left; gold-embroidered and jewelled robe, sewn with pearls, sleeves slashed, and with sable trimming, black and white jewelled head-dress, necklace of pearls on her breast, locket with pendent pearl; pomander hanging from waist, hands folded, rings on the fingers; in background red curtain. Signed H F 1554. Panel 40 × 30 in.

By LUCAS DE HEERE. Lent by The SOCIETY OF ANTIQUARIES.

111. QUEEN MARY (1553-1558).

Three-quarter length, life-size, standing, hands clasped, holding gloves; black fur-lined robe over white red-embroidered dress, jewelled cap. Panel 34 × 27 in.

Lent by The DUKE OF DEVONSHIRE, K.G.

112. PHILIP II. OF SPAIN (1556-1598).

Three-quarter length, standing, to right; black slashed tunic over yellow doublet and trunk hose, right hand resting on chair, left holds gloves, black cap; badge of the Garter suspended round neck. Canvas 44½ × 35 in.

Philip II., King of Spain, and also of England (1554-1558), son of Charles V., Emperor of Germany, and Isabella of Portugal, born at Valladolid, May 21, 1527, succeeded to the Crown of Spain on the abdication of his father in 1556, and in 1580, on the direct male line of Portugal becoming extinct, he laid claim to the throne, and annexed the Portuguese Kingdom to the Spanish monarchy. He died in the Escurial at Madrid, September 13, 1598. Philip married—first, in 1543, Maria, dau. of John III. of Portugal; secondly, in 1554, Mary, Queen of England; thirdly, in 1560, Isabella de Valois, dau. of Henry II. of France; and fourthly, in 1570, Anne, dau. of the Emperor Maximilian II.

By PAUL VERONESE. Lent by The VISCOUNT DILLON.

113. STEPHEN GARDINER, BISHOP OF WINCHESTER (1483-1555).

Half-length, life-size, to left; in black cap and rochet, with fur collar. Panel 21 × 17 in.

Lent by The DUKE OF DEVONSHIRE, K.G.

114. PORTRAIT OF A LADY.

Half-length, life-size, to left; black dress slashed with white, lace lappet, white embroidered ruff, carcanet of jewels on her head, cameo necklace; over shoulders gold chain in five rows with pendent medallion of St. George. Panel 21¼ × 14¾ in.

By MARC GHEERAEDTS. Lent by The DUKE OF DEVONSHIRE, K.G.

115. CÆSARE ADELMARE (d. 1569).

Three-quarter length, standing to right; black cap and black slashed dress with red sleeves, broad gold chain round neck, gloves in right hand, left on hilt of sword; curtain to left, fluted columns to right, on plinth of which is "Ætatis suæ 39 An°· Dm. 1558. Post Tempestatem Pranguillitas." Panel 49½ × 39½ in.

Room IV.] *Portraits.* 39

Cæsare Adelmare, 2nd son of Pietro Maria Adelmare of Treviso, Italy, and of Paola, daughter and co-heiress of Giovanni de Pavolo Cesarino ; came to England in 1550, and was physician to Queen Mary and Queen Elizabeth ; married Margaret, daughter of Martin Perin, Treasurer in Ireland. He died in 1569.

Lent by Capt. Cottrell-Dormer.

116. Ferdinando Stanley, 5th Earl of Derby, K.G. (d. 1594).

Bust ; open-lace edged collar, black doublet. Canvas 30 × 24 in.

Son of Henry, 4th Earl ; married (1579) Alice, daughter of Sir John Spencer, of Althorpe, an accomplished man and a poet. During the alarm of the Spanish invasion was Mayor of Liverpool, being then Lord Strange, and raised a large force of horsemen ; K.G. ; died by witchcraft, as was said, perhaps by poison, 16 April, 1594 ; celebrated by Spenser under the name of "Amyntas."

Lent by The Earl of Derby.

117. Queen Elizabeth as Princess (b. 1533, d. 1603).

Small half-length, to left ; black fur-lined dress, chemise and ruffs embroidered with gold, gold head-dress jewelled, gold necklace, with pendent black ring ; in right hand, book ; in left, glove, resting on cushion ; jewel waist-band. Panel 20 × 14 in.

Lent by The Lord Kenyon.

118. Stephen Gardiner, Bishop of Winchester (1483-1555).

Small life-size to the waist ; episcopal habit ; red book in right hand. Panel 19 × 14 in.

Statesman and divine ; studied at Trinity Hall, Cambridge ; was secretary to Cardinal Wolsey, secured the favour of Henry VIII., and was employed in the matter of his divorce from Queen Katherine ; appointed Bishop of Winchester in 1531 ; opposed the Reformation ; imprisoned in Edward VI.'s reign ; released and made Lord Chancellor by Queen Mary.

Lent by Trinity Hall, Cambridge.

119. Elizabeth, Lady Raleigh (d. 1647).

Three-quarter length, life-size, to left, resting right hand on arm of chair ; lace head-dress with flowers, black and red brocaded velvet robe, rich ruff, chemisette and cuffs of yellow lace. Panel 44 × 31¼ in.

Dau. of Sir Nicholas Throckmorton ; was married in 1590 to Sir Walter Raleigh, by whom she had two sons, Walter and Carew.

Lent by The Lord Sackville.

120. Alice Spencer, Countess of Derby (1556–1636).

Reddish hair ; small black head-dress, large ruff, sleeves and stomacher covered with lace ; feather fan in left hand ; date 1598 ; age 42. Panel 30 × 25 in.

Youngest of six daughters of Sir John Spencer, of Althorpe ; born 1556 ; married (1579)

Ferdinando, 5th Earl of Derby (No. 116); celebrated by Spenser under the name of "Amaryllis"; married, secondly, in 1600, Thomas Egerton, Lord Chancellor Ellesmere, his third wife; received, 1602, a visit at Harefield from Queen Elizabeth; died 26 January, 1635-6. Milton wrote his beautiful little pastoral, "Arcades," to be acted in compliment to her.

Lent by The EARL OF DERBY.

121. MARY, LADY MILDMAY (d. 1576).

Three-quarter length, to left, standing by table; black head-dress and gown, with close-fitting ruff and lace tippet; double gold necklace, looped up on breast; holding Chinese fan with both hands. "An°· Dmi. 1574. Ætatis suæ 46." Panel 32¼ × 24 in.

Daughter of William Walsingham, by Joyce, daughter of Edmund Denny, Baron of Exchequer, and sister of Sir Francis Walsingham.

Lent by EMMANUEL COLLEGE, CAMBRIDGE.

122. QUEEN MARY (1553-1558).

Bust, life-size, to left; close-fitting black dress, with open high collar, showing white lining embroidered with pattern in blue lines, frill around neck, black and white jewelled cap, with black veil; from triple chain of pearls round her neck hangs a richly-chased jewel, with large pendent pearl; on the background is a cartel, inscribed, *Queene Marie.* Panel 19¼ in.

This portrait was probably taken from the celebrated picture at Madrid, painted by Sir Antonio More, at the time of her marriage with Philip II., and which still remains in the gallery there. It represents the Queen life-size, seen to the knees, and seated in a square-back chair, holding a rose in her right hand, and a pair of gloves in her left. More received a gold chain worth £100, and £100 a year as painter to their Majesties for painting the picture. Van Mander states that More made many copies of this picture, and gave them to the nobility, even to Cardinal Granvelle and the Emperor himself. The large jewel in her dress is still in the possession of a family in England which traces its descent from Tudor times.

By SIR ANTONIO MORE. Lent by The DEAN AND CHAPTER OF DURHAM.

123. PORTRAIT OF A MAN.

Three-quarter length, life-size, to right; semi-suit of armour, peascod breastplate, with gorget attached, full arms and pauldrons, edged with jewelled stuff, crested helmet—open cask—bears plumes of jewelled white feathers. He stands in front of his tent, which bears his coat of arms, and holds a commander's baton in his right hand, his left rests on his sword. Panel, 44 × 33½ in.

Lent by The LORD SACKVILLE.

124. SIR WALTER MILDMAY, KNT. (d. 1589).

Full length, life-size, to left; in black doublet, trunks, hose, gown and cap, white ruffs at neck and wrists; right hand on book placed on table; left on hip; view of landscape with castle in background; red curtain, inscribed AN. DNI 1588 ÆTATIS SVÆ 66 VIRTVTE NON VI. Panel 74 × 47 in.

Room IV.] *Portraits.* 41

Sir Walter Mildmay, of Apthorpe, 4th son of Sir Thomas Mildmay, of Moulsham, Essex, was educated at Christ College, Cambridge, and appointed by Henry VIII. one of the Surveyors-General of the Court of Augmentations. He was knighted by Edward VI., February 22, 1547, was included in several commissions for the regulation of the coinage and revenue, and sat in Parliament from 1552-1556. By Elizabeth he was made Chancellor of the Duchy of Lancaster, Under-Treasurer of the Exchequer, Chancellor of the Exchequer, and a Privy Councillor. In 1584 he purchased the suppressed convent of Blackfriars at Cambridge, and founded Emmanuel College. He died May 31, 1589, and was buried in St. Bartholomew's Church, Smithfield.

Lent by EMMANUEL COLLEGE, CAMBRIDGE.

125. THOMAS PERCY, EARL OF NORTHUMBERLAND, K.G. (1528-1572).

Full-length, life-size, kneeling on left knee slightly to left before a stool; in black doublet and trunks, fur-lined surcoat. Garter on knee, and badge suspended from neck; right hand holding book on stool. Inscribed ESPERANCE EN DIEU MAY COMPHORT: ÆTATIS SUÆ 38 AN DNI 1566 ET DIE DEC⁰· IUN. Panel, 48 × 34½ in.

Born 1528, eldest son of Sir Thomas Percy, brother and heir-presumptive of Henry Algernon, 6th Earl of Northumberland, who led the vanguard of the "Pilgrimage of Grace," and for which he was executed, and honours forfeited. Sir Thomas was made Governor of Prudhoe Castle, and created Earl of Northumberland in 1557; married in 1558 Anne Somerset, daughter of the Earl of Worcester. In conjunction with the Earl of Westmoreland, he in 1569 led the rising in the North, the object of which was to restore the Catholic religion. Durham was captured, the altars re-erected, and masses publicly offered up for nearly a month, and the people publicly reconciled to the ancient faith.

The Earl of Sussex, Lord Provost of the North, succeeded in quelling the revolt; and the Earl, who escaped to Scotland, was betrayed into the hands of Mar, the Scottish Regent; imprisoned at Lochleven, and subsequently handed over to Elizabeth for the sum of £2,000. He was imprisoned at York, and on refusing to abjure his religion he was condemned to death, and executed August 22nd, 1572. By a decree of Pope Leo XIII., dated 1895, he was declared to be a martyr.

Lent by CAPTAIN AND MRS. SLINGSBY.

126. SIR ANTONIO MORE (1519-1575).

Three-quarter length; black doublet and trunk hose; massive gold chain; head of large dog to right of picture, on which his left hand rests. Panel 45 × 33 in.
Portrait painter; born 1519, of Dutch family, worked much in England; died 1575.

By Sir ANTONIO MORE. Lent by The EARL SPENCER, K.G.

127. JANE DORMER, DUCHESS OF FERIA (1538-1612).

Nearly full-length, life-size, to right; black dress with gold and silver embroidery, white silk embroidered sleeves, white ruff, pearls in hair, jewelled chain, girdle and bracelets; in right hand lace handkerchief, left on back of chair; red curtain in background; and inscription, ÆTATIS SVÆ 25. Canvas, 66 × 42 in.

Jane Dormer, second dau. of Sir William Dormer and Mary, dau. of Sir William Sidney of Penshurst, born at Heythrop, Oxon, January 6, 1538, was taken at an early age into the household of Princess Mary, and became her constant companion when Queen. She married,

D

December 29, 1558, Don Gomez Suarez de Figueroa, Duke of Feria, whom she joined in Flanders in the following year. From Flanders the Duke and Duchess went to Spain, where he died in 1571, immediately after his appointment as Governor of the Low Countries. The Duchess continued to reside on her late husband's estates, and earned the esteem and regard of all by her liberal and charitable nature. She died at Madrid, January 13, 1612. She not only corresponded with Mary Queen of Scots, whom she met at Amboise, on her way to Spain, Mary signing herself, "Your perfect friend, old acquaintance, and dear cousin," but also at least with four Popes—Gregory XIII., Sixtus V., Clement VIII., and Paul V. Henry Clifford, her servant, thus describes her: "She was somewhat higher than ordinary, of a comely person, a lively aspect, a gracious countenance, very clear skinned, and quick in senses."

Lent by CAPTAIN COTTRELL DORMER.

128. REGINALD, CARDINAL POLE (1500-1558).

Three-quarter size, seated; long grey beard, dark biretta cap and rochet; books to his left, green curtain at back. Canvas 45 × 36 in.

By PERINO DEL VAGA.   Lent by The EARL SPENCER, K.G.

129. SIR THOMAS EGERTON, BARON ELLESMERE, VISCOUNT BRACKLEY, LORD CHANCELLOR (1540?-1617).

Three-quarter length, life-size, to left, seated; he wears Chancellor's robes, and holds a paper in right hand; on a table is the Great Seal. Canvas 48¼ × 38¼ in.

Sir Thomas Egerton, Baron Ellesmere and Viscount Brackley, Lord Chancellor, natural son of Sir Richard Egerton, of Ridley, Cheshire, born about 1540, was educated at Brasenose College, Oxford, called to the bar, became Solicitor-General in 1581, Attorney-General in 1592, and was knighted in the following year. On April 10, 1594, Egerton was appointed Master of the Rolls, and Lord Keeper, May 6, 1596, in which capacity he took a prominent part in the imprisonment and trial of Essex, having been present at the Council when the Queen boxed Essex's ears. On the accession of James I. Egerton was reappointed Lord Keeper, and subsequently promoted to the Lord Chancellorship, with the dignity of Baron Ellesmere, an office which he filled till within a few days of his death. In 1616 he was created Viscount Brackley, and James I. promised him an earldom, but he died before the patent could be made out, March 15, 1617. His only surviving son, John, was created Earl of Bridgewater on May 27 following. Elizabeth familiarly called him her "dromedary."

Lent by The LORD EGERTON OF TATTON.

130. MARY HUNGERFORD, BARONESS HUNGERFORD, AFTERWARDS HASTINGS.

Three-quarter length, life-size, to left; in widow's cap, dark furred robe, red sleeves, coral rosary in left hand; in right, the red rose of Lancaster. Panel 33 × 36 in.

Mary, Baroness Hungerford, was the only dau. and heiress of Sir Thomas Hungerford, son of Robert, 3rd Baron Hungerford, who having espoused the cause of Edward IV., but afterwards exerting himself for the restoration of Henry VI., was seized, tried at Salisbury as a traitor, and executed. She married Edward Hastings, son and heir of William, 1st Lord Hastings, and the attainders of her father and grandfather having been reversed in the first Parliament of Henry VII., she had restoration of the honours and estates of her family, and in consequence bore the titles of Lady Hungerford, Botreaux, Molines, and Moelst. Her son and successor, George Hastings, was created Earl of Huntingdon, December 8, 1529.

Lent by The TRUSTEES OF THE LATE LORD DONINGTON.

131. THE PRINCESS ELIZABETH, OR "THE PERFECT WIFE."

Small, full-length, standing on a tortoise; white dress over crimson-broidered kirtle, white shoes with roses, lace ruff, jewels and feather in hair, dark green sash round left arm, necklace of pearls with pendant. Index finger of the right hand pressed on lips, a dove rests on the left hand. Keys attached to red girdle. She stands on an Eastern carpet; red curtains, chair, and cushions in background. Panel 22 × 17 in.

This picture is described by Granger *(Biogr. Hist. I.*, 101) as having been in the collection of the late James West, Esq. It was engraved in mezzotint by John Faber, jun., in 1742, as "*The most illustrious Princess Elizabeth, crowned Queen of England, anno* 1558, *H. Holbein, pinxt.* 1558." In a letter from Mr. Richard Bull to Granger (now in the College Library at Eton) dated February 23, 1773, he states that Walpole was always uncertain whether it was a portrait of the Princess Elizabeth, and that he himself doubted whether it was a portrait at all. A similar picture is at Stanmer Park, but the figure differs. The latter is enclosed in a (modern?) gilt frame, on which is inscribed round the picture—

Uxor amet, sileat, servet nec ubique vagetur
Hoc Testudo docet, clavis labra juntaque Turtur.

This picture was part of the famous Lexington Collection, and then belonged to Lord George Manners Sutton. It is now in the possession of the Earl of Chichester, great-grandson of Amelia D'Arcy, Countess of Holdernesse, whose great-grandmother, Bridget D'Arcy, was sister of Lord Lexington. In the *Emblemata* of Hadrianus Junius, drawn by Geoffroy Ballain, and published in 1565, there occurs a similar figure with the exception of the dove. It is entitled, "Uxoriæ Virtutes," and below are some appropriate verses in Latin.

Lent by G. E. MARTIN, ESQ.

132. EDWARD, LORD HASTINGS OF LOUGHBOROUGH, K.G. (d. 1558).

Three-quarter length, towards left; black doublet, laced with gold, ermine-lined surcoat, black jewelled cap; around his neck the collar of the Garter with George; right hand on hip, left on hilt of sword; shield of arms to left. Panel 34 × 26 in.

Sir Edward Hastings, created Lord Hastings of Loughborough, was the younger son of Mary, Baroness Hungerford. In 1550 he served the office of sheriff for the counties of Warwick and Leicester, and in the same year took part in an expedition to dislodge the French from a position between Boulogne and Calais. On the death of Edward VI. he supported the cause of Mary, and was made a Privy Councillor, Master of the Horse, and Collector-General of the Queen's Revenues in the City of London. In 1554 he was sent with Sir Thomas Cornwallis to Dartford to remonstrate with Wyat, who had raised a rebellion to oppose the Queen's marriage.

He was appointed one of the commissioners to arrange with the Emperor Charles V. for the reception of Cardinal Pole in this country, and also in 1556 for the inquiry into the Dudley conspiracy. In 1557 Hastings was constituted Chamberlain of the royal household, and was elevated to the peerage, January 15, 1558, as Baron Hastings of Loughborough, but dying the same year at Stoke Pogis the title became extinct.

Lent by The TRUSTEES OF THE LATE LORD DONINGTON.

133. ELIZABETH LEICESTER, LADY TRAFFORD.

Three-quarter size; jewelled head-dress, close frill, fur-lined surcoat, showing oversleeves of gauze; dated 1571, age 36; shield of arms to her right. Panel 45 × 32 in. Wife of Sir Edward Trafford, Kt.

Lent by SIR HUMPHREY DE TRAFFORD, BART.

133*. THOMAS RADCLIFFE, 3RD EARL OF SUSSEX, K.G. (1526–1583).

Small, half-length, to right; black doublet with furred surcoat, white ruffs at neck and wrists, black cap, with jewels; Garter chain with George; right hand holds white staff of office. Panel 16 × 12 in.

Thomas Radclyffe, 4th Lord Fitz-Walter, and 3rd Earl of Sussex, eldest son of Henry Radclyffe, 2nd Earl, and Lady Elizabeth Howard, dau. of Thomas 2nd Duke of Norfolk, born in 1526, was appointed Ambassador by Queen Mary to Charles V. to treat of her marriage with Philip of Spain; constituted in 1555 Lord Deputy of Ireland, and in the next year chief justice of the forests south of Trent. Created a K.G., Sussex was re-appointed Lord Deputy of Ireland, and in 1560 Lord Lieutenant. Elizabeth employed him in the negotiations of the proposed marriage between herself and the Archduke Charles of Austria. In 1569 he was made Lord President of the North, and the next year invaded Scotland. He sat subsequently on the trial of the Duke of Norfolk, and was one of the Commissioners in 1581 to treat of the Queen's marriage with the Duke of Anjou. He died in June, 1583, and was buried at Boreham, in Sussex.

Lent by C. J. RADCLYFFE, ESQ.

ROOM V.

Pictures, Plate, Jewellery, Coins, Seals, and Furniture.

REIGN OF ELIZABETH. (1558-1603.)

Elizabeth, daughter of Henry VIII. and Anne Boleyn, born at Greenwich, September 7, 1533; succeeded November 17, 1558; crowned June 15, 1559; died at Richmond, March 24, 1603, and was buried at Westminster.

134. WILLIAM PAULET, 1ST MARQUESS OF WINCHESTER, K.G. (1476-1572).

Half-length, to left; black cap and gown, collar, and badge of the Garter, holds a staff in his left hand. Panel 15½ × 12½ in.

William Paulet, Earl of Wiltshire and Marquess of Winchester, son of Sir John Paulet, Knt., of Nunny, and Alice, dau. of Sir William Poulett, Knt., of Hinton St. George, Somerset, at an early age stood high in favour with Henry VIII., was knighted, made Comptroller of the King's Household in 1535, Treasurer in 1537, and in the next year created Lord St. John of Basing. In 1541 he was Master of the Wards, in 1542 elected a K.G., in 1544 accompanied Henry at the taking of Boulogne, and was one of the King's executors and a member of his son's Council, in whose first year he had custody of the Great Seal, was Lord Master of the Household and President of the Council. On January 19 he was created Earl of Wiltshire, made Lord High Treasurer, and October 12, 1551, Marquess of Winchester. By his counsels he in a great measure prevented the Duke of Northumberland's attempt to place Lady Jane Grey upon the throne, for which the Queens, Mary and Elizabeth, continued him in his Treasurer's office, which he held for thirty years. Being asked how he preserved his place through so many changes of Government, he replied, "*By being a willow and not an oak.*" He died at Basing, March 10, 1572, in his ninety-seventh year.

Lent by The SOCIETY OF ANTIQUARIES.

135. William Paulet, 1st Marquis of Winchester, K.G. (1476-1572).

Half-length, to left ; black cap and gown, badge of the Garter suspended from a ribbon, staff in left hand. Panel 15 × 11¼ in.

Lent by The Duke of Devonshire, K.G.

136. Court of Wards and Liveries.

View of the interior of a "court," with various personages seated at a table, others standing "without the bar." The seated figure at the head of the table is supposed to be Lord Burghley, Master of the Court from the beginning of the reign of Elizabeth till his death in 1598 ; on either side of him are the Chief Justices, as assessors ; the second figure, on the left, may be Thomas Seckford, the Surveyor, 1580-1589 ; the third, on the left, George Goring, the Receiver-General, reading a scroll ; next to him Marmaduke Servant, the usher of the Court, with rod in his hand. The second figure to the right is probably Richard Kingsmill, attorney ; and next to him William Tooke, the auditor, with a book open before him ; and on his left, Seward Taylor, the messenger. The three persons at the lower end of the table answer to the clerks. Outside the bar, on the left, is the Queen's serjeant in royal robes ; and opposite, on the other side, is a counsellor pleading. At the bottom, without the bar, are two sergeants, Thomas Gent and Edmund Anderson. Canvas 30 × 28 in.

The above particulars are taken from Vertue's engraving, published in the *Vetusta Monumenta*, Vol. I., pl. 70. The names of the various personages are mostly conjectural. The Court of Wards and Liveries was first erected in the reign of Henry VIII. for the administration of the estates of the King's wards during their minority, and for delivery of seisin upon coming of age.

Lent by The Duke of Richmond and Gordon, K.G.

137. Robert Dudley, Earl of Leicester, K.G. (1531-1588).

Three-quarter length, life-size, towards right; white doublet and trunk hose, white sword belt, sword and dagger, black steel gorget, white ruff ; his right hand rests on table ; background inscribed, *Federigo Zucchero, A.D.*, 1575. *Robert Dudley, Earl of Leicester, Ae.* 43. Panel 44 × 32 in.

By Federigo Zucchero.   Lent by G. Milner-Gibson-Cullum, Esq.

138. Sir Thomas Gargrave, Knt. (1495-1579).

Small bust, to left ; black doublet, black surcoat lined with fur, black cap ; gold chain round neck ; background inscribed an. do. 1570 aeta. svæ. 75. Panel 16 × 12½ in.

Sir Thomas Gargrave, Speaker of the House of Commons, son of Thomas Gargrave, of Wakefield, and Elizabeth, dau. of William Levett, of Normanton, Yorkshire, was born in 1495 at Wakefield. Appointed a member of the Council of the North, he accompanied the Earl of Warwick into Scotland in 1547, acted as Treasurer to the Expedition, and was knighted. He represented the City of York in 1547, and again in 1553, but sat for the county in 1555. He was

Room V.]   *Portraits.*   47

chosen Speaker of the House of Commons in 1558-9, and in the following year was made Vice-President of the Council of the North. He took an active part in defeating the rebellion of the North under the Earls of Northumberland and Westmoreland, and held Pontefract Castle and the neighbouring bridges, for which he received the thanks of the Queen. He purchased a large amount of land at Wakefield, including Kingsley Hall, where he resided for some time, and eventually procured Nostell Priory. Gargrave died March 28, 1579, and was buried at Wragley. This portrait of him was formerly in the possession of Sir Levett Hanson, of Normanton, who left it to his sister, Lady Cullum. A similar portrait is said to belong to Viscount Galway at Serlby, in Nottinghamshire.

Lent by G. MILNER-GIBSON-CULLUM, ESQ.

139. THOMAS HOWARD, 4TH DUKE OF NORFOLK, K.G. (1536-1572).

Small bust, to left; black coat, white ruff, black jewelled cap with feather. Panel 11 × 8¼ in.
Lent by The DUKE OF NORFOLK, E.M., K.G.

140. "THE VENERABLE" PHILIP HOWARD, EARL OF ARUNDEL (1557-1595).

Small bust, to right; white doublet with silver lace and buttons, black coat, large white ruff. Panel, circular, 1? in.

Philip Howard, Earl of Arundel, eldest son of Thomas, 4th Duke of Norfolk, who was executed in 1572, and Mary, dau. and heir of Henry Fitzalan, Earl of Arundel, born June 28, 1557, was baptized at Whitehall, Philip II. standing as godfather. He was educated by his father as a Protestant, but at an early age changed this creed for that of his ancestors. He assumed the title of Earl of Arundel in right of his mother, and was accordingly summoned among the peers in 1583, and in the same year restored in blood. At one time he was a great favourite with Queen Elizabeth, but soon fell under suspicion on account of his strong Catholic views. He was in consequence summoned before the Star Chamber, condemned to a fine of £10,000, and imprisoned during the Queen's pleasure. After enduring a year's confinement he was, in 1589, arraigned for high treason, and sentence of death was passed upon him; but Elizabeth, having secretly resolved that he should not be executed, kept him in prison till his death, October 19, 1595, which occurred, as stated on his coffin, *non absque veneni suspitione*. He married, at the age of fourteen, Anne, sister and co-heir of Thomas, last Lord Dacre of Gillesland, by whom he had issue one son, Thomas, known as Lord Maltravers, and one daughter, Elizabeth, who died young. By order of Pope Leo XIII. he was declared a confessor, and styled "Venerable."

By F. ZUCCHERO.   Lent by The DUKE OF NORFOLK, E.M., K.G.

141. MARY SIDNEY, COUNTESS OF PEMBROKE (1550?-1621).

Three-quarter length, life-size, facing; black dress, white lace cap, ruff, and cuffs; she holds a book in her right hand. Panel 35 × 27 in.

Mary, dau. of Sir Henry Sidney, Knt., and Lady Mary, eldest dau. of John, Duke of Northumberland, born about 1550, was the third wife of Henry, 2nd Earl of Pembroke, by whom she had issue two sons, William and Philip, both of whom succeeded to the title, and one

Exhibition of the Royal House of Tudor.

daughter, Anne, who died young. She lived to a very advanced age, and died at her house in Aldersgate Street, September 25, 1621, and was buried near her husband in the chancel of Salisbury Cathedral. Her brother, Sir Philip Sidney, dedicated to her his celebrated romance, the *Arcadia*. She was carefully educated in modern and ancient languages, including Hebrew, wrote many verses, but the small pieces of her prose surpass them. On her death were written the well-known lines—

> "Underneath this sable hearse
> Lies the subject of all verse—
> Sidney's sister, Pembroke's mother:
> Death, ere thou hast slain another
> Learn'd and fair and good as she,
> Time shall cast a dart at thee."

By MARC GHEERAEDTS.   Lent by The EARL OF PEMBROKE.

142. THOMAS SACKVILLE, 1ST EARL OF DORSET, K.G. (1536-1608).

Three-quarter length, life-size, to right; black doublet and fur-lined surcoat, white ruff, black hat, George of the Garter suspended to blue ribbon; right hand holds staff of Treasurer, left rests on table; inscribed, TOVIOVRS LOYALL; name below. Panel 35½ × 29 in.

Thomas Sackville, Lord Buckhurst, Earl of Dorset, poet and statesman, the only son of Sir Richard Sackville, born at Buckhurst, in Sussex, in 1536, was educated at Oxford and Cambridge, and entered at the Inner Temple. Whilst studying law, he wrote with Thomas Norton the tragedy of *Gorboduc*, which was performed in the great hall of the Temple and Whitehall before the Queen in 1561. This is the earliest regular drama in blank verse in the English language. After travelling for some time in France and Italy, Sackville on his return entered public life, was created in 1566 Baron Buckhurst, went on an embassy in 1570 to France to treat of the proposed marriage of the Queen with the Duke of Anjou, and in 1587 was employed as ambassador to the Netherlands to adjust the differences between the Dutch and the Earl of Leicester, whose anger he drew down upon himself, and in consequence was imprisoned till the death of his formidable enemy in 1588. He was elected a K.G., and chosen Chancellor for the University of Oxford in 1589, and in 1598 succeeded Lord Burghley as Lord High Treasurer. On the accession of James I. his patent of office was renewed for life, and in the following year he was created Earl of Dorset. He died suddenly of dropsy in the brain whilst attending at the Council Board, April 19, 1608, and was buried in Westminster Abbey. Besides *Gorboduc*, Dorset wrote several other poems, of which are his *Induction*, a poetical preface to *The Mirrour for Magistrates*, *The Complaint of the Earl of Buckingham*, &c.

By MARC GHEERAEDTS.   Lent by The LORD SACKVILLE.

143. SIR JOHN SPENCER (d. 1599).

Half-length, life-size, to left; dark dress; pendent jewel from dark ribbon; dated 1590. ÆT. 57. Canvas 35 × 28 in.

Father of Robert, 1st Baron Spencer; married Mary, daughter and heir of Sir Robert Catelin, Lord Chief Justice of England.

By G. STRETES.   Lent by The EARL SPENCER, K.G.

144. SIR WILLIAM PADDY (1554–1634).

Three-quarter length, seated; red gown; holds an anatomical drawing of a heart in his right hand. Canvas 53½ × 41½ in.

Physician, educated at St John's College, Oxford; was present at the death of James I. at Theobalds, near Enfield, and wrote an account thereof in a prayer-book preserved in the Library of St. John's; supported the privileges of the College of Physicians successfully before Sir Thos. Middleton, Lord Mayor, and Sir Henry Montagu, Recorder of London.

Lent by ST. JOHN'S COLLEGE, OXFORD.

145. ROBERT DEVEREUX, 2ND EARL OF ESSEX, K.G. (1567–1601).

Half-length, life-size, to right; white doublet and ruff; jewel of K.G.; shield of arms to his left. Panel 41 × 33 in.

Robert Devereux, 2nd Earl of Essex, son of Walter, 1st Earl, born November 10, 1567, was educated at Trinity College, Cambridge. Lord Burghley, to whose guardianship he had been entrusted, introduced him to Court, where "his goodly person" and "innate courtesy" soon procured him the special favour of Elizabeth. In 1585 he accompanied the Earl of Leicester to Holland as General of the Horse, distinguished himself at the battle of Zutphen, and on his return to England was made Master of the Horse, and elected K.G. In 1591 he commanded the forces sent to the assistance of Henry IV. of France against Spain, and in 1596 accompanied Lord Howard in the expedition against Cadiz. In 1597 he was made Earl Marshal, but next year, presuming on Elizabeth's fondness and admiration for him, he rudely turned his back upon her in the Council Chamber, for which she boxed his ears, and told him "to go and be hanged." Essex was thereupon banished from the Court, but being in a measure restored to the Queen's favour, he was sent to Ireland as Lord-Lieutenant. On his concluding a treaty with the Irish Chieftain Tyrone and returning to London without the permission of the Council, he was deprived of his dignities and placed under restraint. In 1601, having attempted to excite an insurrection in London against the Queen, he was imprisoned, tried, found guilty of high treason, and executed February 25, 1601. Essex was rash, bold, and presumptuous; but brave, generous, and affectionate. In 1591, during the campaign in Normandy, Sir Thomas Coningsby (*Journal of the Seige of Rouen*) thus speaks of him: "For such a body hath he made of yron supporting travaile and passioned in all extremities that the following of him did tyre our bodies that are made of flesh and boane." Also in 1596 in the attack on Cadiz the assailants under Essex were on the point of being repulsed, when at the critical moment he rushed forward, seized his own colours, and threw them over the wall, "giving withal a most hot assault unto the gate, where, to save the honour of their ensign, happy was he that could first leap down from the wall and with shot and sword make way through the thickest press of the enemy."

By ISAAC OLIVER. Lent by The EARL SPENCER, K.G.

146. SIR EDWARD HASTINGS (d. 1603).

Three-quarter length, to left; ruff and black dress slashed with red; pendent jewel; small book in right hand, left on hip. Panel 28 × 22 in.

Sir Edward Hastings, third son of Francis, 2nd Earl of Huntingdon, by Catherine Pole, daughter of Lord Montagu, married Barbara, daughter of Sir William Devereux, of Mirevale Abbey, Warwickshire. He died in 1603.

Lent by The TRUSTEES OF THE LATE LORD DONINGTON.

147. Robert Dudley, Earl of Leicester, K.G. (1531–1588).

Full-length, life-size, to right, standing; his right hand resting on a petronel, his left is placed on his helmet, which stands on a table. He wears a white and gold doublet and trunk hose, white stockings and shoes, and the Order of the Garter. The gorget round his neck and his helmet are of steel, richly damaskeened with gold. Through a curtain drawn aside in the background is seen a tent. Canvas 81 × 52 in.

Robert Dudley, Earl of Leicester, favourite of Queen Elizabeth, born 1531, was a younger son of John Dudley, Duke of Northumberland, who was executed for the part which he took in the cause of Lady Jane Grey, and he was himself tried on the same account, but pleading guilty his life was spared, and he was imprisoned for about a year. On his release he went abroad, and was present at the battle of St. Quentin. On the accession of Elizabeth the dawn of his future began, and he was made Master of the Horse, a K.G., a Privy Councillor, High Steward of the University of Cambridge, and on September 28, 1563, was created Lord Denbigh, and the next day Earl of Leicester. For these high honours he seems to have been indebted solely to his handsome person and his courtly manner, since the course of his life shows him not to have been possessed of one single quality either of head or heart deserving of admiration. In 1585 he was sent with almost royal powers into the Low Countries, but he greatly injured the cause of the Dutch by his insolence and incapacity; yet in 1588, Elizabeth appointed him commander-in-chief of the army raised to oppose the Spanish invasion. He died suddenly on the 4th of September of the same year, not without suspicion of poison. Leicester was three times married—first, to Amy Robsart, dau. of Sir John Robsart, to whose murder the general voice of the time has charged him of being an accessory; secondly, to Lady Douglas Howard, whom he divorced; and thirdly, to Lettice, widow of the Earl of Essex, who, it is said, gave him the potion which he himself had prepared for her, and from the effects of which he died. Elizabeth called him her "Sweet Robin."

By Federigo Zucchero.   Lent by The Lord Zouche.

148. Queen Elizabeth (1558–1603).

Full-length, life-size, towards left; black jewelled dress with white silk kirtle, figures with emblems of beasts, birds, fishes, and flowers, white open ruff with gauze wings, coronet and jewels and flowers in the hair, necklet of pearls with pendants; right hand holding glove rests on cushion of throne, feather fan in left; jewelled shoes; standing on steps carpeted. Canvas 88 × 65 in.

There are several portraits of Elizabeth which abound in "concetti," and accompanied by emblems of animals or inanimate things. In a picture at Hampton Court she is represented as issuing out of a palace accompanied by two female attendants; Juno, Pallas, and Minerva seem flying before her; Juno drops her sceptre and Venus her roses; Cupid flings away his bow and arrows, and clings to his mother. Pictures at Hatfield show her in a robe sprinkled with representations of ears and eyes, also with an ermine as the emblem of charity. There is also a picture of her at Hardwick Hall, in which her bust is worked with eyelet holes, having the silk and needle hanging down from each, an allegory much too recondite for common apprehension. The pastoral poems of that age abound in compliments to her beauty, but, as Warton observes, "the present age sees her charms and her character in their proper character."

Lent by The Duke of Devonshire, K.G.

149. CHARLES HOWARD, 1ST EARL OF NOTTINGHAM (1536–1624).

Full-length, life-size, to right; in Garter robes, collar of the Garter with George; right hand resting on white staff, left on hilt of sword; in the background, through an open window is seen the Armada. Canvas 86 × 49 in.

Charles Howard, 2nd Lord Howard of Effingham, Earl of Nottingham, was the son of William, Lord Howard of Effingham, and grandson of Thomas, 2nd Duke of Norfolk. Born in 1536, he went in 1559 to congratulate Francis II. on his accession to the throne, and in 1569 was made General of the Horse in the army sent against the Earls of Northumberland and Westmoreland. In 1573 he succeeded his father in his title and estates, was installed a K.G., and made Lord Chamberlain of the Royal Household, and in 1585 constituted Lord High Admiral of England. He commanded the fleet which defeated and dispersed the Spanish Armada in 1588, and also that which captured Cadiz in 1596. For this latter success Howard was created Earl of Nottingham, and appointed Justice Itinerant of all the forests south of the Trent. In 1601 he suppressed the Earl of Essex's insurrection, and was principally concerned in bringing that nobleman to the block. James I. continued him in all his employments, and at his coronation appointed him Lord High Steward. In 1605 he went as ambassador to Spain, and in 1613 convoyed the Princess Elizabeth on her marriage to Flushing. He died December 14, 1624. The Earl married, first, Catherine Carey, dau. of Henry, Lord Hunsdon, by whom he had issue two sons (his grandson Charles succeeding him in the title) and three daughters; and secondly, Lady Margaret Stewart, dau. of James, Earl of Moray, by whom he had one son, Sir Charles Howard.

Lent by The DUKE OF NORFOLK, E.M., K.G.

150. WILLIAM CAVENDISH, 1ST EARL OF DEVONSHIRE (d. 1626).

Half-length, life-size, to left; white doublet and ruff, black cloak, left hand holds a cap, the arm rests on sword. Inscribed 1ST EARL OF DEVONSHIRE 1576, Æ SUÆ 25. Panel 27 × 21 in.

Second son of Sir William Cavendish, statesman; was created Baron Cavendish of Hardwick in 1605; aided largely in the colonisation of the Bermudas; was created Earl of Devonshire in 1615, for which title he is "reputed to have paid £10,000."

Lent by The DUKE OF DEVONSHIRE, K.G.

151. CHARLES PAGET.

Three-quarter length, life-size, standing, to left; white doublet with collar, and embroidered trunk hose; fur-trimmed cloak over left shoulder, hands on hips; in upper left corner a picture of a man shot by Cupid, and falling from a rock into the sea, with motto "Amantes Dementes," in allusion to Paget's devotion to Mary Queen of Scots; to right, arms, and "ÆTATIS 33, 1595." Panel 44 × 34 in.

Charles Paget, brother of Thomas, 3rd Lord Paget, having conceived a romantic attachment to Mary Queen of Scots, engaged in the Babington conspiracy to murder Queen Elizabeth, 1586, on the discovery of which he fled into Sussex, where he lay concealed under the name of Mope until able to escape abroad.

Lent by The LORD ZOUCHE.

152. LUCY HARRINGTON, COUNTESS OF BEDFORD (d. 1627).

Three-quarter length, life-size, seated to left, head resting on right hand; black dress, white lace ruffs and cuffs; coronet of pearls, pearl earrings, chain over shoulders; left hand holding lace handkerchief, and on third finger ring, attached by cord to waist. Canvas 57 × 41 in.

Lucy Harrington, eldest dau. of John, 1st Lord Harrington, celebrated for her taste and accomplishments, married in 1594 Edward, 3rd Earl of Bedford. Her brother John, 2nd Lord Harrington, dying in 1614, left her his heir. She died May 31, 1627, without issue, having survived her husband only a few weeks. The Countess of Bedford was a great patroness of poets, especially Donne, Ben Jonson, Drayton, and Daniel, who frequently experienced her munificence. Drayton in particular says "she rained upon them her sweet showers of gold," for which they in return wrote verses in praise of her talents and acquirements.

By G. HONTHORST.   Lent by The DUKE OF DEVONSHIRE, K.G.

153. ANNE CLIFFORD, COUNTESS OF DORSET, PEMBROKE, AND MONTGOMERY, AS A CHILD (1590-1676).

Anne Clifford, Countess of Dorset, Pembroke, and Montgomery, was the only surviving child of George, Earl of Cumberland, and Lady Margaret Russell, dau. of Francis, 2nd Earl of Bedford. Born at Skipton Castle, January 30, 1590, she married, February 25, 1609, Richard Sackville, Lord Buckhurst, by whom she had three sons, who died young, and two daughters. Lord Buckhurst dying March 28, 1624, she married, June 3, 1630, Philip Herbert, 4th Earl of Pembroke and Montgomery, by whom she had no issue, and who died in 1660. On the death of Henry Clifford, 5th and last Earl of Cumberland, without male issue, the large family estates in the North reverted to the Countess. Her passion for bricks and mortar was immense. She restored Skipton, Appleby, Brougham, Brough, Pendragon, and Bardon Tower, also several churches and chapels, and built the almshouses at Appleby. It was her custom to reside at each one of her six castles, where she freely dispensed her charity and hospitality. Though generous to her friends and dependents, she was frugal in her personal expenses, dressing after her second widowhood in black serge, living abstemiously, and pleasantly boasting "that she had never tasted wine and physic." She wrote curious memoirs of herself, preserved in the Harleian MSS. She died March 22, 1676, in her 87th year, and was buried in the vault which she had built in Appleby Church.

By F. ZUCCHERO.   Lent by COLONEL CHARLES WYNNE-FINCH.

154. HENRY FITZALAN, 23RD EARL OF ARUNDEL (1511-1580).

Three-quarter length, life-size, facing; black doublet, black ermine-lined cloak, black cap, collar of the Garter with George; in right hand gloves, left grasping hilt of his sword; inscribed A° DNI. 1558, Æ. SVÆ 56. Panel 34½ × 28½ in. Engraved in Lodge.

Lent by The DUKE OF NORFOLK, E.M., K.G.

155. QUEEN ELIZABETH (1558-1603).

Half-length, life-size, to left; black dress, with white bodice and sleeves, embroidered and jewelled, red lily issuing from each shoulder, lace ruff, jewels in hair and earring, necklace of pearls with ruby drop; in right hand, fan; in left, lily. Panel 36 × 30 in. From the Bernal Collection.

By F. ZUCCHERO.   Lent by MRS. DENT of Sudeley.

ROOM V.]   *Portraits.*   53

156. SIR WILLIAM ST. LOE.

Half-length, life-size, to left; black dress with small frill ruff, gloves in right hand. Panel 25¼ × 20½ in.

Sir William St. Loe, captain of Queen Elizabeth's Guard; third husband of "Bess of Hardwick," afterwards Countess of Shrewsbury.

Lent by The DUKE OF DEVONSHIRE, K.G.,

157. PORTRAIT OF A MAN.

Life-size, half-length, in an oval; buff jerkin, broad red sash, lace collar. Panel 23 × 18 in.
By GONZALES?   Lent by G. E. MARTIN, ESQ.

158. SIR WILLIAM CAVENDISH, KNT. (1505–1557).

Three-quarter length, life-size, to left; black coat lined with fur, black cap; ring on first finger of right hand; gloves in left. Inscribed SIR WILLIAM CAVINDISH ÆTATIS SVÆ 44. Panel 33½ × 27 in.

Sir William Cavendish, statesman, born about 1505, was the 2nd son of Thomas Cavendish, of Cavendish. Having been introduced to Court, he was in 1530 appointed a commissioner for the visitation of the monasteries; as such, securing for himself some rich grants. In 1541, he received the office of auditor of the Court of Augmentations, in 1541 became Treasurer of the King's Chamber, was knighted and sworn of the Privy Council. He stood high in favour with Edward VI., was confirmed in his offices, and received additional grants of monastic estates. Under Mary, Cavendish conformed, was reappointed treasurer of the royal chamber, and died October 25, 1557. He was three times married, his third wife being Elizabeth, daughter of John Hardwick, of Hardwick, but better known as "Bess of Hardwick," the builder of Hardwick Hall, Oldcotes, and Chatsworth.

Lent by The DUKE OF DEVONSHIRE, K.G.

159. ELIZABETH HARDWICK, COUNTESS OF SHREWSBURY, "BESS OF HARDWICK" (1519–1607).

Three-quarter length, life-size, to left; black gown and hood, white ruffs at neck and wrists; left hand holding necklace of six strings of pearls, right resting on table. Panel 42 × 32 in.

Elizabeth Hardwick, Countess of Shrewsbury, called "Bess of Hardwick," born 1520, was the dau. and co-heir of John Hardwick of Derbyshire. She married, first, Robert Barley of Barley, Derbyshire; secondly, Sir William Cavendish, Treasurer of the King's Chamber (Edward VI.); thirdly, Sir William St. Loe, Captain of the Guard of Queen Elizabeth; and fourthly, George Talbot, 6th Earl of Shrewsbury (February 9, 1568). She had prevailed upon her first and third husbands, both of whom were very rich, to settle upon her and her heirs all their wealth; and her last marriage with the Earl of Shrewsbury, one of the richest and most powerful peers of his time, added still more to her wealth, as she persuaded him also to bestow upon her a large portion of his property. She had for some time with her husband the custody of Mary Queen of Scots, whom at first she fawned upon and flattered; but her attentions were converted into the most envenomed hatred when she began to entertain ambitious schemes for her grandchild, Lady Arabella Stuart. She lived to a great old age, surviving her husband many years, and died in 1607 immensely rich, and it is said without a friend. Lodge says of her: "She was a woman of masculine understanding and conduct, proud, furious, selfish, and unfeeling, a builder, a buyer and seller of estates, a money-lender, a farmer, and a merchant of lead and coals." She erected or rebuilt Chatsworth, Hardwick, Oldcotes, Bolsover, and Worksop.

Lent by The DUKE OF DEVONSHIRE, K.G.

160. GEORGE TALBOT, 6TH EARL OF SHREWSBURY, K.G. (d. 1590).

Half-length, life-size, to left; dark dress with white ruff and pendent badge of the Garter. Canvas 27 × 21 in.

Son of Francis, 5th Earl; commanded in the North under his father in the reign of Queen Mary, was chosen K.G. in 1561, had the custody of Mary Queen of Scots, and in 1571-2 was Lord High Steward of England. Fourth husband of the celebrated Bess of Hardwick. (See No. 159.)

Lent by The DUKE OF DEVONSHIRE, K.G.

161. PORTRAIT OF A MAN.

Half-length, life-size, to right; black and gold doublet, broad red sash over left shoulder, deep falling lace collar. Panel 23 × 18 in.

By GONZALES?   Lent by G. E. MARTIN, ESQ.

162. GILBERT TALBOT, 7TH EARL OF SHREWSBURY, K.G.

Three-quarter length, life-size, standing, to left; bare-headed; black dress and circular ruff; right hand, with gloves, resting on table. Canvas 40½ × 33 in.

Gilbert Talbot, 7th Earl of Shrewsbury, son of George, 6th Earl, by his first wife, Lady Gertrude Manners; married Mary Cavendish (see No. 167), dau. of his stepmother, Elizabeth Hardwick, Countess of Shrewsbury, by her second husband, Sir William Cavendish.

Lent by The DUKE OF DEVONSHIRE, K.G.

163. SIR HENRY BROMLEY, KNT. (d. 1613).

Life-size, half-length, to right; buff leather jerkin, black steel gorget, falling embroidered collar, black trunks, right hand grasps hilt of sword, left rests on hip; inscribed, "*Anno domini ætatis suæ* 27 *ady* 8th *February.*" In the left upper corner sun hidden by clouds, with the motto, "*Sol occultus meus.*" Panel 24½ × 19½ in.

Sir Henry Bromley, eldest son of Lord Chancellor Bromley, was knighted by Queen Elizabeth in 1592, and in the same year represented the county of Worcester in Parliament. In 1597 he was returned by the county of Salop, and in the Parliament called at the accession of James I.; in 1608 he again represented the county of Worcester, being seated at Holt Castle in that county, where he died May 15, 1613, and was buried in the chancel of that parish church.

Lent by G. E. MARTIN, ESQ.

Room V.]   *Portraits.*   55

164. Lady Grace Talbot, aged 19.

Full-length, standing, to left; black dress with ruff; rose in right hand; feather fan held downwards in left; virginal with music book on table to left; castle seen through a window above. Panel 44½ × 35.

Daughter of George, 6th Earl of Shrewsbury, and sister of Gilbert, 7th Earl.

Lent by The Duke of Devonshire, K.G.

165. Sir Thomas Gresham, Knt. (1519–1579).

Three-quarter length, life-size, to right, black furred surcoat, white ruff at neck and wrists, black cap, jewelled pendant attached to chain; gloves in right hand, left on table. On cartel in background "Sr *Thos. Gresham mercator Londini*, A.M." Panel 46 × 32¼ in.

Sir Thomas Gresham, son of Sir Richard Gresham, an opulent merchant, born in 1519, studied at Gonville College, Cambridge, and in 1552 was sent to Antwerp as King's factor there, his principal duty being to negotiate foreign loans for the Crown. In 1559 he was knighted by Queen Elizabeth, and appointed for a short time ambassador at the Court of the King of Spain's Regent at Brussels. In 1564, having lost his only son, Gresham resolved to devote a portion of his great wealth to the erection of a house or exchange, like that at Antwerp, for the London merchants. The building was formally opened by Elizabeth in 1570, who named it the Royal Exchange. He also under his will founded and endowed Gresham College, and provided for the erection and support of eight almshouses. He died suddenly, November 21, 1579.

By Sir Antonio More.   Lent by Miss Sumner.

166. Sir Christopher-Yelverton, Knt. (1536–1612).

Half-length, life-size, to left; black cap, judge's robes; dated 1602. ÆT. 66. Panel 42 × 31 in.

3rd son of Sir Wm. Yelverton, of Rougham, Norfolk; studied at Gray's Inn, and rose to distinction in the law; Speaker of the House of Commons, 1597; Queen's Sergeant, 1598; Judge of the Queen's Bench, 1602; knighted by James I.

Lent by The Trustees of the late Lord Donington.

167. Mary Cavendish, Countess of Shrewsbury.

Three-quarter length, life-size, to right; black dress and circular lace ruff, long rope of pearls, jewelled badges fastened to stomacher, chinese fan in left hand. Canvas 40 × 33 in.

Mary Cavendish, daughter of Sir William Cavendish and Elizabeth Hardwick, afterwards Countess of Shrewsbury; married Gilbert Talbot, 7th Earl. (See No. 162.)

Lent by The Duke of Devonshire, K.G.

168. Peregrine, Lord Willoughby de Eresby (1554–1601).

Half-length, life-size, to left; buff doublet, white sleeves, and trunks and ruff, black gold-laced surcoat and hat; right hand on hip. Inscribed, *Peregrine Lo. Willoughbye of Erseby.* Panel 36 × 30 in.

Peregrine Bertie, Lord Willoughby de Eresby, son of Richard Bertie and Catherine, Baroness Willoughby de Eresby, born at Lower Wesel, Cleves, October 12, 1555, when his parents were fleeing from England. He was named Peregrine as he was born in *terra peregrina.* He succeeded to the title on the death of his mother in 1580, went to Denmark in 1582 to invest Frederick II. with the Garter, was engaged in the war in the Low Countries, and in 1586 succeeded Sir Philip Sidney in the Governorship of Bergen-op-Zoom. He commanded the expedition to Dieppe in 1589 to aid Henry of Navarre, and in 1598 was made Governor of Berwick, and came into frequent conflict with the Scots. He died June 25, 1601. He married Lady Mary Vere, dau. of John, 16th Earl of Oxford, and through his eldest son Robert became the ancestor of the Earls of Lindsey and Dukes of Ancaster.

Lent by The EARL OF ANCASTER.

169. SIR HENRY UNTON, KNT. (d. 1596).

Half-length, life-size, towards left; white doublet, red gold-laced cloak over left shoulder, large white ruff, black cap with jewel and aigrette; left hand holding hilt of sword; in background shield of arms. Panel 29½ × 23 in.

Sir Henry Unton, son of Sir Edward Unton, of Farringdon, Berks, and Anne, Countess of Warwick, dau. of Edward, Duke of Somerset, the "Protector," born at Wadley, near Farringdon, was educated at Oriel College, Oxford, received early employment under Lord Chancellor Hatton, was present in 1586 at the siege of Zutphen, and for his gallantry on that occasion was knighted by the Earl of Leicester. In 1590 he was made an honorary M.A. of Oxford, and appointed Ambassador to France in 1591, where he "stoutly" challenged the Duke of Guise in defence of his royal mistress, and again in 1593. He died in the camp of the French king at Lafere, March 23, 1596, and was buried at Farringdon. He married Dorothy, eldest dau. of Sir Thomas Wroughton, of Broad Hinton, Wilts, but had no issue. She afterwards married George Shirley, and died in 1634.

There is in the National Portrait Gallery a remarkable picture, painted for his widow, containing a portrait of Unton surrounded by scenes representing not only the most remarkable passages of his life, his birth, education, travels, and marriage, but also his death and burial, and the monument erected to him in Farringdon Church.

Lent by The DUKE OF NORFOLK, E.M., K.G.

170. QUEEN ELIZABETH (1533–1603).

Three-quarter length, life-size, to left; rich open lace ruff, jewelled stomacher and large farthingale; coronet of pearls, long "rope" of pearls suspended from shoulders; feather fan in right hand; red curtain behind. Canvas 49 × 39 in.

Lent by The LORD ZOUCHE.

171. ROBERT DUDLEY, EARL OF LEICESTER, K.G. (1531–1588).

Three-quarter length, life-size, to right; cap with red feather, small ruff, brown doublet with red sleeves and trunk hose, right hand on hip, left touching hilt of sword. Panel 36 × 27 in.

Lent by The TRUSTEES OF THE LATE LORD DONINGTON.

172. SIR PHILIP SIDNEY, KNT. (1554–1586).

Three-quarter length, to right, standing; right hand on hip, left on sword; white doublet and ruff, steel gorget. Canvas 45 × 32½ in.

Sir Philip Sidney, son of Sir Henry Sidney and Mary, sister of Robert, Earl of Leicester, born at Penshurst, November 29, 1554, was educated at Shrewsbury, Christ Church, Oxford, and Trinity College, Cambridge, which he left with a high reputation for scholarship. In 1572 he went abroad on his travels, was in Paris during the massacre of St. Bartholomew, and narrowly escaped being one of its victims; visited Belgium, Germany, Hungary, and Italy, where he formed a friendship with Tasso, and returned to England in 1575. Introduced to Court by his uncle, the Earl of Leicester, he soon became a special favourite of the Queen; but in 1580, owing to a quarrel with the Earl of Oxford, he withdrew from the Court, and resided at Wilton, the seat of his brother-in-law, the Earl of Pembroke, where he wrote a romance for the amusement of his sister, and thence obtained for it the title of *The Countess of Pembroke's Arcadia*. In 1583 he married Frances, dau. of Sir Francis Walsingham, and was knighted; in 1585 he was appointed Governor of Flushing, whither he went to take part in the war of the Dutch against the Spaniards; but at the battle of Zutphen, in Gelderland, he received a musket shot in the thigh, from which he died at Arnheim, October 7, 1586. A beautiful trait of humanity is recorded of him, that as he was borne from the field of battle, languid with the loss of blood, he asked for water, but just as the bottle was put to his lips, seeing a dying soldier looking wistfully at it, he resigned it, saying, "This man's necessity is yet greater than mine." His body was brought to England, and interred in St. Paul's Cathedral, the great grief of the nation being shown by a general mourning.

By PAUL VERONESE? Lent by The VISCOUNT DILLON.

173. SIR FRANCIS WALSINGHAM, K.G. (1536–1590).

Bust, to right, life-size; black coat and cap, white ruff. Panel 23 × 18 in.

Sir Francis Walsingham, statesman, born at Chiselhurst, in Kent, in 1536, was educated at King's College, Cambridge, and afterwards travelled on the Continent, where he acquired an excellent knowledge of languages. In 1570 he went as ambassador to Paris, being there during the massacre of St. Bartholomew; and in 1573 was appointed one of the Secretaries of State, and knighted. In 1583 he went on an embassy to James VI. of Scotland, three years afterwards he sat on the trial of Queen Mary, and in 1587 was elected a K.G. With all these distinctions he died poor, April 6, 1590, and was buried in St. Paul's Cathedral. "Walsingham was a man of subtle policy, sparing neither time, trouble, nor expense in carrying such measures as he thought likely to serve the cause of the Queen and embarrass her enemies." It has been said that he kept fifty-three agents and eighteen spies in foreign courts.

Lent by MRS. DENT of Sudeley.

174. SIR PHILIP SIDNEY.

Full-length, standing, to right; circular lace ruff, black and gold dress, and short crimson cloak with empty sleeves; left hand on hilt of sword. Canvas 79 × 37 in.

Lent by The LORD ZOUCHE.

175. SIR FRANCIS DRAKE, KNT. (1540?–1596).

Three-quarter length, to left; ruff and black dress; pendent badge, with profile of Queen Elizabeth; right hand on globe; arms above to left, to right "ÆTATIS SUÆ 53, ANº 1594;" 16 lines of poetry below. Panel 42 × 32 in.

Sir Francis Drake, circumnavigator and admiral, born about 1540 near Tavistock, in

Devonshire, at an early age made voyages to Zealand and France. Excited by the exploits of Sir John Hawkins in the New World, Drake abandoned his life of a trader and joined that commander in an expedition to the Spanish Main. Upon his return Drake fitted out a vessel, and with it commenced his long series of voyages to the West Indies, in the course of which he sacked the Spanish Colonies, destroyed their ships, and enriched himself with plunder of enormous value. Successive voyages were made in 1570 and 1572, from both of which Drake returned laden with spoil. Under the sanction of Elizabeth, Drake again set sail in 1577 on his famous voyage round the world, which occupied two years and ten months. In spite of the protests of Philip II., Drake was graciously received by Elizabeth, who visited him on board his ship at Deptford, and conferred on him the honour of knighthood. In 1587 he considerably hindered the preparation of the Armada by entering the Roads of Cadiz and destroying over 100 ships, which he afterwards merrily called "singeing the King of Spain's beard." On the approach of the Armada, Drake was appointed vice-admiral under Lord Howard, and made prize of a large galleon commanded by Don Pedro de Valdez. In 1589 he commanded an unsuccessful expedition to Portugal to expel the Spaniards and restore Don Antonio; and in 1595, along with Sir John Hawkins, was sent with a fleet to the West Indies. Both commanders died during the voyage, Hawkins at Puerto Rico, and Drake on board his own ship near the town of Nombre de Dios, June 28, 1596. In person Drake was low of stature, but well formed, had a broad open chest, a very round head, his hair of a fine brown, his beard full and comely, his eyes large and clear, of a fair complexion, with a fresh, cheerful, and engaging countenance.

Lent by The MAYOR AND CORPORATION OF PLYMOUTH.

176. JOHN CASE, M.D. (d. 1600).

Half-length, life-size, to left; black cap and gown; holding book with both hands; skeleton on table before him, skull and hour-glass above; six lines below:—"We have bene flesh and bloode," &c. Panel.

Writer on Aristotle, and physician; was a chorister at New College and Christ Church, Oxford; elected to a scholarship at St. John's College in 1564, and subsequently practised medicine; was collated in 1589 to a canonry at Salisbury, and on his death left various sums to St. John's College. He was buried in the chapel of the College.

Lent by ST. JOHN'S COLLEGE, OXFORD.

177. QUEEN ELIZABETH (1558–1603).

Bust, life-size, facing; white dress, embroidered with flowers, crimson velvet mantle, lace ruff, pearl earring, and cap. Panel 19 × 17 in.

By FEDERIGO ZUCCHERO.   Lent by MRS. DENT of Sudeley.

178. HENRY HASTINGS, 3RD EARL OF HUNTINGDON, K.G. (d. 1595).

Three-quarter length; in rich gold-inlaid suit of armour, bareheaded, with small ruff; dated 1588. ÆT. 52. Panel 43 × 33 in.

Eldest son of Francis, 2nd Earl; created K.G. 1579, Privy Councillor under Elizabeth, President of the North; one of the peers who had charge of Mary Queen of Scots; a benefactor to Emmanuel College, Cambridge; married Katherine, dau. of John Dudley, Duke of Northumberland; died 14 December, 1595.

Lent by The TRUSTEES OF THE LATE LORD DONINGTON.

Room V.] *Portraits.* 59

179. Sir Walter Raleigh, Knt. (1552–1618).

Three-quarter length, standing, to left; right hand resting on staff, left on hip; white doublet, black trunk hose; on table a globe, on which a ship is sailing; above is written "Fata Quo," inscribed Sir Walter Raleigh 1604. Panel 44 × 33 in.

Distinguished in action, in courtly gallantry, and in literature; born at Budleigh; entered at Oxford, but left to assist the French Protestants; rose high in Elizabeth's favour; took an active part in the destruction of the Spanish Armada; was imprisoned for 12 years by James I.; released to undertake an expedition to Guiana; returned unsuccessful, and was executed at Westminster 1618. His *History of the World*, written during his imprisonment, remained unfinished.

By F. Zucchero.   Lent by The Lord Zouche.

180. Robert Cecil, 1st Earl of Salisbury, K.G. (1563–1612).

Three-quarter length, life-size, to left; black doublet and surcoat, white ruff; right hand rests on table, on which are papers and the purse of office; left holds band string. Panel 34¾ × 24¼ in.

Robert Cecil, 1st Earl of Salisbury, youngest son of William Cecil, Lord Burghley, and Mildred, dau. of Sir Anthony Cooke, born in 1563, was knighted in 1601, sworn of the Privy Council, and made Secretary of State, and afterwards Master of the Court of Wards. On the accession of James I. he was created, May 13, 1603, Baron of Essendon, advanced August 20, 1604, to the title of Viscount Cranborne, and in May, 1605, to the Earldom of Salisbury. During this time he continued sole Secretary of State, and on the death of the Earl of Dorset succeeded him as Lord High Treasurer. Worn out with business and the cares of office, he died May 24, 1612. He married Elizabeth, sister of Henry Brooke, Lord Cobham, by whom he had issue one son, William, his successor, and one daughter, Frances, who married Henry Clifford, Earl Cumberland.

Lent by The Duke of Devonshire, K.G.

181. Frances, Lady Sidney (d. 1602).

Full-length, life-size, standing, facing; black dress and ruff, white lace collar and cuffs, right hand rests on a table, left holds a handkerchief. Canvas 79 × 37½in.

Only daughter and heir of Sir Francis Walsingham; married in 1583 Sir Philip Sidney, and subsequently the Earl of Essex and the Earl of Clanricarde. She died at Baron Elms, June 19, 1602, and was buried the next night privately near her first husband in St. Paul's Cathedral.

Lent by The Lord Zouche.

182. William Cecil, Lord Burghley, K.G. (1520–1598).

Three-quarter length; white beard, black cap, high ruff, crimson dress, mantle and collar K.G. Canvas 43 × 34 in.

William Cecil, Lord Burghley, one of England's greatest statesmen, son of Richard Cecil, Master of the Robes to Henry VIII., born at Bourn, Lincolnshire, 15 September, 1520, was educated at the Grammar Schools of Grantham and Stamford, and St. John's College, Cambridge. Allying himself to the Protector Somerset, he was in 1547 appointed Master of Requests, and in the following year Secretary of State. Under Mary, Cecil resigned his office, but was reappointed by Elizabeth on her accession, whose policy he directed for over forty years. He was created Lord Burleigh in 1571, a K.G. in the following year, and succeeded the Marquess of Winchester as Lord High Treasurer, an office which he held until his death, August 15, 1598. Cecil was twice married—first, to Mary, sister of Sir John Cheke, by whom he had Thomas, his successor; and secondly, to Mildred, dau. of Sir Anthony Cooke, and mother of Robert, Earl of Salisbury, When asked how he accomplished so much, Cecil answered that "the shortest way to do many things was by doing only one at a time." Elizabeth was deeply sensible of the loss of such a servant, and it is said that to the end of her life she could never hear or pronounce his name without tears. She always spoke of Burghley as her "spirit," her "leviathan."

Lent by The DUKE OF DEVONSHIRE, K.G.

183. HENRY HASTINGS, 3RD EARL OF HUNTINGDON, K.G.

Half-length; black coat, white ruff collar, and badge of the Garter. Panel 20¼ × 18 in.

Lent by The TRUSTEES OF THE LATE LORD DONINGTON.

184. THOMAS HOWARD, 4TH DUKE OF NORFOLK, K.G. (1536–1572).

Three-quarter length, life-size, to left, in an oval; hand on hip, rich white and gold doublet, blue cloak lined with white, black cap, white feather, pendent jewel, the George heraldry in the four corners. Canvas 52 × 49 in.

Thomas Howard, 4th Duke of Norfolk, son of Henry, Earl of Surrey, and Lady Frances Vere, dau. of John, 15th Earl of Oxford, and grandson of Thomas, 3rd Duke, born in 1536, was restored to his father's title at the coronation of Mary, October 1, 1553, and officiated under his grandfather as Marshal of England. Elected a K.G. in 1559, he commanded the Queen's forces at the siege of Leith in 1560, and in the following year was constituted Lieutenant of the North. He was attainted in June, 1572, of high treason for his intrigues to effect a marriage with Mary Queen of Scots, and being found guilty was executed on Tower Hill on June 2 following. When one reached him a handkerchief to cover his eyes he refused it, saying, "I fear not death." Camden speaks of him as being much loved by the people through his bounty and singular courtesy, and "a man of high nobility, singular goodness of nature, goodly personage, and manly countenance." The Duke was three times married—first, to Mary, dau. and heir of Henry Fitzalan, Earl of Arundel, by whom he had an only son, Philip; secondly, to Margaret, dau. and heir of Thomas, Lord Audley, of Walden; and thirdly to Elizabeth, dau. of Sir James Leybourne.

BY LUCAS DE HEERE.   Lent by The DUKE OF NORFOLK, E.M., K.G.

185. ELEANOR PALMER.

Three-quarter length, life-size, facing; holds a pansy in her right hand, in her left a muff; black dress, richly embroidered with pearls in shape of columns, white ruff, head-dress and necklace of pearls and garnets. Panel 35 × 28¼ in.

Lent by The LORD ZOUCHE.

186. SIR FRANCIS WALSINGHAM, K.G. (1536–1590).

Three-quarter length, seated, to left; skull cap, ruff, and fur-trimmed gown, with pendent medallion of Queen Elizabeth; letter addressed to Lord Burghley in right hand, left on arm of chair. Panel 36 × 29 in.

Lent by The LORD ZOUCHE.

ROOM V.]   *Portraits.*   61

187. THOMAS CECIL, 1ST EARL OF EXETER, K.G. (1542–1622).

Three-quarter length, life-size, standing, to right; black cap and gown, with ruff, and collar of the Garter; right hand on wand, left holding gloves; arms on column to right, with landscape beyond; curtain to left. Panel 30 × 29 in.

Thomas Cecil, eldest son of the great Lord Burghley, by his first wife, the daughter of Sir John Cheke; distinguished himself in the wars in the Low Countries, and served against the Spanish Armada; K.G. 1601; created Earl of Exeter 1605; died 1622, and was buried in Westminster Abbey.

Lent by The LORD ZOUCHE.

188. FRANCIS BACON, VISCOUNT ST. ALBANS (1561–1626).

Half-length, life-size, to right; high crowned hat and embroidered gown. Canvas 26 × 19 in.

Francis Bacon, Lord Verulam, Viscount St. Albans, Lord Chancellor, born January 22, 1561, was the son of Sir Nicholas Bacon. In early childhood, on account of the precociousness of his intelligence, he was called by Elizabeth her "young Lord Keeper." Educated at Trinity College, Cambridge, he continued his studies at Paris, being attached to the suite of Sir Amias Paulet, the English Ambassador. On the death of his father in 1579 he returned to England, betook himself to the study of law, and allied himself with the Earl of Essex, at whose trial for high treason he afterwards appeared as prosecuting counsel. Knighted in 1603, he became Solicitor-General in 1607, Attorney-General in 1613, Lord Keeper of the Great Seal in 1617, and a year later attained the dignity of Lord Chancellor with the title of Lord Verulam. In 1621 he was created Viscount St. Albans, but shortly afterwards being found guilty on his own confession of bribery and corruption was heavily fined and deprived of office by the House of Lords on May 3, 1621. Banished from public life, he devoted himself to literature and science, and died at Highgate in 1626 at the house of his friend the Earl of Arundel. While the public life of Bacon is marked by dishonour and corruption, his literary and scientific works are everywhere illumined by an intellect which towered over those of other men of the time.

Lent by The LORD KENYON.

189. LORD CHANCELLOR BROMLEY (1530–1587).

Bust, to right, life-size; black coat with fur, lace ruff, black cap; dated 1585. Panel 18¼ × 15 in.

Sir Thomas Bromley, Lord Chancellor, son of John Bromley, Justice of Chester, and Elizabeth, dau. of Sir Thomas Lacon, of Willey, in Shropshire, born at Bromley in the same county in 1530, was appointed Recorder of the City of London in 1566, Solicitor-General March 14, 1569, and filled that office for ten years, during which period he acted on the trial of the 4th Duke of Norfolk. On April 26, 1579, he succeeded Sir Nicholas Bacon as Lord Chancellor, and presided over the commission issued in October, 1586, for the trial of Mary Queen of Scots, in which he conducted himself with great delicacy and personal respect towards the unfortunate prisoner, though in subsequent proceedings in Parliament he was the organ of the House to represent to Elizabeth their unanimous request that the judgment might be executed. He died April 12, 1587, and was buried in Westminster Abbey, where his son, Sir Henry, erected a handsome monument to his memory. Bromley married Elizabeth, dau. of Sir Adrian Fortescue, by whom he had four sons and four daughters, one of whom was married to Sir Oliver Cromwell, uncle of the Protector.

Lent by G. E. MARTIN, ESQ.

190. Queen Elizabeth (1533–1603).
In old age; half-length, to left; curled and jewelled hair, high circular ruff of rich lace, white and red dress, the sleeves embroidered with Tudor roses and other flowers. Panel 22 × 17 in.
Lent by The Lord Egerton of Tatton.

191. Henry Fitzalan, 23rd Earl of Arundel (1511–1580).
Small full-length, riding a white horse, full armour; a staff in his right hand, view of Arundel Castle in the background. Dated 1581. Panel 42 × 33 in.
Lent by The Duke of Devonshire, K.G.

192. Matthew Parker, Archbishop of Canterbury (1504–1575).
Half-length, life-size, seated at a table, turned to left; in cap and rochet; hands on open book; bell, seal, and casket on the table; hour-glass by window to left. Panel 26¼ × 21 in.
Matthew Parker, Archbishop of Canterbury, born at Norwich, August 6th, 1504, was educated at Corpus Christi College, Cambridge, made chaplain to Anne Boleyn, Dean of Stoke Clare, in Suffolk, in 1535, and Master of his College in 1544. Three years later he married, and in 1557 became Dean of Lincoln. He lived in retirement under Mary, but when Elizabeth ascended the throne he was appointed Archbishop of Canterbury. On the old Catholic prelates refusing to consecrate him a commission was issued to William Barlow, Miles Coverdale, and other reformed bishops to perform the ceremony, the validity of which has been called in question by some Catholic writers. He died May 17, 1575. Parker was an ardent promoter of the reformed doctrines of the Church, undertook and published at his own expense the *Bishops' Bible*, endowed the University of Cambridge, and particularly his own college, with many fellowships, and founded the Society of Antiquaries, of which he was the first president. Queen Elizabeth, when paying him a visit at his palace, was very much offended at seeing so many married prelates assembled, and on taking leave of his wife said, "Madam I may not call you; mistress I am ashamed to call you; and so I know not what to call you; but howsoever I thank you."
Lent by The Archbishop of Canterbury.

193. Man with a Skull.
By Sir Antonio More. Lent by The Duke of Devonshire, K.G.

193.* William Shakspeare (1564–1616).
Plaster cast, from the monument in the Parish Church of Stratford-on-Avon.

194. Carved Oak Coffer.
Temp. Henry VII. The front is covered with rich panelling and carved rosettes.
Lent by William Sharp Ogden, Esq.

195. Cabinet.
Lent by The Hon. Sir Spencer Ponsonby-Fane, K.C.B.

196. Chair and Footstool in Carved Oak.
Lent by The Science and Art Department.

197. Two Iron Chests, with Original Keys.
Lent by A. Clare, Esq.

CASE A.—ROOM I.

EMBROIDERIES.

198. A COPE OF RED VELVET, with embroidered figures of cherubim angels, fleurs-de-lis, thistles, &c. On the hood is a figure, "3 souls in Abraham's bosom." The orphreys are broad, and executed in feather-stitch and gloss silk layings. The work is "opus phomarium," which has been restored. English. 15th century.

Lent by OSCOTT COLLEGE.

199. RED CHASUBLE, with orphreys, on which are embroidered thistles, cherubim, etc. English.

Lent by OSCOTT COLLEGE.

200. THE BREWERS' MAGNIFICENT HEARSE-CLOTH, the centre of which is of a peculiarly rich cloth of gold, with a deep border of crimson velvet, figured at top and bottom, with St. Thomas of Canterbury in his pontificals. All along the sides are ears of barley, round the stems of which twine inscribed labels; shields of arms, namely, those of the Brewers impaling the arms, assigned to St. Thomas, sab. an archbishop's pall arg. and cross or impaled with arg., three Cornish choughs sab. In the middle, the Assumption of the B. V. Mary is well embroidered. The whole is very fine. Late 15th century. Tissue, Flemish; embroidery, English.

Lent by THE BREWERS' COMPANY.

201. NEEDLEWORK OF QUEEN KATHERINE OF ARAGON, consisting of thirteen pieces of embroidery, cut out of the original canvas, which had become dilapidated. The subjects are flowers, fruits, birds, and insects.

Lent by JOHN HARLEY, ESQ., M.D.

CASE B.—ROOM I.

EMBROIDERIES.

202. FRONTAL OF RED VELVET. This is divided into four panes by three orphreys. It shows traces of repair, and perhaps of alteration, as two of the orphreys differ from the third one. These two are completely worked; both canopy, background, and figure on the same piece of linen. In the third, vacant spaces have been left in the embroidery, and cut figures are stitched there in the usual manner. These figures have gold thread in the cloak, or outer dress, any difference ending there. A few of them may be identified: Moses carrying a rod, and the Tables of the Law. Aaron, or it may be Nathan, with a horn in the right hand. St. Peter can be recognised by the key. Two saints, nimbed, carry what are probably palm-branches. On the velvet panes is found, on each side of the middle orphrey, a cherub. The remainder of the ground is occupied by cut-work flowers of bold designs, in yellow, blue, dark and pale greens, and gold, set off by rays and scroll-floriations of yellow silk, with spangles all stitched on the velvet.

Lent by T. J. WILLSON, ESQ.

203. WHITE CHASUBLE.—A modern mounting of an ancient cross and orphrey, 7 inches in width; the arms of the cross extending 18 inches. This part is occupied with a Crucifixion. The figure of Our Lord follows the later manner of mediæval instances.

The background is of gold thread, stitched down in a lozenge pattern. At the sides is an architectural border of niched piers and mouldings, carrying a vaulted, embattled canopy, overhanging in polygonal form, and all executed in yellow, brown, pink, green, blue, and white.

The orphrey, in divisions about a foot in height, has the same border and canopy repeated; and within, on a similar gold ground, are single figures 7 inches high.

Lent by T. J. WILLSON, ESQ.

204. PURPLE CHASUBLE.—This is plum-coloured or red-purple velvet, with front orphrey and cross at back of ashen-violet velvet, 6½ inches wide. The whole much worn, pieced and cut to very narrow dimensions.

At the intersection of the cross is a figure, presumably St. Margaret, with rays of yellow silk behind.

Two "cut-work" flowers, similar to those on the cope, are upon the cross and orphrey. They are outlined in red, white, and yellow passing. On the lower part of the cross is a fleur-de-lis in gold, outlined in red and yellow silk around the edge of the cut linen.

On the body of the vestment are nine flowers (three in part only), worked in silver thread, and shaded in silk, either blue and white, or green and yellow. The silver part is outlined in red passing, and the silk in white. The sprigs are in yellow and white, with spangles. The silver threads are stitched with dark-yellow silk, either two together, which allows the canvas to be seen, or six threads stitched down with yellow silk on to a sort of soft twine, producing thus an excellent grained or diapered effect.

Lent by T. J. WILLSON, ESQ.

205. CRIMSON VELVET CHASUBLE. It is of the ordinary modern French shape, and measures at back about 25 inches wide. The cross and front orphrey are each 7½ inches wide, and are composed of architectural niches and canopies in coloured silks—three in front, as many at the back, and two additional ones to form the arms of the cross. The back-grounds are of gold thread, stitched in diapered patterns.

The figures are all wrought on finer linen than the ornament and ground, and are cut-work, attached as usual. The linen is allowed to be seen in the flesh, the hands and heads being thus nearly white, with features, hair, and shading of floss silk. The figures are chiefly those of

Apostles—St. Peter, St. Paul, St. John, St. James the Less, and St. Andrew—bearing the usual emblems. Two other figures wearing hats, one carrying a baton, the other a small white scroll—a parchment, perhaps—seem to represent secular personages or characters from the Old Testament. The velvet ground is powdered with twelve flowers, of designs similar to those before described, brightly coloured in pink and green, enriched with gold, and bordered by white, yellow, blue, and gold outlines.

Lent by T. J. WILLSON, ESQ.

206. WHITE SATIN VEIL. This can scarcely be a chalice veil, from its form and enrichment. More probably its use at the altar was during the rite of benediction, as a covering for the platform, or low throne, upon which the monstrance rested.

The work is of an advanced period, perhaps of the earlier part of the seventeenth century. The design is a border, inclosing a meandering stem, the centre filled with a scroll pattern, all traced in lines, formed of three or more plies of gold twist, edged with variegated silk cord. In the thicker lines is a cord made of the twist. The intervening spaces are filled with leaves and flowers of a type approaching the natural, of various hues—of crimson, blue, green, and purple—delicately worked, and the petals outlined by fine silver twist. Outside all is a bordering of crimson and white silk lace. It may be worth remark that the metal twists are of the same sort as in all mediæval instances—that is, of flat, not of round wires.

Lent by T. J. WILLSON, ESQ.

207. AN ANTEPENDIUM, white, charged with a Crucifixion, &c., of 15th century work.

Lent by T. J. WILLSON, ESQ.

207*. PIECE OF NEEDLEWORK, supposed to be the work of Margaret Willoughby, wife of Sir Mathew Arundell. *Temp.* Elizabeth.

Lent by The LORD ARUNDELL OF WARDOUR.

ARMOUR.

Described by S. J. WHAWELL.

208. THREE-QUARTER SUIT OF FLUTED OR CRESTED ARMOUR, commonly known as Maximilian, of the commencement of the reign of Henry VIII. The helmet has a broad skull, rather a blunt and channelled visor, and is laminated at the base of the skull to allow of the head being thrown back with freedom; the gorget has shoulder caps, the globose breastplate has movable gussets and three plates of the large brayette or taces, the bottom one being arched in the centre to admit of the small brayette; backplate with deep garde-rein, medium-sized tassets, full arm guards with espauliéres, condieres, and vambraces, and curious miton gauntlets.

Lent by S. J. WHAWELL, ESQ.

209. A GLOBOSE BREASTPLATE, of bright steel, it has a strong tapul down its centre, thick roped top and roped movable gussets, a small placat at the waist, and three plates of the large brayette or taces. *Temp.* Henry VIII.

Lent by S. J. WHAWELL, ESQ.

210. TWO-HANDLED SWORD, the hilt of blued steel; it has a ringed guard, enclosing smaller rings; the ornamentations consist of scrolls; the long, heavy blade has prongs near the hilt as a first guard, and has the armourer's mark. German. *Circa* 1570.

Lent by S. J. WHAWELL, ESQ.

211. DEMI SUIT OF ENGRAVED ARMOUR, of the end of the reign of Elizabeth, consisting of cabasset, gorget, breastplate, backplate, tassets each made in one piece, full arms, with pauldrons; the decoration represents warriors in Romanesque costumes, trophies of arms, &c.

Lent by S. J. WHAWELL, ESQ.

212. A SPLINTED BREASTPLATE, with part of the gorget attached, it has been richly damaskeened with gold, and is further decorated with chased brass ornaments down the centre. These breastplates are made to wear over a civil costume and under a cloak, and were worn as much against assassination as for show. Italian. Second half of 16th century.

Lent by S. J. WHAWELL, ESQ.

213. DEMI SUIT OF SWISS ARMOUR, of bright steel, of the reign of Henry VIII.; it consists of an open casque with four-sided pointed crown, fixed umbril and cheek pieces, gorget, with espaulieres attached, globose breastplate with tapul, movable gussets and waist piece, lance rest, and three plates of the large brayette, long jointed tassets reaching to just above the knee, and backplate with small garde-rein.

Lent by W. H. SPILLER, ESQ., F.S.A.

214. CAP-A-PIED SUIT OF FLUTED ARMOUR (called Maximilian), of the commencement of the reign of Henry VIII. It consists of close helmet with blunt visor and broad skull, laminated at its base, gorget, globose breastplate, with three plates of the large brayette, short tassets permanently attached, backplate with deep garde-rein, full arms with espaulieres and large condieres, rere and vam braces, miton gauntlets, long cuisses, jambs with broad-toed solerettes.

Lent by The LORD ZOUCHE.

215. CAP-A-PIED SUIT OF ITALIAN GOTHIC ARMOUR, of the middle of the 15th century. It consists of a salad with winged ornaments, gorget; the breastplate is laminated, the edges of each plate pierced and serrated, it has a lance rest and four plates of the large brayette with the small tassets permanently attached; the backplate, which is of graceful form, is also laminated, and has a deep garde-rein; the arms are reinforced on each pauldron with an extra piece, ending in a small pass-garde to turn off the thrust of lance or sword; the gauntlets have long cuffs with gads to the knuckles (the fingers are missing), the long cuisses are jointed, the plates being pierced and serrated to match the rest of the harness; the jambs are of fine form, and are detachable from the long-pointed solerettes; these solerettes were only used when mounted.

Lent by The LORD ZOUCHE.

216. THREE-QUARTER SUIT OF ARMOUR, of the middle of the reign of Elizabeth. It consists of close helmet, gorget, full arms, with pauldrons, rere-braces, small elbows, and vam-braces. Peascod breastplate, backplate, and short broad tassets composed of close splints or plates.

Lent by G. G. KILBOURN, ESQ.

217. CAP-A-PIED SUIT OF ARMOUR, of the reign of Henry VIII. It is of blued steel with gilded roping, portions of which remain. It consists of helmet, with four-sided pointed crown with an acorn at its apex; movable umbril, falling bevor and neck-plates; gorget with shoulder caps; globose breastplate with tapul; movable gussets and lance rest; it is jointed at the waist to give freedom of movement in bending forward, and has three plates of the large brayette, which cover the hips; the tassets are short, and are riveted to the lower plate of the brayette, which is arched in the centre; the backplate is small, and terminates at the waist; the full arms have espauliere-pauldrons, rere-braces, small elbow guards, and vam-braces; the gauntlets have shaped cuffs and separated fingers, cuisses jointed above and below the knee, and jambs with solerettes and semi-rounded toe-caps.

Lent by W. H. SPILLER, ESQ., F.S.A.

218. RAPIER, German, end of the 16th century; the complicated twisted hilt of blackened iron; the pommel fig-shaped; the blade with lozenge-shaped etching in the channels.

Lent by The LORD ZOUCHE.

CASE C.—ROOM I.

Lent by S. J. WHAWELL, Esq.

219. CUIRASS, with the gorget permanently attached, slighly peascod in form, with three laminated plates or splints, back and front, and movable gussets, of the first half of the reign of Elizabeth. This fine specimen of 16th century Milanese work is for parade, and also as a protection against assassination, and not for the purposes of war, as it terminates at the waist. Its decoration consists of three bands of gilt strap-work, the space between being ornamented with large spirited scrolls, with acanthus foliage, tulip flowers, pink blossoms, &c., &c. ; this design is fire gilt on a blue ground, giving the whole a rich effect ; this method of engraving is called pure line, *i.e.*, etched, and not as in later work thrown up in relief by eating away with acid the parts not worked upon, which gave the same appearance as embossing in low relief, as shown on the open casque No. 221.

220. MORION, of russet steel, with high comb, the whole decorated with spirited strap-work, trophies, &c., on a gilt ground. Italian. *Circa* 1570.

221. AN OPEN CASQUE, of classical form ; the outline of this is extremely elegant in design ; it is engraved and gilt on a black enamelled ground, and was made for Cardinal Chigi, and has his portrait and arms on each side, enclosed in broad scrolls, wheat-ears, flowers, &c. ; the high comb has on each side an oval medallion, etched with a winged female warrior, supported on either side with reclining nude figures, holding in their hands palm branches, the top of the comb surmounted with Cardinal's hat. Italian. 16th century.

222. A PEAR-SHAPED MORION, four-sided, and terminating at its apex in a stork ; it is of dark blued steel; this blue was termed in Italy pavonazzo ; it is forged from one piece of metal, the decorations consist of four panels of engraving, representing scrolls, acanthus leaves, griffins, &c., and was originally gilt. The method used in engraving in this manner differs from that called pure line ; the design is painted on with a preparation of vermilion and turpentine varnish, and, when dried, the part left bright is bitten away with diluted aqua fortis. The design is then left in low relief, and has the appearance of being embossed.

223. AN EAR DAGGER, the large circular pommel split in the centre and widening at the top to allow of placing the thumb, the pommel and grip are of horn, riveted to the tang of the blade, which is gilt ; the tapering blade is ridged. Italian Mooresque. Late 16th century.

224. A SMALL STEEL PISTOL OR DAG, with wheel-lock action. It is of Müremburg make, and has that city's and maker's stamp, both on the lock-plate and barrel. *Temp. circa* 1560.

225. HIGH-COMBED MORION, in one piece, engraved with strap-work figures, trophies, &c., the comb with the initial letters, S. P. Q. R. These are the first letters of the words, *Senatus Populus que Romanus*. Italian. Second half of 16th century.

Room I.] *Arms and Armour.* 69

226. POWDER FLASK, of cuir-bouilli, embossed with scrolled foliage, the steel mounts decorated with incised lines. Late Elizabethan.

227. AN OPEN CASQUE, of classical form, forged out of one piece, with the exception of the ear-pieces, engraved with trophies of arms, musical instruments, griffins, &c. Italian. Second half of 16th century.

228. A REPOUSSÉ HUNTING HORN of embossed iron, of the reign of Henry VIII.; one half is embossed in bold relief with foliage, and the other half and band with a spiral wreath of acorns and oak leaves on a granulated ground.

229. PEAR-SHAPED MORION, of the second half of the reign of Elizabeth, and of Italian origin. It is embossed (repoussé) in high relief. On one side is represented a Roman equestrian combat, and on the other Cæsar being offered the head of Pompey after the defeat of the latter's army at the battle of Pharsalia. These subjects are enclosed in strap-work panels, and are surrounded with satyrs, masks, grotesque animals, garlands, fruit, &c., the rim decorated with lozenge-shaped ornaments, trophies, and masks. A fine circular shield preserved in the Armeria Real-de-Turin has a precisely similar subject embossed on it, but is further enriched with damaskeening in gold azziminia on the strap-work borders, which this exhibit, unfortunately, has lost.

230. POWDER FLASK, of wood, inlaid with anular ornaments in ivory, the steel mounts are fire gilt, the front plaque is embossed in relief, with a spirited equestrian combat (*circa* 1590).

231. AN OPEN CASQUE, with buff attached by strap and buckle, engraved with bands of foliated scrolls, trophies, &c., with movable ear-pieces and neck-guard, the lower part of the buff or falling bevor engraved with scrolls and terminal figures. German. Late Henry VIII. or Edward VI. The engraving of this helmet is said to be the work of Peter Speier.

232. PATRON BOX, to hold five cartridges; it is of wood, inlaid with scroll-work in ivory, the mounts are of russet steel. *Temp.* Elizabeth.

233. MORION of russet steel, engraved and gilt, the ornamentation consisting of strap-work panels, containing on one side the subject, Quintus Curtius leaping into the pit, and on the other side Mucius Scævola holding his hand in the flame. Above are the arms of the Elector of Saxony, Augustus I. (1553-86). These helmets were worn by the Elector's bodyguard.

234. A POWDER FLASK, of steel, ribbed and etched. End of the reign of Elizabeth.

235. SPANISH ARMET, of the reign of Philip and Mary. The comb is knotched, the bottom of the visor and the top of the beaver are unusually prominent, and are pierced with many holes for greater freedom in breathing; the neck-plates are missing.

236. CIRCULAR SHIELD, slightly convex; the workmanship is Milanese (*circa* 1565); the centre is embossed in high relief, with a grotesque female head surmounted with a wreath of oak leaves and long curls on each side. The wide border and the eight panels are minutely inlaid with interlaced scrolls and leaves in silver on a blue-black ground, the whole harmonising perfectly; this is a beautiful example of the art of inlaying in silver on steel, a form of decoration introduced into Europe by the Turks and Persians at the end of the 15th century, but was not in general use for embellishing arms until *circa* 1515.

237. CASQUE OF THE REIGN OF PHILIP AND MARY. It is remarkable for its unusual form; it is high in the comb, and the aperture for the face small. This casque, with its fixed umbril and neck-guard, is forged from one piece, and is a good illustration of the skill of the armourers of the 16th century. The ear-pieces are ledged to fit over the umbril to give them greater strength, and are laminated to fit close under the chin. This head-piece was originally of blackened steel; it is strong and heavy, and a most useful helmet for the field.

238. A LARGE POWDER FLASK, of tooled leather, initialed H.L.V., mounts of blackened iron. End of 16th century.

CASE D.—ROOM I.

ARMS AND ARMOUR.

239. CLOSE HELMET (called Maximilian), of the reign of Henry VIII., belonging to a fluted or crested suit; it has a low-roped comb, and is laminated at the base of the skull, the bellows visor is very pointed, and is furnished with a peg to lift it up.

Lent by W. H. SPILLER, ESQ., F.S.A.

240. CLOSE HELMET, of the reign of Philip and Mary, of russet steel, decorated with bands of engraving, which are fire gilt; the ornamentation represents the ducal arms of Savoy (the true-lovers' knot); the helmet is particularly interesting on account of the hollows each side of the skull, which admit the ears, and give greater facilities for hearing.

Lent by W. H. SPILLER, ESQ., F.S.A.

241. CLOSE HELMET, of bright steel, of the beginning of the reign of Henry VIII.; the skull has a low-roped crest, and is laminated at its base, the pig-faced visor formerly belonged to a much earlier headpiece (a basinet) of the end of the 14th century or the commencement of the 15th, but was no doubt converted to fit the other part at the time the skull was made.

Lent by W. H. SPILLER, ESQ., F.S.A.

242. PEAR-SHAPED MORION, Italian, of the latter half of the 16th century; it is of repoussé steel, and is embossed in low relief with grotesque masks, festoons of flowers, fruit, birds, &c., in a scrolled border, the rim chased with acanthus leaves.

Lent by W. H. SPILLER, ESQ., F.S.A.

243. A BLACK AND WHITE OPEN CASQUE, belonging to an armour called Alecret; the pointed skull is four-sided, and has bright raised bands; the movable umbril, cheek pieces, and plate at back of neck ornamented with embossed half circles.

Lent by W. H. SPILLER, ESQ., F.S.A.

244. CLOSE HELMET, of bright steel, Spanish, of the reign of Philip and Mary, the lower part of the visor and the top of the bevor projecting, the comb is knotched.

Lent by G. G. KILBOURN, ESQ.

245. RIBBED STEEL POWDER FLASK, Italian, of the end of the reign of Elizabeth.
Lent by G. G. KILBOURN, ESQ.

246. DAGGER, of the end of the reign of Elizabeth, the guard finely chased with trophies and eagles' heads, the steel grip pierced and chased with scrolls and masks, and with pierced channelled blade.
Lent by S. J. WHAWELL, ESQ.

247. STILETTO, with decorated hilt, blade diamond-sectioned. End of 16th century.
Lent by S. J. WHAWELL, ESQ.

248. DAGGER, of the middle of the reign of Elizabeth, hilt chased with reclining figures, masks, and scrolls; pommel chased with figures standing between columns; blade channelled and pierced.
Lent by S. J. WHAWELL, ESQ.

249. DAGGER, of the early part of the reign of Henry VIII., the ends of the quillons terminating in twisted knobs, pommel shaped like a fleur-de-lis, the blade with strong rib.
Lent by S. J. WHAWELL, ESQ.

250. STILETTO, hilt chased with scrolls, animals, flowers, &c.; pommel and ends of quillons shaped like dolphin heads; the triangular blade etched with scrolled foliage, and numbered with divisions for testing the powder charge in a mortar. Signed CANO. End of the 16th century.
Lent by S. J. WHAWELL, ESQ.

251. CLOSE HELMET, Spanish, of the reign of Philip and Mary; the decorations consist of channels engraved with scrolls, the comb finely engraved in pure line with acanthus leaf scrolls, terminating in rams' heads, &c.
Lent by G. G. KILBOURN, ESQ.

252. A MACE of the second half of the 15th century. It is of blackened steel, and the six flanges are pierced with trefoils, the guard being pierced in a similar manner.
Lent by S. J. WHAWELL, ESQ.

253. HIGH-COMBED MORION, Spanish, second half 16th century; it is engraved in arched panels, with acanthus leaved scrolls, trophies, &c.; on the comb is engraved in the circular medallions the arms, a tree with boar under.
Lent by W. H. SPILLER, ESQ., F.S.A.

254. LARGE CHANFREIN, of bright steel, Spanish, Philip and Mary; it is of good form, and is ornamented in its centre with a shaped shield.
Lent by W. H. SPILLER, ESQ., F.S.A.

255. HIGH-COMBED MORION, Italian, of the second half 16th century; it is engraved in panels representing nude female full-length figures, birds, trophies, warriors in Romanesque costumes, &c., and is furnished with a brass plume-holder.

Lent by G. G. KILBOURN, ESQ.

256. MACE, of the reign of Henry VIII. It has seven flanges, which are reinforced at the points.

Lent by S. J. WHAWELL, ESQ.

257. FLUTED HELMET (called Maximilian), of the beginning of the reign of Henry VIII.; the broad skull has a low crest or comb, and is fluted half way; it has three laminated plates at the base of the skull to allow of the head being thrown back with ease, and has a blunt visor, the lower part of which falls inside the chin-piece.

Lent by W. H. SPILLER, ESQ., F.S.A.

258. DAGGER, of the first half of the reign of Elizabeth; the guard and pommel has a granulated chain-pattern ornament, the pommel being further embellished with a figure fighting with sword and buckler; the stiff blade is serrated.

Lent by G. G. KILBOURN, ESQ.

259. CLOSE HELMET, of the middle of the 16th century; it is of blackened steel, and has a high comb, and a visor and bevor.

Lent by W. H. SPILLER, ESQ., F.S.A.

260. PEASCOD BREASTPLATE, engraved with two portrait medallions and panels of trophies, musical instruments, &c.; movable roped gussets. Spanish. Early Elizabethan.

Lent by S. J. WHAWELL, ESQ.

261. CASQUE, of the reign of Philip and Mary; it is of blackened steel, and remarkable for its outline; the comb is very high and the aperture for the face small; it is strong and heavy, and a most useful headpiece.

Lent by W. H. SPILLER, ESQ., F.S.A.

262. A LEFT-HANDED DAGGER, to be used in conjunction with the rapier. The ringed guard has drooping quillons, and is chased in relief with reclining figures and flowers. It has its original sheath, with the steel lockets chased to correspond with the ornamentations on the hilt. Armourer's mark on the blade. End of 16th century.

Lent by S. J. WHAWELL, ESQ.

263. SMALL POINTED CASQUE, for a foot soldier, of the end of the reign of Henry VIII., with movable umbril.

Lent by G. G. KILBOURN, ESQ.

CASE E.—ROOM II.

Lent by S. J. WHAWELL, Esq.

264. AN ESTOC OR FOINING SWORD, with long, narrow blade, strongly reinforced with a rib down its centre; the hilt, which is blued, has a ribbon-shaped curl to the quillons, the ornamentation consists of incised lines. *Temp.* Henry VIII.

265. SWORD, with blunt back-edge blade; the simple guard has a steel grip, terminating in a bird's beak; the hilt damaskeened with gold tracery, on a russet ground. Venetian. Second half of the reign of Elizabeth.

266. SWORD, with hilt of blued steel, doubled-ringed guard, swept quillons; the guard and pommel decorated with acanthus leaves, plaited wire grip; the blade stamped on each face of the ricasso with the Brescian mark. *Temp.* Edward VI.

267. AN ESTOC OR FOINING SWORD, with stiff quadrangular blade, ringed guard, with shell curved quillons, broadening at the ends, a thumb ring and four-sided pommel. Late 15th century.

268. SWORD, with swept hilt and fish-tailed pommel; brass-wire grip; blade signed PETTIER WIRSBERGH. German. Late Elizabethan.

269. RAPIER, of the second half of the 16th century; the guard has three rings and straight quillons, swelling at the end, and shaped pommel, the whole encrusted with silver, now partly obliterated, the four-sided blade is stamped with the ship mark on each face of the ricasso. Italian.

270. SWORD, of the latter end of the reign of Elizabeth, the swept hilt has short quillons, broad at the ends, and a thumb ring, the guard ornamented with fine dots. Venetian.

271. AN ITALIAN CUP-HILTED RAPIER, the cup elaborately pierced and chased with birds, reptiles, scrolls, &c.; the inside plaque decorated to match the bowl, the quillons and knuckle-guard twisted; the narrow six-sided blade signed SAHAGUM. End of the reign of Elizabeth.

272. SWORD, of the reign of Edward VI.; the double-ringed guard has reversed quillons, and is chased in bold relief with Romanesque trophies of arms, the pommel chased with acanthus leaves; blade signed PHILIP ROSMARCKHT; armourer's mark, negro's head four times repeated on the ricasso.

273. FALCHION, of the beginning of the reign of Elizabeth. This sword is interesting, being intended for a left-handed man. The simple guard has a ring on the outside only, the reversed quillons serving as a protection for both wrist and knuckles. The hilt is entirely decorated with gold and silver inlay, termed in Italy "azziminia," and in France "tauchie." The

delicate designs in gold and silver are hammered on to the hatched surface of the steel or iron. The blade, which is probably of Brescian make, is channelled in two divisions, and has an armourer's mark on each face, a stag with crown over, and is dated Anno 1553.

274. SWORD, with swept hilt and reversed quillons; the guard is faceted and ornamented with escallope shells; the broad channelled blade is signed on each face WIHELM WIRSBERG MEFECIT SOLINGEN, and deeply stamped with the armourer's mark—a pair of pincers with crown over. German. End of 16th century.

275. RAPIER, of the second half of the reign of Elizabeth, with long blade (inscription indistinct), the complicated swept hilt with chased and pierced shells; the whole guard, with its four-sided pommel, inlaid with alternate dots of gold and silver.

276. MACE, of the end of the 15th century, with six flanges, the wooden grip covered with plaited hide.

277. MACE, of the end of the 15th century, with six flanges pierced with trefoil ornaments, the twisted grip bound with leather.

CASE F.—ROOM II.

Lent by W. H. SPILLER, ESQ., F.S.A.

278. SWORD, English, end of the reign of Elizabeth; the hilt has a ringed guard, knuckle-guard, and reversed quillons, and a large globular pommel of unusual dimensions, the whole beautifully encrusted with chased silver on a russet ground, representing winged cherubs, masks, scrolls, &c.; the blade is stamped with the Brescian mark on the ricasso and the wolf marks, which was also the armourer's mark used by the blade makers in Solingen.

279. RAPIER, Italian, of the second half of the reign of Elizabeth; the swept hilt has a treble ringed guard and straight quillons, swelling at the ends, the whole channelled and encrusted with silver, representing wheat-ears on russet ground; the diamond sectional blade is signed on the ricasso FREDRICHO PECIMANO.

280. SWORD, Italian, of the end of the reign of Henry VIII.; the double-ringed hilt has short straight quillons and a knuckle-guard; the decorations consist of twisted knobs, and the ball pommel has a honeysuckle ornament chased in low relief; the blade is back edged, and has the wolf mark on one face only.

281. HAND AND HALF SWORD, Swiss, of the middle of the reign of Elizabeth; the ringed guard and six-sided pommel are etched with a leaf ornament and plated with silver on a hatched ground; the leather grip knotted and partly bound with copper wire; the short broad blade is stamped on each face with the arms of the Arsenal of Zurich.

282. SWORD, Italian, second half of the 16th century; the swept hilt is of great strength; the short broad blade tapering to a point has an armourer's mark on each face of the ricasso; a shaped shield T with S over surmounted with a crown.

283. RAPIER, Italian, of the end of the reign of Elizabeth; it has a ringed swept hilt with reversed quillons; the guard and pommel are thickly encrusted with chased silver, representing masks, trophies, leaves, &c.; the long narrow blade is pierced in the channels, the ricasso bears the armourer's mark on each face.

284. HAND AND HALF SWORD, German, of the end of the reign of Henry VIII.; the hilt has slightly drooping quillons; the ring guard ornamented with welded scroll work; twisted spiral pommel and leather grip; the broad channelled blade signed ANDREA FERARA, and stamped with the wolf mark.

285. RAPIER, Italian, of the end of the reign of Elizabeth, with swept hilt and straight quillons, swelling at the ends; the long six-sided blade is signed in the channel, and has an armourer's mark on each face of the ricasso P. with crown over.

Lent by G. G. KILBOURN, Esq.

286. RAPIER, Spanish, of the end of the 16th century; the bowl hilt, pommel, and ends of quillons are pierced with an open-work pattern; the blade is signed SEBASTIAN HERMANTES.

287. RAPIER, Italian, of the end of the reign of Elizabeth; with bowl hilt and straight quillons, welded to the bowl, which is chased and pierced with birds and foliage; the blade has a diamond section, and is engraved; the name GEROLAMO X. MORATINI is engraved on the blade, and the ricasso has the letters To X. MARSON.

288. RAPIER, Spanish, end of the 16th century; the bowl hilt pierced and chased with scrolls in strap-work panels, the quillons and knuckle-guard twisted and chased; the deeply-grooved blade is inscribed.

289. RAPIER, Spanish, end of the 16th century; the bowl hilt pierced and chased with scrolls in strap-work panels, the quillons and knuckle-guard twisted and chased; the deeply-grooved blade is inscribed.

290. LEFT-HANDED DAGGER, to be used in conjunction with the rapier, of the end of the reign of Elizabeth; the guard has a thumb ring and drooping quillons and fluted pommel; the stiff blade has a diamond section.

291. STILETTO, of the middle of the reign of Elizabeth; it has a small ring and straight quillons and fluted pommel; the slender blade is diamond-sectioned.

292. RAPIER, Italian, of the end of the 16th century; the bowl hilt is pierced in bands, with an open-work border; the straight quillons and knuckle-guard are plain, the pommel chased with acanthus leaves, the shaped grip of steel; the diamond-sectioned blade, which is six-sided near the hilt, is signed JACOB BRACH, Mefecit. Solig, and is incribed SEDEVS * PRONOBIS * QVIS * CONTRANOSS * GVH * DEO * ET * VICT * RICIBVS * ARHISS.

CASE G.—ROOM II.

Lent by G. G. KILBOURN, ESQ.

293. RAPIER, German, of the end of the 16th century; the bowl hilt is pierced and chased with scrolls, the four circular panels chased with dogs hunting the boar, it is further chased with a dragon on each side of the bowl, the straight quillons and knuckle-guard are faceted, the pommel chased with an equestrian combat; blade signed JOHANNIIS WIRSBERGH SOLINGEN.

294. RAPIER, Italian, middle of the reign of Elizabeth; the double-ringed guards are chased with trophies in shaped panels; the ends of the reversed quillons are chased and vase-shaped; the pommels chased with male busts; the blade, which is four-sided, is deeply stamped on the ricasso with armourer's marks.

295. SWORD, Italian, end of the 16th century; the simple hilt has reversed quillons serving as a guard for the wrist and knuckles; the pommel is fig-shaped, and bears an armourer's stamp; the blade is broad and channelled.

296. RAPIER, Italian, of the end of the 16th century; the deep bowl guard consists of a number of pierced and etched plaques, the straight quillons swell slightly at their ends, and the pommel is fluted and ornamented with dots; the blade is long and slender.

297. HAND AND HALF SWORD, Swiss, of the end of the reign of Henry VIII.; the swept hilt has a ringed guard and a thumb-ring at the back, the ends of the reversed quillons and pommel are pear-shaped; the powerful blade is stamped with the Brescian mark.

298. SHORT SWORD, Italian, second half of the 16th century; the hilt, which has a single ring and a knuckle-guard, is chased in relief with leaves, &c.; the pommel is pierced and chased with female busts; the blade is engraved with figures and scrolls.

299. RAPIER, Italian, second half of the reign of Elizabeth; the bold swept hilt is prettily inlaid with an interlaced pattern in gold and silver, on a russet ground; the blade is channelled from hilt to point.

Lent by The LORD ZOUCHE.

300. SWORD, Italian, of the middle of the 15th century. All knights were armed with swords of this description. It has a simple guard, the quillons curving towards the point of the blade; the pommel is large, flat, and circular, and is etched with a male and female bust on a cross-hatched ground; the short grip is covered with fish skin; the blade, which is also engraved, is 32 inches in length and 3 inches wide at the guard, tapering to a sharp point, and is strengthened with a rib down its centre. The object of the point ending in a diamond section was to rend apart the links of the chain mail of an adversary.

301. SWORD, French, second half of the 15th century; it has a simple guard; the quillons curving towards the point; a wooden grip and large wheel pommel; the blade has a tapul or ridge down its centre to strengthen it.

Lent by G. G. KILBOURN, ESQ.

302. BREAST AND BACK PLATE, Spanish, Philip and Mary. It is of the kind called long-waisted; it has movable roped gussets and a small underlapping placat; it has a fixed lance-rest, and is engraved in pure line with interlaced scrolls, winged satyrs, marks, &c.

Lent by S. J. WHAWELL, ESQ.

303. A VENETIAN GLAIVE, of the middle of the 16th century. It is finely engraved with strap-work, enclosing scrolls, &c., and surmounted with a coat of arms on each face.

304. HALBERD, of the reign of Henry VII., with broad blade and reinforced spike.

305. ITALIAN GLAIVE, of the end of the reign of Elizabeth. It is engraved with spirited strap-work, and has two figures in the costumes of the period.

306. HALBERD, of the reign of Henry VII., stamped with the armourer's mark, a crown.

CASE H.—ROOM II.

Lent by The BIRMINGHAM MUSEUM AND ART GALLERY.

307. SMALL WHEEL-LOCK SPORTING GUN, Italian, end 16th century. The ebony stock carved in low relief with scrolls and hunting subjects; the barrel damascened with gold (azziminia) on a hatched russet ground, furnished with fixed back and fore sight. The trigger-guard pierced and chased with a mask surrounded with scrolls.

308. SMALL WHEEL-LOCK SPORTING GUN, German, end of the reign of Elizabeth. The shaped ebony stock prettily inlaid with ivory, representing vases, flowers, and fruit; the barrel with back and fore sight. The lock-plate stamped with an armourer's mark, P. R., with flower under, and the mark of the town of Nürnberg.

ROOM II.]   *Arms and Armour.*   79

309. MATCH-LOCK GUN, end of the reign of Elizabeth. Stock inlaid with engraved mother-of-pearl. The match-lock is the earliest kind of fire-arm that was in use for warlike purposes by any organised body of troops, and was the actual cause of the discontinuance of the use of the long bow, which had hitherto been the most effective infantry weapon. The length and weight of these guns necessitated the use of a rest to support the muzzle end and to ensure an accurate aim.

310. GUN REST, or support for the match-lock gun, German, end of 16th century.

311. WHEEL-LOCK GUN, German, end of 16th century. The shaped stock inlaid with engraved ivory; the spanner is attached for winding.

312. PETRONEL, OR LONG PISTOL, German, end of the 16th century. The stock, which has a pear-shaped butt, is inlaid with ivory; the barrel is long and light, and is stamped with the armourer's mark; the lock-plate also bears the armourer's mark, P. R., and the Nürnberg mark. These pistols were for horsemen.

313. WHEEL-LOCK DAG OR PISTOL, Italian, second half of the 16th century. The ebony stock inlaid with engraved ivory; the short barrel and lock-plate engraved with strapwork and scrolls.

314. DAGGER AND PISTOL COMBINED, Italian, middle of the 16th century. This interesting and rare piece has the wheel-lock action, the hollow blade forms the barrel, the point is kept in position by means of a spring when intended for use as a dagger, but when detached acts also as the ramrod; the hilt, lock, and blade is entirely engraved with a spirited strap-work ornament, &c.

315. WHEEL-LOCK CARBINE, German, end of the 16th century. The short stock inlaid with etched ivory, representing hunting subjects.

316. LARGE WHEEL-LOCK PISTOL, German, end 16th century. Stock inlaid with engraved ivory.

317. WHEEL-LOCK PISTOL, German, second half 16th century. The stock, which has a ball-butt, is inlaid with foliated scrolls. The lock-plate stamped with an armourer's mark, I-O, with flower under.

318. LARGE WHEEL-LOCK PISTOL, German, end of the 16th century. The granulated stock inlaid with etched buck-horn; the ball-butt embellished with a silver plaque, engraved with a Roman Warrior; blued barrel. This particular class of fire-arm were manufactured in Dresden, and came from the arsenal of that city.

CASE I.—ROOM II.

Manuscripts and Printed Books.

At the opening of the Tudor Period the service books in general use in the Church in England were :—

1. The **Missal**, containing the service for the celebration of the Holy Eucharist, with its accompanying Collects, Epistles, Gospels, Sequences, Graduals, Introits, etc.

2. The **Breviary**, containing the office for the recitation of the Psalter at the Canonical Hours of Matins, Lauds, Prime, Terce, Sext, Nones, Vespers and Compline, together with the accompanying Antiphons, Lessons, Hymns, etc.

3. The **Manual**, containing the occasional services which could be performed by a Priest, such as Baptism, Marriage, Burial of the Dead, Churching of Women, Extreme Unction, etc.

4. The **Pontifical**, containing those services, such as Confirmation, Holy Orders, Consecration of Churches, Coronation of Kings, etc., which required to be performed by a Bishop.

To these may be added certain Choir Books, etc., containing selections from one or more of these, as arranged for musical or other purposes, such as the Antiphoner (containing the music of the Breviary), the Grail or Gradual (containing the music of the Missal, the Hymnal, the Processional, etc.), as well as the book of ceremonial directions officially entitled *Directorium Sacerdotale*, but commonly known by what may be called its slang name of *Pica* or *Pie*.

At the beginning of the period to which this Exhibition refers, there were several varieties of these books in use in England, "some following Salisbury use, some Hereford use, some the use of Bangor, some of York, some of Lincoln," but the differences were not very great, nothing like so great as may often be found between the Uses of two churches in the same town at the present day. The Salisbury Use was the most important of these, and was used in a majority of churches. It owed its origin as a distinct Use to St. Osmund, Bishop of Salisbury in the eleventh century, and it has gained a somewhat exaggerated importance through being the direct ancestor of the Anglican Prayer-Book. It has been the fashion with those who wish to minimize the debt due from England to Rome to maintain that the Salisbury Use had an independent origin, and to derive it from a common origin with the Gallican, Mozarabic, and Ephesine family of Liturgies. If the Ancient Celtic Liturgy was of that family (which is by no means certain), there may be some very slight remaining influence, but otherwise the theory is utterly untenable. The Salisbury Liturgy was a mere variety of the Roman, and differed from it no more than did the many German, Italian, Polish, Spanish (non-Mozarabic), and other Western rites, and less than many of the French Uses. If it has a right to an independent position, so has also the Use of Mayence, of Magdeburg, of Halberstadt, or indeed of nearly every diocese in the Latin Church.

The first liturgical change which the Reformation brought about was the omission of the word "Pope" as applied to the Bishop of Rome in 1534, and in 1538 of the offices for the two feasts of St. Thomas of Canterbury. The objectionable words and services were erased in the older books, and a newer and revised edition was printed. Until the reign of Edward VI. these altered books were used, and called *Salisbury* books; but the ideal of Henry VIII. of a Catholic Church of England differing only from the rest of Western Christendom in its independence of Rome was found to be unattainable, and the growing Protestant party demanded a vernacular Liturgy, an article which had only appeared as yet in the Litany of 1544. An instalment was given in the "Order of Communion" (to be used with the Sarum Mass), issued in March, 1548, which was followed the next year by the First Prayer-Book of Edward VI., in which a new Communion Service, founded on the old Liturgy, was contained, together with other services drawn form the Breviary (the eight canonical hours being contracted into two), and occasional services from the Manual. But this book did not satisfy the reforming party, and in 1552 another book of a far more Protestant form was issued, influenced to a great extent by foreign Calvinist reformers, and this, with some modifications effected at the accession of Elizabeth, and still more at the Restoration of Charles II., is substantially the Prayer-Book now in use. The Second Prayer-Book included an Ordinal, which had been published separately late in 1549, and was of such a nature that Queen Mary, in her direction to Bishop Bonner in 1553, directs that those who had been ordained by this "new style and fashion of Order, considering that they be not ordered in very dede" should be reordained, and the careful revisers of 1662 made certain important alterations therein. When Mary came to the throne the Salisbury Use in its old form was restored and several editions were printed; but in 1559, after the accession of Elizabeth, the English Prayer-Book was revived, and with the short interval of extreme Protestantism from 1645 to 1660 has continued ever since.

319. "MISSALE AD USUM SARUM." Printed by William Maynyal, Paris, 1487. Folio.
              Lent by The LORD NEWTON.

319.* "MISSALE," given by Henry VII. to his daughter Margaret, Queen of James IV. of Scotland.
              Lent by The DUKE OF DEVONSHIRE, K.G.

320. "HORÆ BEATÆ MARIÆ VIRGINIS." A late Fifteenth Century MS. of North French or Flemish work, with illuminated borders throughout, and many miniatures. On a flyleaf at the end are the words, "Elizabeth plantaegenct the Queene," *i.e.* Elizabeth of York.
              Lent by STONYHURST COLLEGE.

321. "HORÆ B. V. M. SECUNDUM USUM SERUM CUM ORATIONIBUS BEATE BRIGITTÆ," ETC. Printed by Francis Regnault, Paris, 1550. 8vo.
              Lent by STONYHURST COLLEGE.

322. "MISSALE AD VSUM ECCLESIE SARISBURIESIS optimis formulis ut res ipsa indicat diligentissime cusum atque correctum, etc." Printed by François Regnault, Paris, 1529. 4to.

The word "Papa" following the names of St. Gregory, St. Marcellus, and other Popes, has been carefully erased, and the offices for St. Thomas of Canterbury have been crossed out in ink, in accordance with the royal orders.
              Lent by STONYHURST COLLEGE.

323. "PORTIFORIUM AD USUM ECCLESIÆ SARISBURIENSIS. Pars Æstivalis." Printed by François Regnault, Paris, 1535. 4to.

The Office of St. Thomps of Canterbury (July 7) has not been obliterated, nor has his name been erased from the calendar. The title page has had a new date, 1555, added, which shows this book to have been reissued under Mary.

Lent by STONYHURST COLLEGE.

324. "PORTIFORIUM SECUNDŌ USUM SARŪ NOVITER IMPRESSUM, & a plurimis purgatū mēdis. In quo nomen Romano pontifici falso ascriptum omittit', una cum aliisque christianissimo nostri Regis statuto repugnant." Printed by Edward Whytchurch, London, 1541. 8vo. Pars Æstivalis.

This is the Reformed Salisbury Breviary of the Popeless English Church of Henry VIII. The title of Pope is omitted, and St. Thomas of Canterbury deposed from the rank of Saint. In other respects there is little difference of importance, except in the direction of omission of doubtful legends, &c.

Lent by STONYHURST COLLEGE.

325. "EXPLICUIT HORE B.V.M. SECUNDUM USUM SARUM." Exarsum Londini in Comitorio divi Pauli per Thomasin Petit. Anno. 1541.
A UNIQUE COPY. Lent by OSCOTT COLLEGE.

326. "MANUALE AD USUM INSIGNIS ECCLESIE SARUM." Printed by Christopher van Ruremonde, Antwerp, 1542. 4to.

Lent by The HON. AND REV. KENNETH GIBBS.

327. "MANUALE AD USUM INSIGNIS ECCLESIE SARUM. Iam denuo Antwerpie impressum : et a multis erratis et mēdis quibus scatebat repurgatum ac emunctissime vindicatum." Printed by the widow of Christopher van Ruremonde, Antwerp, 1543. 4to.

Many of the sentences which were given in English, in the earlier manual, are here given in Latin, with directions that they should be spoken "in lingua materna."

Lent by STONYHURST COLLEGE.

328. "MISSALE AD USUM INSIGNIS ECCLESIE SARISBURIENSIS nunc recens typis elegantioribus exaratum, &c." Printed at London, 1557. 4to.

The restored Salisbury missal of Queen Mary. The restoration was complete. The title of Pope was put back, and St. Thomas of Canterbury restored to his former place.

Lent by STONYHURST COLLEGE.

329. "PORTIFORIUM SEU BREVIARIUM ad insignis Sarisburiensis ecclesie usum, &c. Paris Hyemalis." Printed by John Kyngston and Henry Sutton, London, 1556. 4to.
The restored Salisbury Breviary of Queen Mary.

Lent by STONYHURST COLLEGE.

330. "MANUALE AD USUM PERCELEBRIS ECCLESIE SARISBURIENSIS." Londini noviter impressum Anno Domini, 1554. It begins "Benedictis salis et aque." Red and Black. 1554. Without the name of the printer. 4to.

Psalter and Commune. There seems to have been a stock of the Proprium Sanctorum on hand at the time of the abolition of the Pope's supremacy. At the restoration of Catholicity under Queen Mary this stock was used up by printing only the Psalter and Commune, and binding them up with this latter.

Lent by OSCOTT COLLEGE.

331. "BREVIARIUM AD USUM ECCLESIÆ SARISBURIENSIS." Pars Æstivalis. Red and Black. Printed at London (by Robert Caly, late Richard Grafton). 1555. 4to.

Lent by OSCOTT COLLEGE.

332. "HORÆ IN LAUDEM BEATISSIMÆ VIRGINIS MARIÆ AD USUM ROMANUM." Lugdudi, 1558. Printed in "caractères de civilité." This book belonged to Queen Mary Tudor, whose name, arms, and badge are on the cover, and is supposed to have been used by Mary Queen of Scots on the scaffold. According to tradition it came into the hands of the confessor of Mary Queen of Scots, who gave it to the English College at Douai. Thence it was transferred to the Jesuit College at Liège, whence it was brought to Stonyhurst in 1794.

Lent by STONYHURST COLLEGE.

THE LAYMAN'S PRAYER-BOOK.

Besides the public service books of the Church, there have existed from the 14th century certain authorised books of private devotion called by various names, *Horæ, Hours, Prymer, Enchiridion, Hortulus Animæ, Orarium, etc.* These books were substantially the same, though the later ones, especially after the introduction of printing, are considerably fuller than the earlier. The original basis was the service known as the "Hours of Our Lady," to which were added others, such as the "Hours of the Cross," "Of the Trinity," "Of the Blessed Sacrament," etc. These Hours resembled the Breviary Offices in construction, but were shorter and simpler. Their use is somewhat obscure, but they were not only recited in Church, and attended by the laity, but also used for private devotion. Besides these, the Books of Hours included the Seven Penitential Psalms, The Office of the Dead, The Litany, and many miscellaneous prayers, the bulk of which increased considerably as time went on. These "Layman's Prayer-Books," as they may be called, were common in England, France, and Flanders, but comparatively rare elsewhere. They followed the various local Uses of the public service books, those of Paris, Rome, Salisbury, and Rouen being among the commonest of those that have survived. As may be supposed, Henry VIII. was not content with regulating the public services of his kingdom, and soon began to dictate the private devotions also. In 1534 the first reformed Prymer (Marshall's) appeared under the royal sanction. This was chiefly noticeable for the omission of the title of Pope, and for containing Hours of a less direct reference to Our Lady. The invocation of saints was retained, as were also prayers for the departed, and most characteristically Catholic doctrines, except, of course, those relating to the Pope. This was followed by a somewhat simpler book, compiled by John Hilsey, Bishop of Rochester, in 1539, and further changes were introduced in a book set forth by the King in 1545. Here appeared a Litany (which had been already issued in

1544), closely resembling the present Anglican Litany, but including, after the addresses to the Trinity, an invocation of saints, not as in the older Litany individually, but by classes. Edward VI. reissued this Prymer in 1552, but omitted the invocations; and Elizabeth began by a reissue of the Edwardian book, but subsequently, owing to the progress of the Reformation, got rid of the prayers for the dead. Under Mary, the Salisbury Prymer was restored; but even before that it continued in use parallel with the reformed books. It is noticeable that all reformed Prymers down to those of Elizabeth were more Catholic in tone than the public service books.

333. ["PRIMER, OR BOKE OF PRAYERS, &c."] Printed by Nicholas Bourman, London. [1540.] 8vo.

An edition of the reformed Prymer of Hilsey, with a few alterations. The title-page and several other pages are wanting.

Lent by The LORD ALDENHAM.

334. "THE PRYMER IN ENGLISH AND LATYN after the use of Sarum, set out at length with manye goodlye prayers, &c." Printed by Thomas Petyt. London. [1543.] 4to.

A reformed Salisbury Prymer, omitting the title of Pope, and all notice of St. Thomas of Canterbury. The Prymer is followed by the "Epystels and Gospels of every Sonday and holy day in the yeare."

Lent by The LORD ALDENHAM.

335. "THE PRIMER, IN ENGLISHE AND LATYN, set foorth by the Kynges maiestie and his clergie to be taught, learned, and read, and none other used throughout all his dominions." Printed by Richard Grafton, London, 1545. 4to.

The first edition of the Prymer set forth by King Henry VIII. The Litany of 1544, nearly the same as that in the present Prayer-Book, is contained in it, also the Hours, the Dirige, various "godly praiers for sundry purposes," the "seven Psalmes," &c.

Lent by The LORD ALDENHAM.

336. "THE PRIMER AND CATECHISME set forth by the Kynges highness, &c." Printed by Richard Grafton, London, 1552. 8vo.

The Edwardian reprint of the Prymer of Henry VIII. of 1545. There are some alterations of importance, the chief being the omission of invocation of Saints in the Litany. Direct prayers for the dead are retained.

Lent by The LORD ALDENHAM.

337. PRYMER AND CATECHISM, etc., set forth by Queen Elizabeth. Printed by Richard Grafton, London, 1559. 8vo.

The first Prymer of Elizabeth. It closely resembles the Prymer of Edward VI., and is more Catholic than the second Prymer of the same year.

Lent by The LORD ALDENHAM.

338. "THE PRIMER AND CATECHISME set forth at large with many godly Prayers, necessary for al faithful Christians to reade." [Printed at London, 1559.] 8vo.

The second Prymer of Elizabeth. There are here no invocations of Saints in the Litany, but there is a prayer for the departed at the end of the Dirige, though the first and more direct prayer which occurs in the first Prymer of Elizabeth has been omitted.

Lent by The LORD ALDENHAM.

339. "PRECES PRIVATAE, in studiosorum gratiam collectæ, & Regia authoritate approbatæ." Printed by William Seres, London, 1564. 16mo.

This book is arranged much after the fashion of the Prymer, though it is thoroughly purged of all "Popery," except in the calendar, which has saints for every day of the year, and includes St. Thomas of Canterbury. It contains the catechism, morning and evening prayers, modelled on those in the Prayer-book, "Psalmi, lectiones et preces selectæ" for various days, select psalms, and "Precationes aliquot Biblicæ, sanctorum patrum," &c.

Lent by The HON. AND REV. KENNETH GIBBS.

340. "DIVES AND PAUPER." "Here endeth a compendiouse treetise dyalogue of Dives and Pauper, that is to say, the riche and the pore fructuously tretyng upon the X comandmentes, fynisshed the V day of Juyl; the yere of oure lord god M. CCCC. LXXXXIII. Empyntyd by me Richarde Fynson, at the temple barre of London. Deo. gracias."

This is the first edition of this work, and the first book with a date bearing Pynson's name. Our copy is perfect. 1493. London. Folio.

Lent by OSCOTT COLLEGE.

341. "LIBER FESTIVALIS." The first leaf is headed: "Dnica prima adventus." 4to.

This is not Caxton's, but perhaps the Oxford edition of Notary, 1499.

Lent by OSCOTT COLLEGE.

342. "BRITANNIÆ UTRIUSQUE REGÛ et Principum Origo & gesta insignia ab Galfrido Monemutensi ex antiquissimis Britannici sermonis monumentis in latinum traducta." Printed by Jodocus Badius Ascensius [Paris], 1517. 4to.

On one side of the binding are the arms of Henry VIII., on the other the same impaled with those of Katherine of Aragon.

Lent by SIR JOHN EVANS, K.C.B.

343. "LITERARUM, quibus inuictissimus Princeps Henricus octauus rex Angliæ ... respondit ad quandam epistolam Martini Lutheri ad se missam, et ipsius Lutheranæ, quoque epistolæ, exemplum." Printed by Richard Pynson, London, 1527. 8vo.

Lent by The ARCHBISHOP OF CANTERBURY.

344. "ARTICLES devised by the Kynges Highnes Maiestie to stablyshe christen quietness and vnitie amonge vs, and to auoide contentious opiniōs, which articles be also approved by ... the hole clergie of this realme." Printed by Thomas Berthelet, London, 1536. 4to.

These articles are on Faith, Baptism, Penance, the Holy Eucharist, Justification, Images, Honouring and Praying to the Saints, Rites and Ceremonies, and Purgatory. This was one of the earliest steps in the development of Anglican doctrine. The statements of faith differ hardly at all from the Roman Catholic, but the authority on which they are put forth is that of the King, not of the Pope.

Lent by The ARCHBISHOP OF CANTERBURY.

345. "THE INSTITUTION OF A CHRISTEN MAN, conteyning the Exposytion or Interpretation of the Commune Crede, of the seven Sacramentes, of the X. Commandementes, and of the Pater noster and the Ave Maria, Justification, and Purgatory." Printed by Thomas Berthelet, London, 1537. 4to.

This book was set forth by the bishops and clergy. The development of doctrine in a Protestant direction goes a little further than the "Articles" of the preceding year. A great deal of the book is devoted to controverting the claims of the Bishop of Rome to universal jurisdiction. The "Necessary Doctrine," issued in 1543, superseded this treatise.

Lent by The ARCHBISHOP OF CANTERBURY.

346. "THE CHIEFE AND PRYNCYPALL ARTICLES OF THE CHRISTEN FAYTHE, to holde againste the Pope and al the Papistes, and the gates of hell, with other thre very profitable... bokes... made by Doctor Marten Luther. To the Reader. In thys boke shall you fynde... the righte probation of the righte Old Catholyke Churche, etc." Printed by Gwalter Lynne, London, 1548. 8vo.

Lent by The HON. AND REV. KENNETH GIBBS.

347. A COLLECTION OF STATUTES, made during the reigns of Henry VIII. and Edward VI. They contain, among others :—

An Acte concernynge the atteyndre of Elizabeth Barton and other.
An Acte for the punishment of heresie.
An Acte concerning the submission of the clergie to the Kinges maiestie.
An Acte restrainynge the payment of Annates or first fruits to the Bishop of Rome.
An Acte auctorizing the Kynges maiestie to make byshoppes by his letters patentes.
An Acte for abholyshyng of diversitie of opinion in certaine articles concerning Christen religion.
An Acte for the abholyshynge and puttynge awaye of diuerse Bookes and Images.
An Acte against fond and phantasticall prophecies.

Lent by The HON. AND REV. KENNETH GIBBS.

348. "THE SHEPHARDES KALENDER." The first leaf marked Aiii. begins ¶ "a ballat howe princes and states," &c.

This is probably the same edition as the one in the Bodleian, without date, but about 1550. Folio.

Lent by OSCOTT COLLEGE.

349. THE VISION OF PIERS PLOWMAN. (Edited by Robert Crowley, London, 1550).

Lent by OSCOTT COLLEGE.

350. "THE PASSAGE OF OUR MOST DRAD SOUERAIGNE LADY QUENE ELYZABETH, through the citie of London to Westminster the daye before her coronacion." Printed by Richard Tottill, London, 1558. 4to.
                                                          Lent by The ARCHBISHOP OF CANTERBURY.

351. BIBLE, the second edition of the Bishops' Bible. Printed by Richard Jugge, London, 1572. Fol. Formerly belonged to Robert Dudley, Earl of Leicester, whose signature is on the inside of the cover, and whose badge—the bear and ragged staff—appears on the binding. In the calendar are entries recording births and marriages of members of the families of Sir Thomas Dilke, Sir Clement Fisher, Sir Edward Littleton, and Sir Clement Throckmorton.
                                    Lent by The RIGHT HON. SIR CHARLES DILKE, BART., M.P.

352. BIBLE, first edition, present translation 1611.
                                                                   Lent by WILLIAM SHARP OGDEN, ESQ.

353. BINDING, 1557, fine example. "Sententiæ."
                                                                   Lent by WILLIAM SHARP OGDEN, ESQ.

354. BINDING, 1563, embossed pigskin. "Cæsar."
                                                                   Lent by WILLIAM SHARP OGDEN, ESQ.

355. FERNES "BLAZON OF GENTRIE," 1586. London.
                                                                   Lent by WILLIAM SHARP OGDEN, ESQ.

356. GUAGGOS "CIVILE CONVERSATION," 1586. London.
                                                                   Lent by WILLIAM SHARP OGDEN, ESQ.

357. SPENSER "FAIRY QUEEN," imp^d. and Cohn clout imp^d. 1595, both first editions.
                                                                   Lent by WILLIAM SHARP OGDEN, ESQ.

358. BIBLE, 1621. This is a very interesting example, the Common Prayer bindings being in wood, with the sides covered with calf and embossed with Tudor emblems and arms of England previous to the Union. It has also massive brass bosses, &c.
                                                                   Lent by WILLIAM SHARP OGDEN, ESQ.

358a. THE BIRTH OF MANKINDE, otherwise named THE WOMAN'S BOOKE. Printed by Richarde Watkins, 1598.   Lent by W. H. WATTS, ESQ.

358b. THE ARTE OF RHETORICKE, by Thomas Wilson, 1553. Printed by John Kingston, London, 1584.   Lent by W. H. WATTS, ESQ.

358c. A BOOKE OF PRESIDENTS. Printed by John Charlewood, London, 1583.   Lent by W. H. WATTS, ESQ.

358d. PRAXIS FRANCISCI CLARKE. MSS. 1596.
                                                                    Lent by CHETHAM COLLEGE.

358e. PRAYERS AND MEDITATIONS, by Rev. John Bradford, who was put to death at Smithfield, July 1, 1555.
                                                                      Lent by CHETHAM COLLEGE.

CASE J.—ROOM III.

RELICS.

359. ROBE AND MANTLE IN WHITE EMBROIDERED SATIN, said to have been worn by Princess Elizabeth.

Lent by MRS. DENT *of Sudeley.*

360. HAT OF HENRY VIII.

Nicholas Bristowe, a favourite courtier of Henry VIII., was riding with the King and Queen Anne Boleyn in Hertfordshire. Passing Ayot St. Lawrence he greatly admired the place, wondering whose it was. The King said, "It is mine, but now shall be yours." Bristowe asking what evidence he was to produce of the gift, the King gave him the hat he was wearing and asked the Queen for her slippers (see No. 361), saying, "Bring me these in London, and I will give you the Title Deeds." The Hat and Slippers have since always gone with the estate.

Lent by LT.-COLONEL AMES.

361. SHOES OF ANNE BOLEYN, presented by her to Nicholas Bristowe (see No. 360).

Lent by LT.-COLONEL AMES.

362. A LACE CANOPY, said to have been worked by Queen Anne Boleyn, and used at the christening of Princess Elizabeth.

Lent by MRS. DENT *of Sudeley.*

363. NEEDLEWORK OF QUEEN KATHERINE OF ARAGON, consisting of thirteen pieces of embroidery, cut out of the original canvas, which had become dilapidated. The subjects are flowers, fruits, birds, and insects.

Lent by JOHN HARLEY, ESQ., M.D.

Lent by The EARL OF DENBIGH.

364. A BELT OF ELIZABETH.
365. PORTIONS OF FOUR EMBROIDERED VESTS OF ELIZABETH.
366. A PINCUSHION OF ELIZABETH.
367. A CAP OF ELIZABETH.
368. PAIR OF GAUNTLETS.
369. PAIR OF GAUNTLETS.

369.* CASE containing the first volume (manuscript) of the Court Leet Records of the Manor of Manchester, commencing in the year 1552, and printed copy of the volume open at the same page as the manuscript. The other deeds in this case relate to the Manor of Manchester, and range in date from Henry VII. to Elizabeth.

Lent by The LORD MAYOR AND CORPORATION OF MANCHESTER.

CASE K.—ROOM III.

RELICS.

Lent by MRS. DENT of Sudeley.

370. LOCK OF QUEEN KATHERINE PARR'S HAIR, taken from her coffin in 1782, in plain round gold locket.

In the summer of 1782, the earth in which Queen Katherine Parr lay interred was removed and at the depth of about two feet her leaden coffin or chest was found quite whole, and on the lid it when well cleaned there appeared the following rude but legible inscription: "K.P. Here Lyethe quene Kateryn Wife to Kyng Henry the VIII and Last the Wife of Thomas Lord of Sudeley high Admiyrall of Englond and Unkle to Kyng Edward the VI dyed 5 September MCCCCCXLVIII." The coffin was again opened in 1784 and 1786, the spot at that time where the body lay being used for the keeping of rabbits, which made holes and scratched about the royal tomb. Again in 1792 the tomb was violated; the tenant then occupying the Castle allowing a party of inebriated men to dig a fresh grave for the coffin. A tradition lingers in Winchcombe that each one of that band met with an untimely and horrible end. In 1817, the frequent violations of Queen Katherine's tomb were terminated by the then Rector of Sudeley, the Rev. John Lates, taking upon himself to remove the coffin into the stone vault of the Chandos family, there at last to find a shelter from the eye of the inquisitive and vulgar.

371. LOCK OF QUEEN KATHERINE PARR'S HAIR, taken from her coffin in 1792, delicately mounted in gold brooch; the letters "Q. C. P." worked in hair, surrounded with pearls.

372. LOCK OF QUEEN KATHERINE PARR'S HAIR, taken from her coffin in 1782, in heart-shaped gold locket.

373. LOCK OF QUEEN KATHERINE PARR'S HAIR, taken from her coffin in 1817, mounted in silver filagree frame, surmounted by a crown.

374. A TOOTH OF QUEEN KATHERINE PARR, taken from her coffin in 1792.

375. LOCK OF QUEEN KATHERINE PARR'S HAIR, taken from her coffin in 1792, mounted in black oval frame, and presented to the Sudeley Collection by John Hopton, Esq., of Canon Frane Court, in 1880.

376. A PIECE OF NEEDLEWORK, authenticated as part of a dress worn by Queen Katherine Parr.

G

377. Three Small Volumes of Queen Katherine Parr's Compositions. The *first* published in 1547; the *second* in March, 1548—just six months before her death; and the *third* in 1563.

378. Queen Katherine Parr's Book, entitled *Devotional Tracts*, containing:—

1. "A Sermon of St. Chrysostome," translated into Englishe, &c., by Thomas Lupsete, Londoner, 1534. At the bottom of the title-page is the Queen's signature, "Kateryn the Queen, K. P."
2. "A Swete and Devoute Sermon of Holy Saynet Ciprian," &c., translated by Sir T. Elyot, London, 1539.
3. "An Exhortation to Younge Men," &c., by Thomas Lupsete, 1534.
4. "On Charitie," 1534.
5. "Here be Gathered Counsailes of Sainte Isidoire," &c., 1539.
6. "A Compendious Treatise on Dyenge Well," &c., by Thomas Lupsete, Londoner, 1541.

The volume is a small duodecimo, bound in red velvet, with gilt leaves, and has had ornamental borders and clasps. On the fly-leaf opposite the first page are Scriptural sentences written by the Queen herself. On the opposite side of the fly-leaf are some verses, probably from the royal pen of Henry VIII., addressed to Katherine.

This book was given to Dr. E. Charlton, of Newcastle-on-Tyne, by the sister of the late President of the English College at Valladolid, who obtained it during his residence in Spain. It is not unlikely that it was carried thither by some of the English Catholics who resorted to that country for education. In 1625 it seems to have belonged to John Sherrott.

379. Autograph Letter of Thomas, Lord Seymour of Sudeley.

380. Autograph Letter from Queen Katherine Parr to Thomas, Lord Seymour of Sudeley, accepting his offer of marriage.

This letter is signed "Katherine the Queen, K.P.," and was purchased at the Strawberry Hill sale by John Coucher Dent, Esq. It has two indorsements. One in the handwriting of the time: "The Queen's letter from Chelsea to my Lord Admiral. The answer to the Lord Admiral of his former loves." The other, in a modern hand: "Q. K. Parr's letter, with the year she died, which was 1548, to her consort, Thomas Seymour, Lord High Admiral."

381. A Piece of Cere-Cloth, taken from Queen Katherine Parr's coffin in 1799.

382. Small Book of *Prayers or Meditations*, 1545, composed by Queen Katherine Parr. The binding was embroidered by the nuns of Gidding.

Room III.]   *Relics.*   91

383. SILVER WATCH, dated 1597,, formerly belonging to Queen Elizabeth. Maker's name, "*Johannes Bargis*," Londini.
Lent by REV. F. BINGHAM.

383*. MEDAL OF ERASMUS.
Lent by W. S. CHURCHILL, ESQ.

384. MATRIX OF SEAL OF THE PRIORY of St. Bartholomew the Great, in copper.
Lent by ROBERT DAY, ESQ.

385. A SMALL GOLD ETUI, formerly belonging to Anne Boleyn, in the form of a pistol, the barre serving the purpose of a whistle, and enclosing a set of toothpicks; round the handle is coiled a serpent.

A *family* tradition represents that this interesting trinket was a love token given by Henry VIII. to Anne Boleyn, and that the unfortunate Queen on the morning of her execution presented it to Captain Gwyn, the officer on guard, in token of her sense of his respectful conduct towards her. On presenting it, she told him "it was the first token the King had given her," bidding the officer observe "that a serpent formed part of the device, and a serpent," she said, "the giver had proved to her" (see Strickland's *Lives of the Queens of England*).
Lent by The REV. CANON W. S. BEVAN.

386. MATRIX OF SEAL OF CARDINAL CAMPEGGIO, Bishop of Bologna (1474-1539).
Lent by ROBERT DAY, ESQ.

387. ROSARY OF HENRY VIII.
Lent by The DUKE OF DEVONSHIRE, K.G.

388. AN INKSTAND, carved from a beam from Shakspeare's barn at New Place.
Lent by ALFRED HUTH, ESQ.

389. JEWEL OF AGATE INTAGLIO, given by Queen Elizabeth to Archbishop Parker.
Lent by GRANVILLE E. LLOYD BAKER, ESQ.

390. A CARVED IVORY BOX, rose turned, containing parchment with miniature of Queen Elizabeth and a description in Latin of an agate.

The particular agate referred to in this document may possibly be the intaglio described under No. 389, as it has always been preserved in this box.
Lent by GRANVILLE E. LLOYD BAKER, ESQ.

391. METAL-GILT WATCH, the lid engraved with the Crucifixion. "*W. Vibrech Leovardiæ fecit;*" about 1550.
>Lent by T. WHITCOMBE GREENE, ESQ.

392. METAL-GILT WATCH, the lid engraved with the head of a Roman Emperor. Maker's name, "*Jacques Bulcke;*" about 1550.
>Lent by T. WHITCOMBE GREENE, ESQ.

393. METAL-GILT WATCH, with portrait of a lady wearing the Order of the Golden Fleece; the works entirely of iron. (16th cent.)
>Lent by T. WHITCOMBE GREENE, ESQ.

394. ONE METAL-GILT WATCH, by Metzkr of Augsburg, A.D. 1550-1560.
>Lent by T. WHITCOMBE GREENE, ESQ.

395. SMALL METAL-GILT WATCH; the works entirely of iron. (1st half 16th century.)
>Lent by T. WHITCOMBE GREENE, ESQ.

396. METAL-GILT WATCH with Inscription "Sr Wm *Cooper to Eleanor, Daughter of Sr Mich^l Stanhope, wife to Thos Cooper his son of Thurgarten, co. Nots* 1539:" the lid is engraved with Coat of Arms.
>Lent by T. WHITCOMBE GREENE, ESQ.

397. A GOLD WATCH, stated to have belonged to Queen Elizabeth.
>Lent by MISS M. LLOYD.

398. A MELON-SHAPED SILVER WATCH in shagreen case, said to have belonged to Queen Elizabeth.
>Lent by MRS. CHARLES STUART.

399. PURSE worked by Queen Elizabeth.
>Lent by The EARL OF DENBIGH.

400. PURSE worked by Queen Elizabeth.
>Lent by The EARL OF DENBIGH.

401. A BUST OF SHAKSPEARE carved from a piece of Herne's Oak.
>Lent by ALFRED HUTH, ESQ.

402. AN IRON-GILT KEY, the handle formed by two winged sirens. (Italian, 16th cent.)
>Lent by T. WHITCOMBE GREENE, ESQ.

Relics.

403. AN IRON KEY, the handle formed by two griffins. (Italian, 16th cent.)
Lent by T. WHITCOMBE GREENE, ESQ.

404. AN IRON KEY, the stem surmounted by a Corinthian capital, supporting two dolphins, which form the handle. (Italian, 16th cent.)
Lent by T. WHITCOMBE GREENE, ESQ.

405. IRON KEY, the handle formed by two sirens, *temp.* Elizabeth.
Lent by T. WHITCOMBE GREENE, ESQ.

406. AN IRON KEY, with busts, masts, dolphins, &c., forming the handle. (Italian, 16th cent.)
Lent by T. WHITCOMBE GREENE, ESQ.

407. AN IRON KEY, with open-work handle. (French, 1540-1560.)
Lent by T. WHITCOMBE GREENE, ESQ.

408. ENGRAVED SHOE HORN, 1600. By Robert Mindum.
Lent by SIR JOHN EVANS, K.C.B.

409. ENGRAVED SHOE HORN, 1593. By Robert Mindum.
Lent by SIR JOHN EVANS, K.C.B.

410. ENGRAVED POWDER HORN, 1601. By Robert Mindum.
Lent by SIR JOHN EVANS, K.C.B.

411. WALKING-STAFF OF SIR NICHOLAS BACON.

When Sir Nicholas Bacon grew old he was very corpulent, and walked with difficulty, and in taking his seat on the bench used to give three taps with his staff on the floor, as a sign that he had recovered his breath, and that business might proceed.
Lent by SIR J. C. ROBINSON.

412. WALKING-STICK OF SIR FRANCIS DRAKE.
Lent by COLONEL HAROLD MALET.

413. SILVER RING, found near Armagh. (16th century.)
Lent by ROBERT DAY, ESQ.

414. A JETON to commemorate the victories of Captain Robert Blake, made to be worn in the cap. It is believed to be the first instance of a medal given for valour.
Lent by The REV. FRANCIS HOPKINSON.

415. PHŒNIX BADGE OF QUEEN ELIZABETH in silver (A.D. 1558).

    The Phœnix was early adopted by Elizabeth as her device: it was the symbol of celibacy; and she told her first Parliament that she wished her monument to inform posterity, "Here lies a Queen that lived and died a Virgin."
    Lent by ROBERT DAY, ESQ.

416. SEALED QUART, with Tudor rose and supporters, indicating the *quart*, and a lead seal with the letters "qt."
    Lent by W. H. WATTS, ESQ.

417. STIRRUP OF STEEL, said to have been used by Queen Elizabeth.
    Lent by JESUS COLLEGE, OXFORD.

418. IVORY WALKING-STICK, SILVER MOUNTED. The main part of the stick is in the form of a cable; at the ferrule end it is whipped. (16th cent.)
    Lent by WILLIAM GRIFFITHS, ESQ.

419. A SILVER-GILT MEDAL ON THE DESTRUCTION OF THE SPANISH ARMADA, 1588.

    It represents on one side the Pope, kings, bishops, and others seated in Council, and on the other the Spanish fleet driven against rocks.
    Lent by ROBERT DAY, ESQ.

420. ELEVEN GOLD POSY RINGS, *temp.* Henry VIII.—Elizabeth, with the following mottoes:— *As you yous me you shale find me; Kepe faith till Death; once myne and ever Thine; God I pray your happinesse inioy, etc.*
    Lent by ROBERT DAY, ESQ.

421. A MASSIVE GOLD RING set with a Carbuncle, *temp.* Elizabeth.
    Lent by ROBERT DAY, ESQ.

422. CASKET, made from Shakespeare's Mulberry tree.
    Lent by NATHAN HEYWOOD, ESQ.

423. SLIPPERS OF CATHERINE DE BERAIN, ward of Queen Elizabeth, and wife of Sir Richard Clough.
    Lent by MRS. GRIFFITHS.

424. PIECE OF EMBROIDERY, part of Queen Elizabeth's wardrobe.
    Lent by The EARL OF DENBIGH.

425. SILVER SIGNET RING, with crowned letter R and "Bacchal."
    Lent by ROBERT DAY, ESQ.

Room III.] Relics.

426. Matrix of Seal of Winchester, "Sigillum Commissarii Kynton."
Lent by Robert Day, Esq.

427. Copper Matrix of Seal of "Sigillu Thome Fynyon Abbatis de Cumbennere."
Lent by Robert Day, Esq.

428. Two Sergeants' Rings. Mottoes: FEAR AND LOVE GOD (Silver gilt). HONOR GOD IN EVERI PLASE (Gold).
Lent by Robert Day, Esq.

429. Massive Gold Ring, with letter R crowned.
Lent by Robert Day, Esq.

430. Two Silver Circular Mediæval Brooches, inscribed "JESUS NASARERUS, and AVE MARIA GRACIA RENA."
Lent by Robert Day, Esq.

431. Gold Mediæval Brooch, inscribed "AVE MARIA GRACIA PLENA DOMINUS." On the pin are the letters H crowned and A crowned, for Henry VIII. and Anne Boleyn.
Lent by Robert Day, Esq.

432. Heart Shaped Wrot Iron Stand (16th century).
Lent by William Sharp Ogden, Esq.

433. Mother of Pearl Jewel Casket, painted figures inside (16th century).
Lent by William Sharp Ogden, Esq.

434. The Badge of the Pilgrimage of Grace, embroidered in red velvet, consisting of a chalice, a host, five wounds, a crown of thorns, and the sacred monogram i b s. Thes are within a shield, below which are the letters I G *(Itinerarium Gratiæ)*. This badge was made up into a burse, and belonged to the domestic chapel of Kingerby Hall, North Lincolnshire.

The sudden and violent changes which Henry VIII. had brought about in the matter of Church government and the dissolution of the monasteries did not pass by without opposition from the populace. In many parts of the country this feeling showed itself in open rebellion. The most serious insurrection was that in the north, known as the *Pilgrimage of Grace*, in 1536-7. The first rising was in Lincolnshire, but was put down by the Duke of Suffolk without much difficulty. A subsequent insurrection in Yorkshire and the northern counties was much more serious, and was joined by about 40,000 men. The insurgents were under the command of Robert Aske, a Yorkshire gentleman, and at their head marched several priests in the habits of their order, bearing crosses and banners, in which were worked a plough (to encourage the husbandmen), a chalice and host (in remembrance of the spoiling of the Church), and the five wounds of Christ (to signify that they were fighting for Christ's sake). The rebels succeeded in taking Hull and York, as well as Pomfret Castle, into which the Archbishop of York and Lord D'Arcy had thrown themselves; both of whom with seeming reluctance surrendered, but afterwards joined the insurrection. The insurgents were at length dispersed, partly by the negotiations of the Duke of Norfolk and partly by the swelling of the River Don, which prevented their attacking the King's forces. Acting under Henry's special written orders, Norfolk executed martial law in the punishment of the offenders. Seventy-four persons, laity and clergy, were hanged in various towns in Westmoreland and Cumberland, and their leaders, including Aske, Lord D'Arcy, Sir John Bulmer, and Sir Francis Bigod, were brought to London, tried, condemned, and executed, some at Tyburn, others at York and Hull. Lady Bulmer, who had sympathized with the insurgents, died the dreadful death awarded by the English to female treason, and was burnt at the stake in Smithfield.

Lent by The LORD HERRIES.

435. GOLD RING, found on the Field of the Cloth of Gold. Very richly chased with scroll and foliated ornament. At present set with a large emerald, surrounded by brilliants. The ring is of early 16th century work.

Lent by HIS EMINENCE CARDINAL VAUGHAN.

436. IVORY AND SILVER HILTED KNIFE AND FORK IN CASE. 16th century.

Lent by WILLIAM SHARP OGDEN, ESQ.

437. SCISSORS, folding grip, inlaid with gold. 16th century.

Lent by WILLIAM SHARP OGDEN, ESQ.

CASE L.—ROOM III.

MINIATURES.

438. SIR FRANCIS DRAKE, KNT. Inscribed ÆTATIS SUÆ 42 ANO DMI 1581.
By NICHOLAS HILLIARD. Lent by The EARL OF DERBY.

439. LETTICE, COUNTESS OF ESSEX.
By ISAAC OLIVER. Lent by The EARL OF DERBY.

440. ARTHUR, PRINCE OF WALES.
By E. Edwards, after a picture in the possession of the Earl of Jersey. See description by Sir George Scharf, K.C.B. *Archæologia*, vol. xxxix., p. 457.
From the Strawberry Hill Collection.
Lent by The EARL OF DERBY.

441. QUEEN ELIZABETH.
By N. HILLIARD. Lent by The EARL OF DERBY.

442. ROBERT DEVEREUX, EARL OF ESSEX. From the Strawberry Hill Collection.
By ISAAC OLIVER. Lent by The EARL OF DERBY.

443. ISAAC OLIVER. From the Strawberry Hill Collection.
By HIMSELF. Lent by The EARL OF DERBY.

444. PORTRAIT OF A MAN.
By HANS HOLBEIN. Lent by The DUKE OF DEVONSHIRE., K.G.

445. THOMAS CROMWELL, EARL OF ESSEX. Dated 1515.
By HANS HOLBEIN. Lent by The DUKE OF DEVONSHIRE, K.G.

446. PORTRAIT OF A MAN. Dated 1588, aged 45.
Lent by The SOCIETY OF ANTIQUARIES.

447. SIR PHILIP SIDNEY, KNT.
By I. OLIVER. Lent by The RT. HON. SIR CHARLES DILKE, BART., M.P.

448. QUEEN ELIZABETH. Formerly belonged to Mary Queen of Scots.
Lent by SIR JAMES FERGUSSON, BART., M.P.

449. Procession of Queen Elizabeth to Blackfriars, June 9, 1600, on the occasion of the Marriage of Lord Herbert and Lady Anne Russell.

Queen Elizabeth is seated in a canopy chair of state. The six noblemen preceding her, all Knights of the Garter, are, Charles, Earl of Nottingham, Lord High Admiral; George Carey, second Lord Hunsdon, Lord Chamberlain; Henry, sixth Lord Cobham, Warden of the Cinque Ports; George Clifford, Earl of Cumberland; Thomas, Earl of Suffolk; and Edward, fourth Earl of Worcester.

Following the litter is Lady Anne Russell, the bride, dau. of John, Lord Russell. The bridegroom, Lord Herbert, is one of the four knights carrying the canopy.

Lent by A. Campbell Blair, Esq.

454. Sir John Boling and his Mother. Inscribed L 1525.
By Lucas de Heere.   *Lent by Earl Spencer, K.G.*

455. Henry Howard, Earl of Surrey. From the Stowe Collection.
After Holbein.   *Lent by The Duke of Norfolk, E.M., K.G.*

456. Edward de Vere, 17th Earl of Oxford (1540–1604).
Lent by John Harley, Esq., M.D.

457. An Impression in Grey Paper taken from Queen Katherine Parr's Coffin, by Edmund T. Bourne, Esq., of Winchcombe, in 1817.
Lent by Mrs. Dent of Sudeley.

458. Henry VIII.
Lent by Mrs. Dent of Sudeley.

459. Queen Katherine Parr. The brooch which she wears bears a portrait of Henry VIII. From the Strawberry Hill Collection.
By Hans Holbein.   *Lent by Mrs. Dent of Sudeley.*

460. Thomas, Lord Seymour of Sudeley (d. 1549). Bust facing, wearing dark mantle, and cap with feather; long beard.
By Hans Holbein.   *Lent by Mrs. Dent of Sudeley.*

461. Edward VI.
Lent by Mrs. Dent of Sudeley.

ROOM III.] *Miniatures.*

462. QUEEN JANE SEYMOUR. From the Strawberry Hill Collection.
By HOLBEIN. Lent by MRS. DENT of Sudeley.

463. QUEEN ANNE BOLEYN. From the Strawberry Hill Collection.
Lent by MRS. DENT of Sudeley.

464. HENRY VIII. Carving in Boxwood.

This carving also came from the Strawberry Hill Collection. Walpole (*Anecdotes*) does not say whence he obtained it, but he writes: "Holbein cut his own head in wood, and I have another by his hand of the King, in which about his neck, instead of a fringe, he wears a watch."
By HANS HOLBEIN. Lent by MRS. DENT of Sudeley.

465. SIR WALTER RALEIGH, KNT.
Lent by MRS. DENT of Sudeley.

466. EDWARD SEYMOUR, DUKE OF SOMERSET, K.G.
Lent by MRS. DENT of Sudeley.

467. QUEEN MARY.
Lent by MRS. DENT of Sudeley.

468. HENRY VIII. Carving in Hone-stone.

This carving in hone-stone by Holbein is considered to be one of the finest portraits of the King. In Vertue's Catalogue of King Charles I.'s Collection of Pictures, &c., London, 1757, it is described as carved in King Henry VIII.'s time. "Item, A picture carved in grey soft stone, representing King Henry VIII., at length, an entire figure in a curious little carved frame, which the King had when Prince." It was purchased by Horace Walpole at the sale of Lady Elizabeth Germayn's property in 1777, having formerly been in the Arundel Collection. Walpole (*Anecdotes*) describes it as "A fine little figure of Henry cut in stone, whole length." In 1842 it was sold at the Strawberry Hill sale to J. Coucher Dent, Esq. Two other figures carved in stone by Holbein were in the Museum of Tradescant at Lambeth.
By HANS HOLBEIN. Lent by MRS. DENT of Sudeley.

469. SILVER REPOUSSÉ PLAQUE OF QUEEN ELIZABETH, after the Engraving by Crispin de Passe, with her Autograph.
Lent by MRS. DENT of Sudeley.

CASES M & N—ROOM IV.

AUTOGRAPHS.

470. LETTER FROM FERDINAND V., King of Aragon, and Isabella of Castile his Queen, conveying an order to the Spanish Ambassador at Rome to offer to Pope Innocent VIII. the expression of their great regret at not being able to pay him their personal homage on his elevation to the chair of St. Peter, in consequence of their being at that time seriously engaged in expelling the Moors from their country. Dated Alcala, 8th Feb., 1486. Signatures of Ferdinand and Isabella.
Lent by GEORGE PRITCHARD, ESQ.

471. WARRANT ON SIR ROBERT LITTON, Keeper of the Great Wardrobe, &c., for a riding gown of black satin, "hacched and furred." Dated Shene, 14th December, 1498. Signature of King Henry VII.
Lent by GEORGE PRITCHARD, ESQ.

472. END OF A BOOK OF ACCOUNTS, signed by King Henry VII. Dated Michaelmas, 1506.
Lent by GEORGE PRITCHARD, ESQ.

473. LETTER FROM HENRY VII. to Louis XII. of France. A letter of compliment, acknowledging letters received from Louis by his "valet de chambre Mace de Villebresme," and assuring Louis "que nous desirons voullons et entendons demourer & continuer tousjours vre bon cousin, loyal frere, bon confedere e allie." "Escript en nre manoir de Waynstede, le XII° jour daoust lan XV*c.* & six."
Lent by ALFRED HUTH, ESQ.

474. ORDER OF HENRY VIII., dated 3rd of January, 2nd year of his reign, 1510, at the Manor of Richmond, for "five yards of London Russet" to be delivered to each one of thirteen yeomen of the King's Chamber attending within the Tower of London for their waiting clothing, "to be as good a suete as it hath ben of olde time."
Lent by GEORGE PRITCHARD, ESQ.

475. WARRANT FROM HENRY VIII. to Sir Andrew Wyndesore, Keeper of the Great Wardrobe, to deliver certain apparel to the bearer. Dated Greenwich, 14th April, 2 Henry VIII. [1511]. Autograph signature.
Lent by G. MILNER-GIBSON-CULLUM, ESQ.

Autographs.

476. WARRANT BY LOUIS XII., KING OF FRANCE, for payment of 2,200 livres to Laurens de Quenteuille. Dated 2nd November, 1513. Autograph signature.

Lent by G. MILNER-GIBSON-CULLUM, ESQ.

477. RECEIPT FOR THE PAYMENT OF £113 6s. 8d., commanded by King Henry VIII. to be paid to the "Popys Ambassador, whiche brought to the Kinge the cappe of mayntenance in reward £100, and to Mounsier de Pyssener in reward 20 marks," in all £113 6s. 8d. Dated 15th September, 1514. Signed by T. Lincoln, post Ebor [Cardinal Wolsey].

Lent by GEORGE PRITCHARD, ESQ.

478. WARRANT FROM HENRY VIII., reciting that "Our trusty and right well beloved Councillor Thomas Wolsey our elemosyner delivered unto Sir Thomas Knyvet, Kt.," the sum of 200 marks, by way of loan on his departing to sea, and directing that the bond be given to his widow, Viscountess Lisle, to be cancelled. Westminster, 13th November, 1512.

Lent by GEORGE PRITCHARD, ESQ.

479. LETTER FROM THOMAS WOLSEY, CARDINAL, ARCHBISHOP OF YORK, to Pope Leo X., announcing the death of John [Hatton], Bishop of Negropont, suffragan of York, and recommending Richard [Wilson], Prior of Drax, to be appointed in his place. Dated London, 3 June, 1516.

Lent by ALFRED HUTH, ESQ.

480. LETTERS OF THE EMPEROR CHARLES V. to the Abbot and Convent of St. Vincent at Metz, directing them to admit John Thevene to the Monastery "ad quendam præbendam laycalem." Dated at Ratisbon, 3 May, 1532. Autograph signature.

Lent by G. MILNER-GIBSON-CULLUM, ESQ.

481. LETTER FROM CARDINAL LORENZO CAMPEGGIO, the Papal Legate in the cause of the divorce of Henry VIII. and Katherine of Aragon, to Francis II., Duke of Milan. Dated 24 Aug., 1533. Autograph signature.

Lent by G. MILNER-GIBSON-CULLUM, ESQ.

482. AUTOGRAPH LETTER FROM QUEEN KATHARINE OF ARAGON in Spanish to her nephew, the Emperor Charles V., respecting the divorce of herself and Henry VIII. She complains of the delay, and asks the Emperor to take action in the matter to persuade the Pope to give his decision, and for his help generally. Dated at Buckden, 8 Feb., 1534.

Lent by ALFRED HUTH, ESQ.

483. LETTER OF ANNE BOLEYN, Queen of England, addressed "To o' trusty and right wellbeloued Thomas Cromwell, esquer, Secretary to my Lord." Dated March 8 (1535 ?). Autograph signature, "Anne the quene."

Lent by ALFRED HUTH, ESQ.

484. LETTER FROM HENRY VIII. to [Grace] Lady Bedingfeld, concerning the burial of Katherine of Aragon, his wife, spoken of in the letter as "widow and douagier of the right excellent prince our dearest and naturall brother Prince Arthur." Dated at Greenwich, 10 Jan., 1536. With the King's signature.

Lent by SIR HENRY BEDINGFELD, BART.

485. GRANT BY ANNE OF CLEVES, LATE QUEEN OF ENGLAND, to Philip Chewte, Esq., of the office of Bailiff of the Manor of Frossenden, co. Suffolk. Dated March 4th, 1552. Autograph signature, "Anna the dowghter off Cleves."

Lent by ALFRED HUTH, ESQ.

486. LETTER FROM THOMAS CROMWELL, afterwards EARL OF ESSEX, in French, to the French Ambassador in London. He announces the arrival of the Ambassadors of Denmark and Norway at the Court of the Queen Dowager of Hungary to conclude and sign a treaty of alliance. Dated Stepney, September 15th [1534].

Lent by ALFRED HUTH, ESQ.

487. RECEIPT FOR CLOTH OF GOLD, tinsel satin, velvet satin, sarcenet, chamblette, etc., from Messrs. de Bardy, Merchants, of Florence. Signed "Andrew Wyndsor, Keeper of the Great Wardrobe. 12 Feb., 1529."

Lent by GEORGE PRITCHARD, ESQ.

488. LETTER FROM KATHERINE PARR, Queen of Henry VIII., to her brother on the occasion of her marriage to the King. Dated July 20, 35 Hen. VIII. [1543]. Signed "Kateryn the Queene."

Lent by ALFRED HUTH, ESQ.

489. WARRANT BY QUEEN MARY I. appointing Sir Henry Bedingfeld Lieutenant of the Tower: Dated 28 Oct. 2 & 3 Phil & Mar. [1555] with signature "Marye the Queene."

It was remarked at the time that as the Lieutenant of the Tower had been changed before the murder of Edward V. and his brother, so this change might portend evil to the Princess Elizabeth, who was then a prisoner. Nothing, however, came of it.

Lent by SIR HENRY BEDINGFELD, BART.

490. ORDER issued by Mary for £50 to be paid to the footman of her late "father and brother—, whose soul God pardon." Signed: Thomas Berry. 16 May, 1554.

Lent by GEORGE PRITCHARD, ESQ.

491. SIGN-MANUAL OF PHILIP AND MARY, ordering Sir Henry Tirrell, Knt., to muster levy all under his rule, both horse and foot, to put down tumult, stir, or rebellion. 20 April, 1555.

Lent by GEORGE PRITCHARD, ESQ.

492. INSTRUCTIONS FROM QUEEN MARY to Ant. Hussy to act as Governor of ye Merchants in ye Low Countries, etc. Signed: June, 1556.

Lent by ALFRED HUTH, ESQ.

493. LETTER FROM QUEEN ELIZABETH to Sir Henry Bedingfeld, calling upon him to supply "one hable man," armed and mounted, to go to Newcastle, in case of French designs upon Berwick. Dated Dec. 26th, 2 Eliz. [1560]. With autograph signature.

Lent by SIR HENRY BEDINGFELD, BART.

494. AUTOGRAPH LETTER OF QUEEN ELIZABETH, in French, addressed to Henry IV. of France, with seals and silk. No date. Thanks him for the portrait he has sent, but says the friendship of which his messenger assures her is even more valuable to her, who rejoices in seeing that "a good tree continues to bear good fruit."

Lent by ALFRED HUTH, ESQ.

495. LETTER FROM REGINALD POLE, CARDINAL, ARCHBISHOP OF CANTERBURY, in Italian, to Cardinal Sant' Angelo. Dated London, January 14th, 1555.

Lent by ALFRED HUTH, ESQ.

496. LETTER OF QUEEN ELIZABETH to Sir Henry Sidney, Knt., Deputy Governor of Ireland, sparing the life of the Earl of Thomond. Dated Hampton Court, November 20th, 1570.

Lent by GEORGE PRITCHARD, ESQ.

497. LETTER OF WILLIAM CECIL, Lord Burghley, to Robert Peter, auditor of the receipts at the Exchequer, September 26th, 1574, on financial matters, and mentioning the receipt of a packet of letters by Secretary Walsingham. Autograph signatures.

Lent by ALFRED HUTH, ESQ.

498. LETTER FROM SIR PHILIP SIDNEY to Lord Burghley, Lord High Treasurer, praying an advance of £200 for Sir Nicholas Bagnoll. Dated Leyston House, February 8th, 1576.

Lent by ALFRED HUTH, ESQ.

499. LETTER FROM ROBERT DUDLEY, EARL OF LEICESTER, to the Lord Treasurer and Sir Walter Mildmay, requiring five thousand pounds beforehand, while his assurances are being prepared. Dated at the Court, November 28th, 1576.

Lent by ALFRED HUTH, ESQ.

500. ORDER TO PAY SIR FRANCIS DRAKE, JOHN HAWKINS, and two others, certain sums of money. Sir Fr. Drake being away his money to be paid to John Hawkins. Signed, Lord Burghley and Francis Walsingham. 4 August, 1584.

Lent by GEORGE PRITCHARD, ESQ.

501. ORDER BY THE PRIVY COUNCIL, directing a sum of £30 to be paid to George Constable, muster-master in co. of Lincoln. Signed by John Whitgift (Archbishop of Canterbury), George Talbot (6th Earl of Shrewsbury), Henry Stanley (4th Earl of Derby), Lord Hounsdon, William Brooke (4th Lord Cobham), Thomas Sackville (1st Lord Buckhurst), and William Burghley. 12 March, 1586.
Lent by GEORGE PRITCHARD, ESQ.

502. LETTER FROM SIR FRANCIS DRAKE to the Earl of Essex, evidently relating to the expedition against Spain, though very guardedly expressed. Dated February 16, 1587.
Lent by ALFRED HUTH, ESQ.

503. LETTER OF SIR FRANCIS DRAKE, being a note of armour, provisions, and other necessaries to be made in the Low Countries, amounting to £20,723 13s. 4d., with an order for shipping. Dated October 12, 1588. Signatures of Sir Francis Drake, Sir John Norris, Edward Fenton.
Lent by GEORGE PRITCHARD, ESQ.

504. ORDER FROM QUEEN ELIZABETH TO THE SHERIFF OF NORFOLK to prepare the soldiers and all the bands in the County of Norfolk at an hour's warning, as the Spanish Armada was approaching our shores. Signed by William Haydon, Sheriff, 21 June, 1588.
Lent by GEORGE PRITCHARD, ESQ.

505. ORDER IN COUNCIL to Sir Julius Corsar, to consider the legality of the Placart granted by the States forming the Dutch Republic as to the recognition of their independence. Signed by Sir Thomas Bromley, Lord Burghley, Lord Howard of Effingham, Sir Francis Knollys, and Sir Christopher Hatton. 28 Dec., 1585.
Lent by GEORGE PRITCHARD, ESQ.

506. MINUTE OF THE PRIVY COUNCIL, ordering £10,000 for victualling ships preparing for the capture of Cadiz. Signed by Lord Burghley, Earl of Essex, and Lord Howard. 19th Feb., 1596.
Lent by GEORGE PRITCHARD, ESQ.

507. LETTER FROM ROBERT DEVEREUX, Earl of Essex, in French, to Henry IV. of France. Endorsed "Le comte d'Essex, Janvier, 1595." With the original seal.
Lent by ALFRED HUTH, ESQ.

508. LETTERS FROM SIR WALTER RALEIGH to his nephew, Sir John Gilbert, Knight, of July 14th (a little before the sailing of the Island expedition under Essex, on August 17th, 1597), with address and seal.
Lent by ALFRED HUTH, ESQ.

509. LETTER FROM HENRY WRIOTHESLEY, Earl of Southampton, to Lord Spencer, relating to the expedition to the Netherlands.
Lent by ALFRED HUTH, ESQ.

510. RECEIPT BY FRANCIS, Duke of Anjou, for a sum of money received from Pierre Chenoule. Dated Dunkirk, June 16th, 1580. Autograph signature.
Lent by G. MILNER-GIBSON-CULLUM, ESQ.

511. WARRANT BY FRANCIS I., KING OF FRANCE. Dated June 20th, 1540. Imperfect. Autograph signature.
Lent by G. MILNER-GIBSON-CULLUM, ESQ.

512. LETTER TO POPE PAUL III. BY MARY OF AUSTRIA, Queen of the Netherlands, sister of Charles V.
Lent by G. MILNER-GIBSON-CULLUM, ESQ.

513. DEED OF GRANT, by which Sir William Stanley, Knt., of Hooton, co. Chester, sells land at Ewlowe, Hawarden, in co. of Flint, to Margaret Both for five pounds in silver. Dated 1482.
Lent by NATHAN HEYWOOD, ESQ.

CASE O.—ROOM V.

ELECTROTYPES.

LENT BY THE SCIENCE AND ART DEPARTMENT.

514. SALVER. The original, of silver-gilt, the gift of Archbishop Parker in 1570, is the property of Corpus Christi College, Cambridge. Engraved with floriated arabesques, with lobes radiating from a central boss bearing a shield in champlevé enamel of the arms of Archbishop Parker. *English.* Hall-mark, 1545.

515. TANKARD AND COVER. The original, of silver-gilt, the gift of Archbishop Parker in 1571, is the property of Corpus Christi College, Cambridge. The drum has bands of arabesque ornament in repoussé, and medallions with masks in high relief within laurel leaves. The lid is similarly ornamented, and has three helmeted masks. *English.* Hall-mark, 1570-1.

516. EWER. The original, of silver-gilt, the gift of Archbishop Parker in 1570, is the property of Corpus Christi College, Cambridge. Decorated with an arabesque pattern in repoussé on the octagonal bowl and base. The lid has a boss with the arms of the college and of the donor, with his motto, initials, and the date, 1570, in enamel. *English.* Hall-mark, 1545.

517. EWER. Copper-gilt, chased with strap-work, cartouches, &c. The original, of silver-gilt, is the property of Her Majesty the Queen, and forms part of the collection of Royal plate at Windsor Castle. *English.* Date 1597.

518. CUP. The original, a cocoanut mounted in silver-gilt, the gift of Katherine Baylye, is the property of New College, Oxford. The base ornamented in repoussé, with fruit and strap-work, the stem engraved in leaf-pattern. Tooth-edged bands and a rim engraved with an inscription and floral ornament enclose the nut. *English.* Hall-mark, 1584.

519. SPOON. The original, one of a set of thirteen silver-gilt Apostle spoons, is the property of Corpus Christi College, Cambridge. It has a flat, wide bowl, and a figure of St. Paul. *English.* Hall-mark, 1515.

520. SALVER. The original, of silver parcel-gilt, is the property of the Merchant Taylors' Company. The boss in the centre bears the arms of the family of May, surrounded by panels of dolphins and flowers in repoussé, and engraved with flowers, scrolls, and strap-work. *English.* 1597.

521. SPOON. The original, one of a set of thirteen silver-gilt Apostle spoons, is the property of Corpus Christi College, Cambridge. It has a flat, wide bowl, and a figure of the Saviour. *English.* Hall-mark, 1566.

522. WINE WAGGON AND TUN. The original, of silver-gilt, is the property of the Mercers' Company. The waggon, on four wheels, with discs of arms at the sides in enamel, is elaborately engraved and chased with arabesques. Boxes for spices at the ends are surmounted by figures on pedestals, and in front of the car is the figure of the Master; between the stages is a medallion engraved with Judith and Holofernes.

The tun, on a richly-engraved oblong base with bosses of enamel, is surmounted by a column having a band of enamel, dolphin brackets and gargoyles, surmounted by an eagle on a globe. *English.* First half of 16th century.

523. CUP AND COVER. The original, of silver-gilt, the gift of John Campernowne, is the property of Corpus Christi College, Cambridge. A baluster stem with three brackets supports a straight-sided bowl, engraved with floral ornament, three skulls, and the arms of the donor. The cover is surmounted by the figure of a warrior with spear and shield. *English.* Hall-mark, 1602-3.

524. CUP AND COVER. The original, a cocoanut, mounted in silver-gilt, is the property of Exeter College, Oxford. The stem is formed by thin bars, resting on leaves ; the cover has a crested rim, and a ball enclosed in leaves of openwork tracery. *English.* 16th century.

525. TANKARD. The original, of serpentine mounted in silver-gilt, is the property of Clare College, Cambridge. Repoussé and engraved with strap-work, masks, birds, fruit, and flowers. *English.* 16th century.

526. CUP AND COVER. The original, of gold, the gift of George Hall, Bishop of Chester, is the property of Exeter College, Oxford. It has two handles, and is decorated in repoussé with lozenge-shaped gadroons, and engraved with flowers and an inscription. *English.* 16th century.

527. MACE. The original, of silver-gilt, is the property of the Merchant Taylors' Company. It has shields of arms, and two plain rims. Made by Duckett, a goldsmith, in 1597. *English.* 16th century.

528. PATEN. The original, of silver-gilt, from the Kearney Abbey Collection, is in the South Kensington Museum, Reg. No. 737.-1877. Punched with a Tudor rose, circlets, chevrons, trefoils, and shamrock leaves. *English.* Hall-mark, 1562-3.

529. CUP. The original, a cocoanut cup, mounted in silver-gilt, is the property of Queen's College, Oxford. Three lions support the base and trumpet-shaped stem ; the nut is enclosed by three bands of trefoil ornament. *English.* 16th century.

530. SALT-CELLAR. The original, of silver, is the property of South Kensington Museum. The base and stem are ornamented with fruit, flowers, and strap-work in repoussé. *English.* 17th century.

531. SALVER. Copper-gilt, chased with strap-work, cartouches, &c. The original, of silver-gilt, is the property of Her Majesty the Queen, and forms part of the collection of royal plate at Windsor Castle. *English.* Date 1597.

532. EWER. The original, of silver-gilt, is the property of the Corporation of Bristol, the gift of Alderman Robert Kitchen. The foot and stems with bands of chased ornament support a vase-shaped bowl engraved with arabesques, festoons of fruit, and marine monsters; in front in relief is a cherub head; a Medusa mask supports the plain curved handle, on which is an arabesque figure. *English.* Plate mark of 1595.

533. SALVER. The original, of silver-gilt, is the property of the Corporation of Bristol, the gift of Alderman Robert Kitchen. Engraved and chased with the Tudor rose, arabesques, festoons of fruit, and sea monsters in medallions. In the centre a raised medallion bears the arms of the donor. *English.* Plate mark of 1595.

534. REGALIA.—SALT-CELLAR on high pedestal, copper gilt, chased with foliage and allegorical figure subjects in circular medallions, the summit crowned by a small statuette of a warrior. The original, of silver gilt, forms part of the regalia in the Tower of London. *English.* Date about 1560.

535. SALVER. The original, of silver parcel-gilt, the gift of William Ofley, is the property of the Merchant Taylors' Company. On a boss in the centre are the arms of the donor, surrounded with repoussé panels of lions' heads, flowers, and fruit. On the rim are shields of arms of the Company, and of the donor, with his merchant mark, and an inscription. *English.* 1590.

536. SALT-CELLAR and COVER. The original, of silver-gilt, repoussé and engraved, is the property of Corpus Christi College, Oxford. The bowl has cartouches, with central bosses and engraved foliated scroll-work; the lid, similarly ornamented, is surrounded with a figure with staff and shield. *English.* Hall-mark, 1554.

CASE P.—ROOM V.

LENT BY THE SCIENCE AND ART DEPARTMENT.

537. WATCH. Silver, elliptic, the cases engraved with Scriptural subjects, gilt dial; maker, "Barnes at Dorcest" (Dorchester). *English.* About 1600.

538. CUP. Silver. The shallow bowl is supported by a baluster-shaped stem, standing on a spreading foot. Found in a rabbit burrow at Stoke Prior, near Leominster, Herefordshire. *English.* London hall-mark for 1578-9.

ROOM V.] *Plate.* 109

539. JUG. Mottled brown German stoneware. The neck mounted with broad silver band of strap-work, foliage, and masks. The mounting *English*. About 1580.

540. JUG OR TEA POT. Chinese porcelain, octagonal form; with blue mandarins and ornaments; mounted in silver-gilt, the foot and cover chased with birds, flowers, and cartouches. The mounting *English*. Hall-marks for the year 1585.

541. SALT-CELLAR WITH COVER. A small "standing salt"; silver-gilt, cylindrical, repoussé with strap-work, fruit, and masks, the projecting top and base chased with bands of diaper ornament. The cover, which is similarly decorated, is surmounted with the figure of a warrior with shield and spear. *English*. Hall-mark for 1566-7.

542. SALT. Silver-gilt, circular, bell-shaped, in three tiers, the two lower ones having compartments for salt, and the upper one forming a pepper-caster. The salt is repoussé with strap-work and floral designs, and rests on three claw and ball feet. Two shields are engraved respectively with the letters F. E. A. and a fox. Found in a rabbit burrow at Stoke Prior, near Leominster, Herefordshire. *English*. London hall-mark for 1594-5.

543. MAZER BOWL. Walnutwood, decagonal, with chased silver rim and foot, united at the back by five silver demi-figures of females. *English*. Hall-mark of 1595. (Robinson Collection.)

544. TANKARD, OR BLACK JACK. Leather, with rim of silver, slightly ornamented, bearing an inscription. *English*. Early 17th century.

545. PEPPER CASTER. Silver-gilt, vase-shaped, repoussé with strap-work and fruit, and chased with bands of diaper ornament. *English*. Hall-mark for 1563-4.

546. JUG. Stoneware, with silver-gilt lid and silver-gilt bands round the mouth and foot. The lid is repoussé with scrolls and masks, and the upper band chased with foliations. *English*. About 1580.

547. JEWEL. Gold, enamelled; a "Memento mori," in form of a coffin with scrolls and arabesques on black ground, inscribed round the sides "Through the resurrection of Christe we be all sanctified." Within the coffin is an enamelled skeleton. *English*. About 1600. (Found at Tor Abbey, Devonshire.)

548. SALT. Silver-gilt, circular, bell-shaped, engraved with a floral pattern. The dome-shaped cover is surmounted by a ring handle. Found in a rabbit burrow at Stoke Prior, near Leominster, Herefordshire. *English*. London hall-mark for 1596-7.

549. RING. Gold. With circular bezel, deeply chased with representation of a cradle; the shoulders chased with flowers, the hoop with spiral flutes separated by beading, inscribed within "My . wille . were"; the letters nielloed. *English*. 16th century. (Waterton Collection.)

550. RING. Gold, massive. With hexagonal bezel chased with an eagle, the shoulders engraved with the Virgin and Child, and S. John; inside, the initials J. K., with a true-lovers' knot. *English.* Early 16th century. (Waterton Collection.)

551. RING. Gold, signet. The bezel engraved with shield of arms, and the initials C. P. *English.* 16th century. (Waterton Collection.)

552. RING. Gold. The hoop chased with rich floriated ornament, and two scrolls, inscribed "Nul sans peyn"; inside "sans mal desyr." *English.* Early 16th century. (Waterton Collection.)

553. RING. Gold, with traces of enamel. With circular bezel, uninscribed, the shoulders fluted, the centre groove containing the figure of a saint, the others engraved with marguerites, inscribed within "De bon cor." *English.* Early 16th century. Found near York, 1855. (Waterton Collection.)

554. RING. Gold. The bezel set with a crystal, engraved with an escutcheon, above which are the initials W. G.; the date 1555 beneath the crystal. *English.* 16th century. (Waterton Collection.)

555. RING. Gold. With revolving bezel; on one side a hawk, on the other a shield of arms with three lions passant gardant. *English.* 16th century. (Waterton Collection.)

556. RING. Gold. With hexagonal bezel with death's head in white enamel, and the inscription " + Nosse te ypsum," the edge of the bezel inscribed in enamelled letters " + DYE TO LYVE;" the shoulders chased with scrolls and enriched with black enamel. *English.* 16th century. (Waterton Collection).

557. RING. Gold. With octagonal bezel engraved with shield of arms. *English.* Late 16th century. (Waterton Collection.)

558. RING. Gold. The bezel engraved with a lion rampant, and the letters A·H above it. *English.* 16th century. (Waterton Collection.)

559. RING. Gold, massive. The bezel chased with representation of a castle, the shoulders engraved with figures of the Virgin and Child, and S. Christopher; inscribed within "En bon an." *English.* Early 16th century. (Waterton Collection.)

560. RING. Silver. The hoop inscribed outside with the words " + Quant. dieu. plera. melior. sera." *English.* Early 16th century. (Waterton Collection.)

561. RING. Gold. The bezel nearly circular, set with crystal over crimson foil, engraved with an escutcheon of arms; beneath the crystal are the letters V.M.N., and the date 1572. *English.* (Waterton Collection.)

562. RING. Gold. With projecting bezel set with a sharp-pointed writing diamond; traces of black enamel round bezel and on shoulders. *English.* 16th century. (Waterton Collection.)

563. RING. Gold. The bezel deeply chased with shield of arms, the shoulders formed of caryatid figures boldly chased; inside the monogram C.B. *English.* 16th century. (Waterton Collection.)

564. RING. Gold. With circular bezel chased with hound couchant beneath a tree, and initials I.L. *English.* 16th century. (Waterton Collection.)

565. RING. Gold. The bezel set with a crystal, engraved with an escutcheon, crest, and mantling; dated beneath the crystal, 159(?)7. *English.* Late 16th century. (Waterton Collection.)

566. RING. Silver gilt. Hollow, with six rounded projections on the hoop, chased in relief with the words "Je. le de. sir," alternating with coronets. *English.* Late 15th century. (Waterton Collection.)

567. RING. Bronze. With circular bezel chased with a merchant's mark, with traces of spiral gilding on the hoop. *English.* 16th century. (Waterton Collection.)

568. RING. Gold. With circular bezel, set with crystal intaglio of helmeted head, profile to right, the ground foiled crimson. *English.* Late 16th century. (Waterton Collection.)

569. RING. Silver, signet. With octagonal bezel, engraved with the letter I beneath a coronet, the hoop spirally fluted. *English.* 16th century. (Waterton Collection.)

570. RING. Gold. The bezel set with crystal, engraved with an escutcheon bearing a merchant's mark, viz., the monogram E.M. surmounted by a double cross. *English.* 16th century. (Waterton Collection.)

571. RING. Silver. Hoop, with traces of gilding; inscribed outside "Cest mon plaisir"; the words divided by two trefoils each. *English.* Early 16th century. (Waterton Collection.)

572. RING. Gold. The bezel set with a crystal, engraved with an escutcheon. *English.* Late 16th century. (Waterton Collection.)

573. RING. Gold. The bezel engraved with shield of arms, crest, and motto; the shoulder chased with thistles. *English.* 16th century. (Waterton Collection.)

574. RING. Gold. With circular bezel chased with a rebus, a tree; on one side W Y, on the other O T reading (if the tree be an elm) "Wy elm ot"; on the root an R. From the Coleby Hall sale. *English.* 16th century. (Waterton Collection.)

575. COFFER. Iron, clamped with cross bands, and painted with flowers; a toy model of a strong box. *German.* Early 16th century. Given by the Rev. R. Brooke.

576. GLOVES (a pair). Leather, the cuff embroidered with silk, gold thread, and seed pearls, on a satin ground, and fringed with gold and silver lace. Given by King Henry VIII. to Sir Anthony Denny, Kt., Privy Councillor, a friend of the King, and one of his executors. Given by Sir Edward Denny, Bart.

577. PANEL OF EMBROIDERY. English work of the early part of the 16th century.

578. GLOVES OR MITTENS (a pair). Crimson velvet, embroidered with gold and silver thread and silk, the cuff also richly embroidered on white satin ground. Given by Queen Elizabeth to her Maid of Honour, Margaret Edgcumbe, wife of Sir Edward Denny, Kt., Banneret. Given by Sir Edward Denny, Bart.

579. STATUETTE. Carved oak. Figure of a man wearing a cloak and a flat cap. *English*. Early 16th century.

580. LOCK AND HASP, WITH KEY. Wrought iron. With incised scrolls, rosettes in relief, and pierced border; the key with trefoil bow. *English* (from Somersetshire). 16th century.

581. BUST. Carved jet. Portrait of King Henry VIII., with paste emerald fastening to the ruff. *English* or *German*. Dated at back, "A° D$\overline{NI}$ 1528."

582. FRAGMENT OF A RETABLE OF CARVED ALABASTER. Found in the churchyard wall at Milton, Cambridgeshire, in 1889. Nottingham School of Sculpture. *English*. Late 15th century.

583. STATUETTE. Carved oak. Figure of St. Andrew. *English*. Early 16th century.

584. BADGE. Wrought iron; a portcullis badge of the Tudor family. *English*. 16th century.

585. BADGE. Wrought iron; a portcullis badge of the Tudor family. *English*. 16th century.

CASE Q.—ROOM V.

586. VIRGINAL. Formerly belonging to Queen Elizabeth. Cedarwood, the interior decorated with a band of arabesques painted in carmine and blue on a gold ground, and the front with panels of similar ornament, having also on the left the royal arms of Queen Elizabeth, and on the right a dove, crowned, holding a sceptre, and standing on a root of an oak tree. There are fifty keys with jacks and quills, thirty of them mounted with ebony, with stamped and gilt ornament on the ends, and the rest inlaid with

silver, ivory, and various kinds of wood. The outer case is deal, covered with crimson velvet and lined with yellow silk, fitted with three engraved and gilt lock plates, and the inside of the rising flaps ornamented with flowers and tendrils in gold on a gold-sprinkled black ground. This instrument is described in the *Gentleman's Magazine* for 1815 as having been sold about the year 1803 at Lord Spencer Chichester's sale at Fisherwick, Staffordshire; it was purchased by the late owner about 1842 from a person who stated that it came from Fisherwick. *Italian*. Second half of 16th century.

CASE R.—ROOM V.

PLATE.

587. SILVER STANDING CUP WITH COVER, 1570-71, known as the "Berry Cup."

In the form of a gourd, chased with fruit and flowers, and arabesques; the foot in form of a twisted and branched stem. On a band surrounding the brim of the cup is pounced, "*This sweet berry from beniamen did fall then good Sr beniamin berry it call*," and in the depressed part near the centre of the bowl, "*Multa cadunt inter calicem supremaq labra*," and "*viuiti ad extremū.*"

Hall-marks: London, 1570-1.

A cup of similar design but of later date, and about half the weight, is in the possession of the Corporation of Portsmouth, said to be the gift of Sir Benjamin Berry, who was Lieutenant-Governor of Portsmouth in the reign of Elizabeth.

Lent by CHARLES J. JACKSON, ESQ.

588. STONE POT, with silver-gilt mounts, 1575-76.

Body of brown mottled ware, with rim, lid, and foot of silver-gilt, wrought with flowers, fruit, and cartouches in high relief.

Hall-marks: London, 1575-76.

Lent by MRS. DENT of Sudeley.

589. QUEEN KATHERINE PARR'S JUG, of Venetian lace glass, with English silver mounts.

Lent by MRS. DENT of Sudeley.

590. IVORY "GRACE CUP," which belonged to St. Thomas of Canterbury (Thomas à Becket), mounted in silver-gilt. 1525-6.

The original small ivory cup has been surmounted by a broad band of silver-gilt, and lined with the same metal. A jewelled foot of silver-gilt has also been fixed on to the ivory foot. On the band is the inscription, VINVM . TVVM . BIBE . CVM . GAVDIO. The metal foot is encircled by a broad band of arabesque pierced foliage, above which is a cavetto filled originally with jewels and leaves alternately; above this again is a coronet or cresting of strawberry leaves.

The cover encloses the original ivory lid, which is lined with silver-gilt and encircled by a richly-wrought band of pierced leaf-work, on which are fixed silver-gilt vases alternating with groups of pearls and jewels. On the flat part of the ivory lid is a band, inscribed ESTOTE SOBRII, the words alternating with the letters T B entwined with the labels of a mitre placed between them. On the centre of the cover is a vertical ring of pierced work like that on the foot of the cup, from which rises a gadrooned pedestal with reeded belts and bands of large pearls, supporting a figure of St. George on foot overcoming the Dragon.

The silver-gilt mounts of this cup bear the London hall-marks for 1525-6.

This cup belonged to Sir Edward Howard, standard-bearer to Henry VIII., and was left by him to Katherine of Aragon, who left it back to the Howard family.

Lent by The DUKE OF NORFOLK, E.M., K.G.

591. ST. GEORGE AND THE DRAGON: A group in silver, chased in high relief, the horse trappings set in coloured stones, the border chased with arms, masks, and salamanders under a palm tree, with leaves formed of carved rock crystal, mounted with silver, from which is suspended an enamelled shield, 18 in. high. Said to have been presented by Francis I. to Henry VIII. on the Field of the Cloth of Gold. (From the Hamilton Palace Collection.)

Lent by RICHARD HOLT, ESQ.

592. STONE POT, mounted in silver-gilt, 1582-3.

The rim, lid, and foot are ornamented with strap-work, fruit, and flowers in relief.
Hall-marks: London, 1582-3.

Lent by COLONEL A. J. COPELAND.

593. SILVER-GILT BOX, 1610-11.

Made in the form of a scallop shell, with four snails for feet.
Hall-marks: London, 1610-11.

Lent by The DUKE OF WESTMINSTER, K.G.

594. MAZER, *circa*.

Maple-wood bowl, with plain silver-gilt band, and in the bottom a silver-gilt print with monogram i b s on field of dark-blue enamel and encircled with rays.

Lent by ALL SOULS' COLLEGE, OXFORD.

595. STANDING MAZER, 1529-30.

Maple-wood bowl, with band and foot of silver-gilt. The band is plain, with reeded belts; the foot has a gadrooned stem, and is encircled round the base by an open floral cresting. The print is lost. Hall-marks: London, 1529-30.

Lent by ALL SOULS' COLLEGE, OXFORD.

596. SMALL SILVER DISH. Hall-marks, 1570-1.

Lent by MRS. DENT of Sudeley.

ROOM V.] *Plate.* 115

597. CUP, formed of a shell, mounted in silver-gilt, 1570-71.

The body of the cup is in the form of a great fish with a figure of Jonah in the mouth, the under part being a shell, with head, tail, back, and fins of silver-gilt. Astride the fish's back is a sea-monster with trident. The metal-work of the body is connected with the foot by four bands in the form of fishes. The stem consists of four boldly modelled fishes, resting on a base, with shells and sea-monsters in repoussé. Hall-marks: London, 1570-71.

Lent by ALFRED DE ROTHSCHILD, ESQ.

598. JUG OF BROWN STONEWARE, mounted in silver-gilt.

Dark brown jug, silver-gilt mount, decorated with strap-work design, enclosing masks and bunches of fruit, with lions' heads frequently repeated. Date 1586.

Lent by SIR SAMUEL MONTAGU, BART., M.P.

599. SALT-CELLAR AND COVER OF SILVER-GILT.

Decorated on body and cover with strap-work, fruit, and masks, horse-shaped feet. The cover is terminated by a three-handled vase, upon which stands a figure armed with a spear or club. Date *circa* 1566-67.

Lent by SIR SAMUEL MONTAGU, BART., M.P.

600. SILVER CUP, ornamented with engraved work. Hall-marked, 1587.

Lent by SIR SAMUEL MONTAGU, BART., M.P.

601. CUP AND COVER on stem, with plain knop and circular-ridged foot, engraved with the arms and motto of the City of Exeter, and inscribed "Ye gufte of ye good Queene, 1585," with a medallion bust of Queen Elizabeth in robes of state in relief. Maker's mark, R.W., over a vase in shaped shield.

Lent by RICHARD HOLT, ESQ.

602. SILVER BOX, made in the form of a scallop-shell.

Lent by The DUKE OF WESTMINSTER, K.G.

603. SILVER BOX, made in the form of a scallop-shell

Lent by The DUKE OF WESTMINSTER, K.G.

604. SILVER CUP AND COVER, with double handle, said to have belonged to Dr. Dee the astrologer, and to have been used by him as a divining cup. It bears the initials IV. D.

Lent by MRS. TEMPLE FRERE.

605. SILVER MUG, *temp.* Elizabeth.

Lent by MRS. TEMPLE FRERE.

806. CHAMBERLAIN'S MACE OF ROCK CRYSTAL, mounted in silver-gilt, and jewelled. This remarkable and beautiful specimen of goldsmith's work consists of a stem, on which have been originally threaded seven pieces of rock crystal, diminishing in size from the base upwards, the largest about 3¼ inches long and 1½ inches diameter ; the places of several are now supplied by cut glass. Six knops of the same material in chased and jewelled mounts served to divide the longitudinal portions ; of these, the lower two remain, and are facet cut into octahedrons, the others have been supplied by glass. The head of the mace is formed of an imperial crown, jewelled, and having arches with a crocket ornament, bearing the orb and cross ; beneath the head, and supporting it, are four brackets formed of dragons and lions bearing blank shields, the supporters of Edward VI., whose arms, or those of Queen Elizabeth, are engraved in a roundel encompassed by a corded ornament on the top of the mace within the crown. The mountings, portions of which seem to have been renewed, are variously chased. This mace, perhaps the most remarkable of its kind existing in England, is stated to have been presented to the City of Norwich by Queen Elizabeth ; it is figured in the "Art Treasures of the United Kingdom." English 16th century work. Length, 3ft. 2in.

. Lent by The MAYOR AND CORPORATION OF NORWICH.

607. SILVER-GILT TAZZA-CUP.

On short baluster stem ; the stem and base ornamented with gadroons and other repoussé work, and with stamped and chased borders ; round the edge is engraved in cusped letters the following inscription :

THE . MOST . HERE . OF . IS . DVNE . BY . PETER . PETERSON.

He was an eminent goldsmith at Norwich, in the reign of Queen Elizabeth.

In the bottom of the bowl are engraved, within a circle, the arms of the City of Norwich, viz., gu. a castle surmounted with a tower ar., in base a lion passant guardant or. Two plate-marks have existed on the edge of the bowl, one of these seems to bear the arms of the city in an escutcheon, which was used to distinguish the plate made and assayed at Norwich, and the other a cross-mound. English work, the latter half of the 16th century.

Lent by The MAYOR AND CORPORATION OF NORWICH.

608. SILVER-GILT SALT AND COVER.

The circular base, drum, and cover richly ornamented with repoussé of masks, strap-work, flowers, and fruit ; round the base of the drum in pounced letters is the following inscription, THE GYFTE OF PETAR READE ESQVIAR; and round the top, ASPERANSE IN DEO.

On the drum are three shields of arms : those of Reade, those of Blennerhasset, and the honourable augmentation granted to Reade by the Emperor Charles V. at the siege of Tunis. The cover is surmounted by an urn-shaped ornament bearing a statuette in antique costume, resting on a spear and holding a shield with the arms of Norwich ; within is pounced the crest of Reade, a goat's (or stag's ?) head erased, ducally gorged, and the motto as before, ASPERANSE IN DEO. The plate-marks are a Roman capital D, the arms of Norwich, and a cross-mound within a lozenge ; it was therefore made at Norwich, and its date is not later than 1568, for Peter Reade died in that year. Height 15¼ inches, diameter 6¼ inches.

Lent by The MAYOR AND CORPORATION OF NORWICH.

ROOM V.] *Plate.*

609. STATE SWORD OF THE CITY OF CHESTER, given by Henry VII., in 1506.
    Lent by The MAYOR AND CORPORATION OF CHESTER.

610. A STATE SWORD; two-edged blade, 3ft. 1in. long, 2in. wide, straight cross hilt 13¼in. long, the ends widened, mounted in coloured stones, and engraved with a running pattern; the handle, 10in. long, ends in a cut-glass pommel 3⅛in. in diameter, mounted in silver-gilt bands with female bust and fleurs-de-lis. On the blade is an inscription, "SYR MARTYN BOWES KNYGHT BORNE WITHIN THIS CITIE OF YORKE AND MAIOR OF THE CITIE OF LONDON 1545. FOR A REMEMBRANCE." Continued on the other side, "GAVE THIS S .... TO THE MAIOR AND COMMUNALTIE OF THIS SAID HONORABLE CITIE."
    The scabbard is of crimson velvet, edged with gold lace, and on a mounting at each end of back and front are the arms of Bowes; these shields are united by two therm satyrs; above, on both sides, in circular medallions under glass, are the arms of York city emblazoned. Two other mountings on each side are engraved with stiff tracery of the period, and having on them cut pebbles. There is no mark upon the sword, which appears to be in its genuine state; time of Henry VIII.
    Lent by The LORD MAYOR AND CORPORATION OF YORK.

Lent by C. J. JACKSON, ESQ.

611. AN ELIZABETHAN SILVER COMMUNION CUP AND COVER, 8¼ inches high, somewhat different in form from the common type of the period, inasmuch as the bowl is rounded in its upward outline and less bell-shaped. It is also more ornamented with engraving. The cover is also deeper, and is ornamented with cursive ornament of arabesque foliage, engraved between two plain bands running round the cover. Date engraved on the top of cover, 1576.

612. AN ELIZABETHAN GREY STONEWARE VASE, with three handles, and shield of arms in medallions in relief, dated 1588 and 1594, mounted with silver rim, foot and cover, chased with cherubs' heads, foliage, rosettes, and other ornaments—14¾ inches high. Maker's mark, I.M., with line and dot beneath, in plain shield. *Circa* 1594.

613. AN APOSTLE SPOON (St. Thomas), *temp.* Henry VIII. Hall-marks, 1523.

614. APOSTLE SPOON (St. John), *temp.* Elizabeth. Hall-marks, 1562.

615. SPOON, with a lion segant holding shield at end of stem, *temp.* Elizabeth. Hall-marks, 1592.

616. A MAIDENHEAD SPOON, *temp.* Elizabeth. Hall-marks, 1598.

617. APOSTLE SPOON (St. Andrew), *temp.* Elizabeth. Hall-marks, 1599.

618. SEAL-TOPPED SPOON, *temp.* Elizabeth. Hall-marks, 1601.

619. BALUSTER-TOPPED SPOON, *temp*. Elizabeth. Hall-marks, 1601.

620. AN APOSTLE SPOON (St. Bartholomew), *temp*. Henry VIII. Hall-marks, 1534.

621. SPOON, with ornamental knop at end of stem, *temp*. Edward VI. Hall-marks, 1551.

622. A MAIDENHEAD SPOON, *i.e.*, having the head and bust of the Blessed Virgin at the end of stem, *temp*. Mary. Hall-marks, 1553.

623. SPOON, with Baluster top, *temp*. Elizabeth. Hall-marks, 1560.

624. SPOON, with figure of the Blessed Virgin at the end, *temp*. Elizabeth. Hall-marks, 1561.

625. SPOON, with seal top, *temp*. Elizabeth. Hall-marks, 1562.

626. STANDING CUP AND COVER, silver gilt, c. 1562.

Round body of Cup rings of plain mouldings and broad band of arabesque work; bottom of cup, cover, and foot escalloped; stem baluster-shaped, ornamented with acanthus.

Inscribed: + MATTHAEUS CANTAUR, DEDIT, AULA . 51. TRINITATIS . CANTAB. 1º JAN ANNO 1569. CONSEC SUAE XIº ET AETATIS SUAE 60.

Lent by TRINITY HALL, CAMBRIDGE.

627. TANKARD, silver gilt, 1571.

Round tankard raised bands enriched with Elizabethan ornament; between centre bands are panels formed of arabesque, with plaques of similar design in the centres. Dome-shaped lid, surmounted by a vase-shaped knob.

Inscribed: + MATTHÆVS ARCHIEPS: CANTUAR: 1º IAN. A.D. 1571, with arms of Archbishop Parker.

Lent by TRINITY HALL, CAMBRIDGE.

CASE S.—ROOM V.

Casts and Impressions of Tudor Seals.

LENT BY THE SOCIETY OF ANTIQUARIES.

630. HENRY VII. (1485-1509). GREAT SEAL.

In use from 1485 to 1509.

Obverse.—Sitting figure of the King under a canopy, with two side canopied compartments, containing shields with the royal arms, and a lion below. Beyond these two small niches, each containing a man-at-arms. Legend : HENRICUS : DEI : GRACIA : ANGLIE : : & : FRANCIE : & : DOMINUS : HIBERNIE.

Reverse.—The King on horseback, in armour, with royal arms on surcoat and shield. The horse has a trapper with the royal arms, a plume of feathers on the head, and a small shield on the chamfron. The field is covered with a lattice diaper, enclosing roses, with fleurs-de-lis on the intersections. Legend, as on obverse, but with roses for stops.

631. HENRY VII. GREAT SEAL FOR FRENCH AFFAIRS.

Only known impression appended to the confirmation of the Treaty of Etaples, sealed at Calais, November 11, 1492.

Obverse.—The King enthroned beneath a canopy, with two lions under his feet. On either side a panelled and canopied compartment containing a crowned shield, the dexter with the arms of France, the sinister with the royal arms of England. The dexter half of the seal has the field diapered with fleurs-de-lis, the sinister half with roses. Legend : HENRICUS DEI GRACIA REX FRACIE ET ANGLIE ET DÑS HIB'E.

Reverse.—Small round counter-seal, with an angel with outstretched wings holding a sceptre in each hand, and supporting two shields—one of France, the other of the royal arms of England. No legend.

632. PRIVY SEAL USED BY HENRY VII. AND HENRY VIII.

A circular seal with the royal arms surmounted by a beautiful coronet of fleurs-de-lis and small roses, and flanked on either side by a lion holding up an ostrich feather struck through a scroll. Legend beginning with a large fleur-de-lis ; SECRETUM : HENRICI DEI : GRACIA : REGIS : ANGLIE ET FRANCIE ET : DOMINUS : HIBERNIE.

633. SIGNET OF HENRY VII. AND HENRY VIII.

A small round seal, surrounded by a twisted rush or ender, and bearing a shield of the royal arms, between the letters H R, surmounted by a coronet of crosses and fleurs-de-lis, and encircled by a collar of SS with pendent rose between two portcullises.

634. SIGNET OF HENRY VIII.

Same device as before, but somewhat differently treated.

635. Henry VIII. (1509-1547). First Great Seal.

In use from 1509 to 1536, and perhaps later.

Identical with the great seal of Henry VII., but on the reverse a lion rampant has been added behind the King, and a fleur-de-lis before the horse.

636. Henry VIII. Second Great Seal.

In use from 1532 to 1542.

Obverse.—The King enthroned beneath a rich canopy. At the sides are the royal arms within the Garter, and crowned. Encircling the device, and passing behind the throne, is an ornate band with roses and fleurs-de-lis in loops. Legend : . HENRICVS . OCTAV' . DEI . GRA . ANGLIE . ET . FRANCIE REX . FIDEI . DEFENSOR . ET . DOMIN . HIBERNIE, with roses and fleurs-de-lis for stops.

Reverse.—The King on horseback in armour, with shield, etc. The horse has a diapered trapper with large Tudor roses, and a spike on the chamfron. Behind the King is a large rose, and in base a greyhound courant. The field is encircled by a band with roses and fleurs-de-lis, as on obverse. Legend, same as on obverse.

637. Henry VIII. Third Great Seal.

In use from 1542 to 1547. Also used for a few months by Edward VI.

Obverse.—The King in robes of state, sitting on throne of Renaissance character. On either side the royal arms within the Garter, and crowned. Legend: HENRIC . OCTAVVS . DEI . GRATIA . ANGLIE . FRANCIE . ET . HIBERNIE . REX . FIDEI . DEFESOR . ET . I . TERA . ECCLESIÆ . ĀGLICANE . ET . HIBERNICE . SVPREMV̄ CAPVT.

Reverse.—Almost identical with the reverse of the second great seal, but the field is not diapered. Legend, as on obverse.

638. Henry VIII. Seal, *AD CAUSAS ECCLESIASTICAS.*

Obverse.—The King, enthroned beneath a tester, and holding a sword. On either side the royal arms within the Garter, and crowned. Legend, same as on third great seal.

Reverse.—[Imperfect.]—The King enthroned, and holding a sword. On his right hand kneel a number of archbishops and bishops, in copes and mitres, with their crosses and crosiers. On the left hand is, seemingly, a corresponding group of the clergy. Above, on either side the throne, are figures of Justice, &c. In base are the royal arms within the Garter, and crowned. Legend .

S HEN[RICI OCTAVI ETC. . . FIDEI DEFENSO] RIS POST DEVM ECCLESIE ANGL' SVPREMI CAPITIS [AD CAVSAS ECCLESIAS]TICAS.

639. Golden Bulla of Henry VIII.

Appended to the Confirmation of the Treaty of the Field of the Cloth of Gold, dated at London, September 18th, 1527, now in the Archives Nationales at Paris.

Obverse.—The King in robes of state, sitting on a throne of very rich and elaborate character, with cherubs, festoons of flowers, &c. In base are two cherubs holding a shield charged with a Tudor rose. Legend : HERIC' . 8 . D.G. ĀGLIE . Z . FRĀCIE . R . FIDEI . DEFĒSOR . Z . DÑS . HIB.'

Reverse.—A crowned shield of the royal arms within the collar of the Order of the Garter. Legend, with roses for stops : . . ORDINE . IVNGVNTVR . ET . PERSTANT . FEDERE CVNCTA.

640. EDWARD VI. (1547—1553). GREAT SEAL.

In use from 1547 to 1553; also used for a few months by Queen Mary.

Obverse.—The King enthroned. On either side the royal arms within the Garter, and crowned. Legend: EDWARD'. SEXT' &c., as on third great seal of his father.

Reverse.—The King, in armour with shield, riding at full speed. The horse has a trapper embroidered with the royal arms and large roses on a diapered ground. In base is a greyhound courant. Behind the King is a crowned Tudor rose, and in front of the horse a crowned fleur-de-lis. The field diapered with scrollwork and small roses and fleurs-de-lis. Legend, as on obverse.

641. MARY (1553-1558). GREAT SEAL.

In use from 1553-1556.

Obverse.—The Queen enthroned, between, on the dexter a crowned shield of the royal arms, and on the sinister a crowned rose. In base the motto: TEMPORIS FILIA VERITAS. Legend, with fleurs-de-lis for stops: MARIA . D . G . ANGLIE . FRACIE . ET . HIBERNIE . REGINA . EIVS . NOMINIS . PRIMA . FIDEI . DEFENSOR.

Reverse.—The Queen on horseback, the foot-cloth diapered with pomegranates and castles. Behind her a crowned fleur-de-lis, and on the ground in front of the horse a rose bush in full bloom. In base the motto: TEMPORIS FILIA VERITAS. Legend, as on obverse.

642. PHILIP AND MARY (1554-1558). GREAT SEAL.

In use from 1556 to 1558.

Obverse.—The King in royal robes with sword, and the Queen in royal robes with sceptre, seated under a canopy, and holding the orb and cross, which rests on a pedestal with the initials PM embroidered on the front. Between the heads of the figures is a large shield of Spain and England impaled within the Garter, and crowned. Legend, with roses for stops: ⚜ PHILIP . ET . MARIA . D . G . REX . ET . REGINA . ANGL' . HISPANIAR . FRANC' . VTRIVSQ' . SICILIE . IERVSALEM . ET . HIB' . FIDEI . DEFENSOR.

Reverse.—The King and Queen both riding on horseback to the left. The King is in armour, but with a round cap instead of a helmet, and holds a drawn sword. The Queen holds a sceptre, and is facing her husband. The King's horse has a handsome trapper fringed with tassels. Behind the King, on a field diapered with loops containing roses, fleurs-de-lis, castles, and pomegranates, is a shield of the arms of Spain impaling England within the Garter, and crowned. Legend, with roses for stops: ARCHIDVCES . AVSTRIE . DVCES . BVRGVNDIE . MEDIOLANI . ET . BRABANCIE . COMITES . HASPVRGI . FLANDRIE . ET . TIROLIS.

643. ELIZABETH (1558-1603). FIRST GREAT SEAL.

In use from January 26th, 1558, to 1587, and perhaps later.

Obverse.—The Queen in robes of state, enthroned beneath a domed circular canopy with curtains. On the base of the throne is the motto: PVLCHRVM PRO PATRIA PATI. On either side of the Queen the royal arms within the Garter and crowned. Legend: + ELIZABETH. DEI. GRACIA. ANGLIE. FRANCIE. ET. HIBERNIE. REGINA. FIDEI. DEFENSOR.

Reverse.—The Queen in embroidered gown and holding a sceptre, riding on horseback to the left. The foot-cloth is richly embroidered, and before and behind the horse is a flowering rose bush. In the field on either side the Queen are a fleur-de-lis and Tudor rose, both crowned. Legend, as on obverse.

644. ELIZABETH. SECOND GREAT SEAL. [*Two original impressions.*]

In use from 1586 to 1603. Also used for a few weeks by James I.

Obverse.—The Queen crowned, in plain gown with mantle and ruff, and holding the orb and sceptre, sitting on a throne. On each side is a hand and arm issuing from clouds and holding back the royal mantle. On either side of the throne is a shield of the royal arms within the Garter, and crowned, and above the hands a Tudor rose. Legend, as on first great seal.

Reverse.—The Queen, crowned, with the orb and sceptre, and wearing a gown with puffed sleeves, and a large ruff, riding on horseback to the left. Above her head are rays issuing from the clouds, and the field is powdered with small flowers and the royal badges, viz., the rose, fleur-de-lis, and harp, severally crowned. The ground is covered with flowers, and in front of the horse is a flowering rose bush. Legend, as on the first great seal.

646. CHARLES, LORD HOWARD OF EFFINGHAM (1585). SEAL AS LORD HIGH ADMIRAL.

Large round seal, with three-masted ship, having on the mainsail Lord Howard's arms within the Garter. From the mastheads fly two armorial standards, and at the sides of the seal are a lion and a dragon, each holding a banner of St. George. The ship is a fine and elaborate example of the period. Legend + SIGILL D' CAROLI HOWARD BARON : D'EFFINGHAM . . . . . TIS MAGNI ADMIRALI ANGLIÆ. ETCET, A° 1585.

647. HENRY VIII. SEAL FOR COURT OF EXCHEQUER.

Obverse.—The King crowned and in armour, with drawn sword, riding at full speed. The horse has a trapper with the royal arms, and a chamfron and crinière of plate. The upper half of the field is covered with a checky pattern of plain squares, alternating with others charged with fleurs-de-lis.

Reverse.—A shield of the royal arms, crowned, and supported by an antelope and a stag gorged with coronets and chained. In base is a scroll lettered : SIGILLY . SCACARII DOMINI REGIS. The legend begins with a portcullis between two fleurs-de-lis on the obverse, and is continued on the reverse, with fleurs-de-lis for stops : HENRIC'. VIII'. DEI . GRA . ANGLIE . FRANC . ET HIBERNIE . REX . FIDEI . DEFENSOR . ET . IN . TERRA . ECCLESIE . ANGLICANE . ET . HIBERNIE . SVPREMVM . CAPVT.

648. EDWARD VI. SEAL FOR COURT OF COMMON PLEAS.

Obverse.—The King in royal robes sitting on a handsome throne of Renaissance character. On either side are the initials E K crowned.

Reverse.—A shield of the royal arms, with crown above, supported by cords by a crowned lion and a greyhound. Round the field is a scroll, lettered : SIGILLVM PRO BREVIBVS CORAM IVSTICIARIIS. The legend begins on the obverse and is continued on the reverse, and is the same as that on the great seal.

ROOM V.] *Seals.* 123

649. MARY. SEAL FOR COURT OF EXCHEQUER. In use in 2 Philip and Mary.

Obverse.—The Queen enthroned, between the royal arms and a Tudor rose, both crowned. In base the motto: TEMPORIS . FILIA . VERITAS. Legend, as on the great seal.

Reverse.—A crowned shield of the royal arms supported by an antelope and a stag, gorged with coronets and chained. In base a scroll, lettered : SIGILLVM SCACCARII DOMINÆ REGINÆ. Legend, as on the great seal.

650. ELIZABETH. SEAL FOR COURT OF COMMON PLEAS.

Obverse.—The Queen enthroned beneath a canopy, with side curtains. On the dexter side of the field is a crowned Tudor rose, and on the sinister a crowned fleur-de-lis. Legend, as on great seals.

Reverse.—A crowned shield of the royal arms, supported by a dragon and greyhound. On a scroll in base : .S. PRO. BREVIBVS. CORAM. IVSTICIARIIS. Legend, as on the great seals.

651. ELIZABETH. SEAL FOR EXCHEQUER OF PLEAS (1559).

Obverse.—On a carpet, covered with a lozengy pattern of roses and fleurs-de-lis, the Queen enthroned beneath a circular canopy, with looped curtains. The field is diapered with a lattice, enclosing Tudor roses and fleurs-de-lis. In base are the initials E. R. Legend, as on the great seals.

Reverse.—On a field, covered with a lattice, enclosing Tudor roses and fleurs-de-lis, a shield of the royal arms, surmounted by a crown, and supported by two stags, the dexter gorged with a collar, the sinister with a coronet, and both chained. Legend, with roses for stops : + SIGILLVM. SCACARII. DOMINE. REGINE. ANNO. D'. M.D.LIX.

652. THE LADY MARGARET (BEAUFORT), MOTHER OF HENRY VII.

1. Large round seal with a shield of the arms of Beaufort, supported by two antelopes guttées, behind each of which is an ostrich feather struck through a scroll and with a chain along the quill. On the top of the shield stands an eagle displayed and gorged with a coronet, holding in his beak a scroll encircling the seal, inscribed : SIGILLUM : [DOMINE : MARGARETE :] COMITISSE : RICHEMOUND' : AC : FILIE : . . . . EDE : IOHIS : . . . . . DUCIS : SOM'S.

2. Large round seal bearing a shield, the arms of Beaufort, supported by two antelopes, behind each of which is a small feather struck through a scroll. Upon the shield rests a beautiful coronet of roses and fleur-de-lis, from which rises a demi-eagle with wings expanded and gorged with a coronet with pendent chain. The eagle holds in his beak a scroll encircling the seal, inscribed : S' : DÑE : M'GARETE : CM̃ITISSE : RICHEMŨDIE ⚜ DERBI FILIE ⚜ HER' ⚜ IOHIS DUC' : SOM'SET : AC MATR' HẼR'VIJ REG' ANGL ⚜ FR'

653. QUEEN KATHERINE OF ARAGON.

A round seal with a large shield of England impaling Aragon suspended from a royal crown. On either side is a characteristic knot. Legend : [KATHERINA . RE]GINA . ANGLIE . E . FRANCIE . E . DNA . HIBER[NIE].

656. Thomas Cranmer, Archbishop of Canterbury (1533-56).

Type 1. Altered from the seal of Archbishop Warham. Pointed oval, with figure of the Holy Trinity between two Archbishops, all under canopies. At the top, a niche with a figure of the Blessed Virgin and Child, flanked by two angels. In base, the Archbishop between two shields of arms. Legend : [SIGILLUM : THOME] : CRANMER . : . DEI GRACIA : CANTUARIEN-ARCHIEPI.

Type 2. In centre, the martyrdom of St. Thomas of Canterbury, with small figures at the sides in niches. Above, three niches with Our Lord in Majesty between two kneeling saints. In base, a kneeling figure of the Archbishop under an arch, between two shields. Legend : SIGILLV : . : THOME : . : CRANMER : . : DEI : . : GRA : . : CANTUARIEN . ARCHIEPI.

Type 3. The same matrix, but with the crucifixion instead of the martyrdom of St. Thomas.

657. Reginald Pole, Cardinal, and Archbishop of Canterbury (1556-58).

Large pointed oval with, in the upper half, which has a diapered field, a figure of the Holy Trinity with Our Lady and Child in the clouds above, under a canopy. On each side in a niche is the figure of a patriarch. The lower half has a large shield of the archbishop's arms, with a cross pattée over and a cardinal's hat; on either side are the arms of Christchurch, Canterbury, and the See of Canterbury. Legend : + SIGILL: REGINALDI . POLI . CARDINAL' . CAT . ARCHIEPI | TOTIVS . ANGL' . PRIMATIS . ET . APLICE . SEDIS . LEGATI . NATI.

658. Matthew Parker, Archbishop of Canterbury (1552-75).

Pointed oval, with representation of the Doom. In base, a shield of the arms of Parker. Legend : + SIGILLV . MATTHÆ . PARKER CANTVARIEN . ARCHI . EPI.

659. Cuthbert Tunstall, Bishop of Durham (1530-32 and 1553-59).

Pointed oval, with Our Lady and Child, between SS. Cuthbert and Oswald, under canopies. In base, a mitred shield of the arms of Tunstall between two shields of the city and See of Durham. Legend : SIGILLVM : CVTHBERTI : DVNELMENSIS : EPISCOPI.

660. Stephen Gardiner, Bishop of Winchester (1531-50 and 1553-55).

Pointed oval, with St. Swithin between SS. Peter and Paul, with the Holy Trinity above, all under canopies. In base, a mitred shield of the See of Winchester impaling Gardiner, within the Garter. Legend : SIGILLVM STE͜PHANI PERMISSIONE] DIVINA [WINTON]EPI.

661. John Scory, Bishop of Rochester (1551-52).

Pointed oval, with the bishop preaching from a pulpit to a lot of people. In base, a shield with a saltire impaling the words NON ASPERNOR GRA[TIA]M. Legend : SIGILLVM . IOHANNIS . SCORY . EPISCOPI . ROFFENSIS . ANNO . DNI . 1551.

661a. John Jewell, Bishop of Salisbury (1560-1571).

Pointed oval with figure of the Good Shepherd under a canopy. Background diapered with floral scrolls. In base, a shield of the arms of Jewell. Legend : SIGILLVM . . IOHANNIS . IEWELL . EPISCOPI . SARISBVRIENSIS.

ROOM VI.

Drawings, Books, Needlework, Engravings, Etc.

662. SEVEN MEDALLIONS.
     By HANS HOLBEIN.   Lent by The DUKE OF DEVONSHIRE, K.G.

663. MUSICAL PARTY.
     By F. ZUCCHERO.   Lent by The DUKE OF DEVONSHIRE, K.G.

664. HEAD OF A MAN.
     By HANS HOLBEIN.   Lent by The DUKE OF DEVONSHIRE, K.G.

665. A GROUP OF FIGURES BETWEEN COLUMNS.
     By F. ZUCCHERO.   Lent by The DUKE OF DEVONSHIRE, K.G.

666. THOMAS CROMWELL, EARL OF ESSEX.
     By HANS HOLBEIN.   Lent by The EARL OF PEMBROKE.

667. LADY HOLDING A SHIELD.
     By HANS HOLBEIN.   Lent by The DUKE OF DEVONSHIRE, K.G.

668. HEAD OF A MAN.
     By HANS HOLBEIN.   Lent by The DUKE OF DEVONSHIRE, K.G.

669. GROUP OF FIGURES IN LANDSCAPE.
     By F. ZUCCHERO.   Lent by The DUKE OF DEVONSHIRE, K.G.

670. HEAD OF MAN.
     By HANS HOLBEIN.   Lent by The DUKE OF DEVONSHIRE, K.G.

Fifty-four Facsimile Reproductions of the Drawings by Hans Holbein, in the Collection of Her Majesty.

Lent by Mr. FRANZ HANFSTAENGL.

671. QUEEN JANE SEYMOUR, WIFE OF HENRY VIII.

672. EDWARD, PRINCE OF WALES, AFTERWARDS EDWARD VI.

673. Sir Thomas More, Lord Chancellor.
674. Sir John More, father of Sir Thomas More.
675. Elizabeth Dancy, daughter of Sir Thomas More.
676. Cicely Heron, daughter of Sir Thomas More.
677. John More, son of Sir Thomas More.
678. Anne Cresacre, wife of John More.
679. Margaret Clement, a relative of Sir Thomas More.
680. (?) Mother Jack, Nurse to Edward VI.
681. Sir Henry Guildford, K.G.
682. William Warham, Archbishop of Canterbury.
683. John Cardinal Fisher, Bishop of Rochester.
684. John Russell, Earl of Bedford, K.G.
685. William Parr, Marquis of Northampton, K.G.
686. Thomas Boleyn, Earl of Wiltshire and Ormonde, K.G. (?)
687. William Fitzwilliam, Earl of Southampton, K.G.
688. Edward Stanley, Earl of Derby, K.G.
689. George Brooke, Lord Cobham, K.G.
690. Thomas Howard, Earl of Surrey, afterwards Duke of Norfolk, K.G.
691. Thomas Howard, Earl of Surrey, afterwards Duke of Norfolk, K.G.
692. Frances, wife of Henry Howard, Earl of Surrey.
693. Thomas, Lord Vaux.
694. Lady Vaux.
695. An Unknown Lady.
696. Catherine, 4th wife of Ch. Brandon, Duke of Suffolk.
697. Elizabeth, wife of Sir Henry Parker.
698. Jane, wife of Sir R. Lister.

[Room VI.] *Drawings.*

699. Lady Ratcliffe.
700. Joan, wife of R. Zouch (?).
701. Thomas, Lord Vaux.
702. Sir Thomas Wiatt.
703. Sir John Gage, K.G.
704. Sir Richard Southwell.
705. Charles Wingfield (?)
706. Sir John Godsalve.
707. Sir Nicholas Pointz.
708. Sir Thomas Elyot.
709. Margaret, wife of Sir T. Elyot.
710. Sir Philip Hobby.
711. Elizabeth, wife of Sir Thomas Hobby.
712. An Unknown Lady.
713. An Unknown Lady.
714. An Unknown Lady.
715. An Unknown Lady.
716. Sir Thomas Parry.
717. John Poyntz.
718. John Reskimer.
719. Simon George of Quocote.
720. An Unknown Man.
721. An Unknown Man.
722. An Unknown Man.
723. John Colet, Dean of St. Paul's (?)
724. Nicholas Bourbon (?)

Photographs of Portraits by Hans Holbein.

Lent by F. HANFSTAENGL.

725. THE AMBASSADORS. (The National Gallery.)
726. THOMAS HOWARD, 3rd DUKE OF NORFOLK, K.G. (Windsor Castle.)
727. SIR HENRY GUILDFORD. (Windsor Castle.)
730. SIR BRYAN TUKE. (Munich.)

740. EDWARD VI. Lithograph.
Lent by The MARQUESS OF HERTFORD.

741. QUEEN JANE SEYMOUR. Lithograph.
Lent by The MARQUESS OF HERTFORD.

Lent by THE SOCIETY OF ANTIQUARIES.

742. SIEGE OF BOULOGNE BY HENRY VIII. 1544.
Engraving of a Picture destroyed in a fire at Cowdray.

743. ENCAMPMENT OF HENRY VIII. AT MARQUISON, JULY, 1544.
Engraving of a Picture destroyed by fire at Cowdray.

744. DEPARTURE OF HENRY VIII. FROM CALAIS, JULY 25TH, 1544.
Engraving of a Picture destroyed by fire at Cowdray.

745. ENCAMPMENT OF THE ENGLISH FORCES NEAR PORTSMOUTH, JULY, 1545.
Engraving of a Picture destroyed by fire at Cowdray.

---

746. PIECE OF NEEDLEWORK. Worked by Elizabeth Cavendish, Countess of Shrewsbury.
Lent by The DUKE OF DEVONSHIRE, K.G.

747. PIECE OF NEEDLEWORK, REPRESENTING OLD CHATSWORTH HOUSE. Worked by Elizabeth Cavendish, Countess of Shrewsbury.
Lent by The DUKE OF DEVONSHIRE, K.G.

748. PIECE OF NEEDLEWORK. Worked by Elizabeth Cavendish, Countess of Shrewsbury.
Lent by The DUKE OF DEVONSHIRE, K.G.

Room VI.]   *Needlework, &c.*   129

749. Piece of Needlework. Worked by Elizabeth Cavendish, Countess of Shrewsbury.
Lent by The Duke of Devonshire, K.G.

750. Piece of Needlework. Worked by Mary Queen of Scots.
Lent by The Duke of Devonshire, K.G.

751. Piece of Needlework. Worked by Mary Queen of Scots.
Lent by The Duke of Devonshire, K.G.

752. Roundels (eleven). Beechwood, painted on one side in various colours, with devices enclosing scriptural and other mottoes in old English characters. In a circular box, on the lid of which is painted a shield of arms. *English.* First half of 16th century.
Lent by The Science and Art Department.

753. Roundels (twelve). Beechwood; painted and gilt on one side with strap-work and floral ornament; in the centre a posy inscription in old English characters. *English.* 16th century. Given by the Rev. R. Brooke.
Lent by The Science and Art Department.

CASE T.—ROOM VI.

754. Sir Thomas Gresham's Steel Yard or Weighing Machine.
Lent by Miss Sumner.

755. Wedding Ring of Sir Thomas Gresham.
Lent by C. Leveson-Gower, Esq.

756. Miniature of Sir Thomas Gresham.
Lent by C. Leveson-Gower, Esq.

757. Six Pieces of Glass with badge of the Gresham's.
Lent by C. Leveson-Gower, Esq.

LOSELY MANUSCRIPTS.

Lent by W. MORE MOLYNEUX, Esq.
(In Eight Frames.)

758. FRAME I.

1. Letter from Edmund (Grindal), Bishop of London, to William More, Esq., relating to the examination of Symon Pembroke, a wizard or conjuror, whose practices, "seme to tende to coniuracon by casting of figures, telling of thinges lost, hidde, or stolen," &c. Dated Fulham, July 20th, 1564. Signature of the Bishop.

2. LETTER FROM JOHN (WATSON), BISHOP OF WINCHESTER, to Sir William Moore, Knight, appointing him, with Mr. Browne and others, to examine, "those are fallen into the hereasye termed the famelie of love." Dated St. Crosse (Winchester), December 30th, 1580. Signature of the Bishop.

3. LETTER FROM JOHN (WHITGIFT), ARCHBISHOP OF CANTERBURY, to the Lord Chamberlain, begging that Mr. Marsh, a servant, may be excused from furnishing a horse and armour. Dated Croydon, September 28th, 1584. Signature of the Archbishop.

FRAME II.

1. LETTER FROM ROBERT (HOME), BISHOP OF WINCHESTER, to Mr. More, of Losely, giving advice as to the stocking the new pond with the best kind of carp, "thos be of a litle heade, broade side, and not long; soche as be great headed and longe, made after the fashion of an hearing (herring) ar not good, nether will ever be." Dated Waltham, January 5th. Holograph.

2. WARRANT TO WILLIAM MORE, ESQ., for the apprehension of David Oreb, ringleader of certain sectaries, who are about to hold conventicles in the approaching fair at Kateryn Hill. Dated Lambeth, September 19th, 1560. Signatures of Matthew (Parker), Archbishop of Canterbury, Edmund (Grindal), Bishop of London, and Thomas Huycke.

3. LETTER FROM JOHN (WATSON), BISHOP OF WINCHESTER, to Sir William More, Knt.; speaks of his illness, and promises to take the best order for redressing the disorders of the Vicar of Farnham. Dated Southwark House, May 4th, 1581. Signature of the Bishop.

4. LETTER FROM ALEXANDER NOWELL, DEAN OF ST. PAUL'S, to Sir William More, thanking him for his exertions to recover a stolen nag. Dated February 23rd, 1581 (1582). Holograph.

5. LETTER FROM THOMAS (COOPER), BISHOP OF WINCHESTER, to Sir William More of Losely, apologizing for not coming to Losely, "as he was forced to travaile in his hors litter, and fears the fowlenes of the waie and hardnes of passage for the said litter." Dated March 10th, 1585 (1586). Signature of the Bishop.

6. RECEIPT BY DR. JOHN DONNE, afterwards Dean of St. Paul's, to Sir Thomas Egerton, Knt. Lord Keeper of the Great Seal of England, for £100, given by Lady Egerton to "her neece, Anne, the daughter of Sir George More, now wyfe" of Dr. Donne. Dated July 6th, 1703. Holograph.

7. LETTER FROM WILLIAM (DAY), BISHOP OF WINCHESTER, to Sir William More, informing him that he intends to fish the Little Pond at Frensham. Dated August 10th, 1596. Signature of the Bishop.

FRAME III.

1. COMMISSION FROM THE LORDS OF THE COUNCIL to William Moore, Thomas Browne, John Agmondesham, and Thomas Leyfelde, Esqrs., of the county of Surrey, empowering them to

try the information exhibited by Richard Dunsse, of Godalming, against John Tanner, *alias* Bell, sub-bailiff of Godalming, and to report the result. Dated Westminster, June 4th, 1567. Signatures of Sir Nicholas Bacon, Lord Keeper; Sir W(illiam) Parr, Marquess of) Northampton; (Sir William Herbert, Earl of) Pembroke; R(obert Dudley, Earl of) Leicester; E(dward Fynes) Clynton; Lord William Howard; Sir Francis Knollys, Treasurer of the Household; W(illiam) Cecill; Sir Walter Mildmay, K.G., Treasurer and Chancellor of the Exchequer, &c.

2. WARRANT FROM THE LORDS OF THE COUNCIL to the General Receiver of Her Majesty's Revenue and the Collector of the Loan in the county of Surrey, and others, commanding them to deliver certain sums on demand to the Lord Lieutenant of the County, to be applied to the expenses of fitting out and forwarding to France a certain number of soldiers levied within the county. Dated Court of Greenwich, June 25th, 1571. Signatures of the Archbishop of Canterbury; Sir Christopher Hatton, Lord Chancellor; William Cecil, Lord Burghley; Henry Stanley, Earl of Derby; C(harles Howard, Baron) Howard of Effingham; (Henry Carey) Baron Hunsdon; (William Brooke) Baron Cobham; (Thomas Sackville) Baron Buckhurst; J. Wolley; and Sir J(ohn) Fortescue.

FRAME IV.

1. WARRANT TO CHRISTOPHER MOORE, ESQ., Sheriff of the county of Sussex, to deliver to "Katheryn Howarde, one of oure quene's maidens, all the goods, cattall movable and unmovable, fermes, leasses for terme of lyff and yere, dettes, condemnacions," &c., forfeited to the King by William Lidbeter the elder, and William Lidbeter the younger, for the murder of Richard Bolockherde. Dated May 10, 32 Henry VIII. (1540). Signature of King Henry VIII.

2. WRIT TO SIR CHRISTOPHER MORE, Knight, Ulnager of the counties of Surrey and Sussex, touching the collection in the said counties of the grant to the King of eightpence in the pound of value of every cloth. Dated Westminster Palace, July 31st, 3 Edward VI. (1549). Signature of King Edward VI., with counter-signature of (Edward Seymour, Earl of Hertford and Duke of) Somerset, Lord Protector.

3. WARRANT to raise and equip one hundred able men. Dated November 21st, 1 Elizabeth (1558). Signature of Queen Elizabeth.

4. WRIT TO SIR GEORGE MORE, Knight, collector of the loan in the county of Surrey, deferring for six months the promised payment of the loan. Dated February 23rd, 1597. Signature of Queen Elizabeth.

FRAME V.

1. LETTER FROM WILLIAM CECIL, LORD BURGHLEY, to Mr. William Moore and another, magistrates of the county of Surrey, respecting the confession of George Eliott inculpating Sir Edward Bray, &c. Dated Westminster, October 29th, 1573. Holograph. Seal of Lord Burghley.

2. LETTER FROM SIR WALTER RALEGH to Sir William More and other magistrates of Surrey, desiring to know the cause of the law-suit vexatiously brought by Edward Owen against Robert Sharpe, "one of her highnes servauntes of my band." Dated Court at Greenwich, May 20th, 1598. Signature of Sir Walter Ralegh.

3. LETTER FROM SIR NICHOLAS THROCKMORTON to his father-in-law, Sir George More, relating to the settlement of his estate. Dated Ranesbury, Tuesday,——, 1603. Holograph.

4. LETTER FROM SIR ROBERT CECYLL to Sir William More, Knight, announcing the committal of a prisoner by "their Lordships," who " doe lyke very well of your proceedinges ; so that now there remayneth no more but that you return your thanks." Dated The Court, June 3rd, 1597. Signature of Sir Robert Cecyll.

FRAME VI.

1. LETTER FROM G(EORGE CAREY, BARON) HUNSDON to Sir William More, Knight, and others, magistrates of Surrey, desiring them to stay the vexatious litigation with which Edward Owen and one Sheers molest the bearer, Robert Sharpe. Dated Court at Greenwich, May 26th, 1598. Signature of Lord Hunsdon.

2. LETTER FROM THOMAS EGERTON, C.S. (*Custos Sigilli*), Lord Keeper of the Great Seal, to Sir William and Sir George More, Knights, desiring them to examine into the matter of a petition preferred by Israell Bowtell against Edward Owen. Dated November 15th, 1598. Signature of the Lord Keeper.

3. LETTER FROM T(HOMAS EGERTON, BARON) ELLESMERE, Lord Chancellor, to Sir George Moore, expressing his congratulations to Sir George at his recovery from illness, and advising him to be careful of his health. Not dated. Signature of Lord Ellesmere, Chancellor.

4. LETTER FROM (HENRY PERCY, EIGHTH EARL OF) NORTHUMBERLAND, K.G. to Sir George More, acknowledging the receipt of a dispensation for his appearance at the feast of the celebration of the Order of the Garter, though he thinks it had not been needful, considering his restraint from absolute liberty. Dated Petworth, May 12 (? 1585). Holograph.

5. LETTER FROM E(DWARD SOMERSET, FOURTH EARL OF) WORCESTER, to Sir George More and Laurence Stoughton, Esq., respecting the yearly contribution of oats for the provision of Her Majesty's stables, from the Hundred of Farnham. Dated Court at Whitehall, November 17, 1602. Signature of Lord Worcester.

6. WARRANT OF (CHARLES HOWARD) EARL OF NOTTINGHAM to the Reguarders of the Royal Forest of Windsor, to certify the number of acres contained in "Spring Grove" Coppice, and whether it may "convenientlye be incopsed and felled this yeare without prejudice and annoyance of the vert and game of venison there." Dated Arundel, December 8, 1604. Signature and seal of arms of the Earl of Nottingham.

FRAME VII.

1. LETTER FROM SIR NICHOLAS BACON, Lord Keeper of the Seal, to Sir William More, Knt., announcing the reform of the disorders of the " protection men " and " clarkes whom they have corrupted," and desiring him to punish Thomas Manne "for his offence in caryeng abought a harlott in stead of his wief." Dated Gorhambury, December 8, 1573. Signature of Sir N. Bacon, C.S. (*Custos Sigilli*).

2. LETTER FROM (CHARLES) HOWARD, LORD HOWARD OF EFFINGHAM, to the Deputy Lieutenant of the County of Surrey, enclosing letters from the Lords of the Council, and desiring a certificate of their action in the matters contained. Dated Court at Windsor, August 16, 1586. Signature of Lord Howard.

3. LETTER FROM ROBERT DUDLEY, EARL OF LEICESTER, to the Deputy Lieutenants of the County of Surrey, announcing the appointment of the writer's nephew, Sir Robert Sidney, Knt., to take charge of certain levies now being raised in the county. Dated Leicester, June 8, 1857. Signature of the Earl of Leicester.

4. LETTER FROM SIR JULIUS CÆSAR, KNT., Judge of the Admiralty, and afterwards Master of the Rolls, desiring him not to remove Mr. John Young from his office of Deputy Vice-Admiral of Sussex until he is able to confer with him upon the matter. Dated London, April, 1588. Signature of Sir Julius Cæsar.

5. WARRANT FROM SIR CHRISTOPHER HATTON, Lord Chancellor, to Sir William Moore, Knt., and others, magistrates of Surrey, desiring them to certify to the Court of Chancery the causes which moved them to differ from certain other Commissioners appointed to try the suit of Edward Gateward against Richard Bostocke. Dated Ely Place (Holborn), February 7, 1589. Signature and seal of Sir Christopher Hatton.

FRAME VIII.

1. WARRANT under Lady Jane Grey's signature to Sir Thomas Camerdine to deliver four tents to her beloved father and counsellor the Duke of Suffolk. Dated 19 July. I Jane the Queene.

2. WARRANT under the sign manual of Philip and Mary, in 1st and 2nd years of their reign, to deliver canvas from the office of the tents to Sir John Lyndsey of Dunbar.

---

759. WOODCUT AND ADVERTISEMENT of "A very rich Lotterie, generall, without any Blanckes, containing a great number of good Prices, as wel of redy money as of plate and certaine sorts of Marchaundiyes, hauing been valued and priced by the commaundment of the queenees most excellent Maieste, by men expert and skielful; and the same Lotterie is erected by her Maiesties order, to the intent that suche commodite as may chaunce to arise thereof after the charges borne, may be converted towards the reparation of the Hawens, and strength of the Realme, and towards such other publique good works. The number of Lots shall be Foure hundredth thousand and no moe : and euery Lot shall be the summe of Tenne shillings sterling onely, and no more." The first Prize in this Royal Lottery was £5,000, the second £3,500, &c.

The woodcut at the head represents a shield of the Royal Arms of Queen Elizabeth, encircled in a Garter bearing the motto of the Order, ensigned with a Royal Crown and supported by a Lion rampant guardant crowned, and a griffin. To the left, a view of the City of London. "Civitas Londinium." Below, in compartments, a large variety of articles of plate, chests, and bags of money, and a tableau representing the "Judgment of Solomon."

Lent by W. MORE MOLYNEUX, ESQ.

760. PROCLAMATION BY THE MAYOR OF LONDON, fixing the date of the "Readyng of the sayde Lotterie" to the Feast of the Purification of St. Mary the Virgin, 1568, at Cates. Printed by Henrie Bynneman, in Paternoster Row, at the sign of the "Mermaid," September 13, 1567.
    Lent by W. MORE MOLYNEUX, ESQ.

761. LIST OF MOTTOES used in the above lottery.
    Lent by W. MORE MOLYNEUX, ESQ.

762. AUTOGRAPH LETTER of Sir Walter Raleigh, dated June, 1591, to the Steward of the Manor of Crematon or to his deputie.
    Lent by CHETHAM COLLEGE.

762. FRUITFULL SERMONS preached by the right reuerend Father, and constant Martyr of Jesus Christ, M. Hugh Latimer.
    At London. Printed by John Daye, dwelling ouer Alders-gate. 1584.
    Lent by W. S. CHURCHILL, ESQ.

ROOM VI.

BOOKS.

(Illustrating the Drama of the Tudor period.)

Lent by The DUKE OF DEVONSHIRE, K.G.

765. A NEW ENTERLUDE no lesse wittie : then pleasant, entituled new Custome, deuised of late, and for diuerse causes nowe set forthe ; neuer before this tyme Imprinted. 1573.
    Among the "players' names" are : 'Peruerse Doctrine, an olde Popishe priest'; 'Ignorance, an other, but elder'; 'New custome, a minister'; 'Light of the gospell, a minister.'

766. A RYGHT PITHY, PLEASAUNT AND MERIE COMEDIE : Intytuled Gammergurtons Nedle : Played on Stage not longe ago in Christes Colledge in Cambridge.
    Made by Mr. [JOHN] S[TILL]. Mr. of Art. 1575.

767. THE RIGHT EXCELLENT AND FAMOUS HISTORYE, OF PROMOS AND CASSANDRA : Deuided into two Commicall Discourses.
    The worke of GEORGE WHETSTONES, Gent. 1578.

768. AN EXCELLENT NEW COMMEDIE, Intituled The Conflict of Conscience. Compiled, by Nathaniell Woodes, minister, in Norwich. 1581.

769. THE ARAYGNEMENT OF PARIS a Pastorall. Presented before the Queenes Maiestie, by the children of her chappell.
    [By GEORGE PEEL.] 1584.

Room VI.] Books. 135

770. A BRIEFE REHEARSALL, or rather a true copie of as much as was presented before her maiesties at Kenelworth, during her last aboade there.
[By GEORGE GASCOIGNE.] 1587.

771. POLYHYMNIA Describing, the honourable Triumph at Tylt, before her maiestie, on the 17. of Nouember, last past, being the first day of the three and thirtith yeare of her Highnesse raigne.
[By GEORGE PEELE.] 1590.

772. THE COUNTESSE OF PEMBROKE'S YUYCHURCH. Conteining the affectionate life, and vnfortunate death of Phillis and Amyntas: That in a Pastorall; This in a Funerall: both in English Hexameters.
By ABRAHAM FRAVNCE. 1591.

773. GALLATHEA. As it was playde before the Queenes Maiestie at Greene-wiche, on Newyeeres day at night.
By The CHYLDREN OF PAULES. 1592.

774. THE TRAGEDIE OF TANCRED AND GISMUND. Compiled by the Gentlemen of the Inner Temple. and by them presented before her Maiestie.
By R. W[ILMOT]. London. 1592.
[Contains: A Preface to the Queene's Maidens of Honor.]

775. SPEECHES delivered to Her Maiestie this last Progresse, at the Right Honorable the Lady Rvssels, at Bissam, the Right Honorable the Lorde Chandos at Sudley, at the Right Honorable the Lord Norris, at Ricorte. 1592.

776. THE BATTELL OF ALCAZAR, fovght in Barbarie, betweene Sebastian King of Portugall, and Abdelmelec King of Marocco. With the death of Captaine Stukeley. 1594.

777. THE RAPE OF LVCRECE. 1594.

778. THE TRUE TRAGEDIE OF RICHARD THE THIRD. As it was playd by the Queenes Maiesties Players. 1594.

779. THE COBLER'S PROPHESIE. Written by ROBERT WILSON. Gent. 1594.

780. THE TRAGEDIE OF DIDO QUEENE OF CARTHAGE: Played by the children of her Maiesties Chappell.
Written by CHRISTOPHER MARLOWE and THOMAS NASH. Gent. 1594.

781. THE WARRES OF CYRUS KING OF PERSIA, against Antiochus King of Assyria, with the Tragicall ende of Panthœa. Played by the children of her Maiesties Chappell. 1594.

782. A MOST PLEASANT AND MERIE NEW COMEDIE, Intituled, A Knacke to Knowe a Knaue. Newlie set foorth, as it hath sundrie tymes bene played by Ed. Allen and his Companie. 1594.

783. THE TRAGEDIE OF ANTONIE. Doone into English by the Countesse of Pembroke. 1595.

784. A PLEASANT CONCEITED COMEDIE, called Loues labors lost. As it was presented before her Highnes this last Christmas.
By W. SHAKESPERE. 1598.

785. THE BLIND BEGGER OF ALEXANDRIA. . . . . . As it hath beene sundry times publickly acted in London by the right honorable the Earle of Nottingham, Lord High Admirall his seruantes.
By GEORGE CHAPMAN. Gentleman. 1598.

786. THE FAMOVS VICTORIES OF HENRY THE FIFTH: containing the Honourable Battell of Agin--cour: As it was plaide by the Queenes Maiesties players. 1598.

787. THE HISTORY OF HENRIE THE FOVRTH; With the battell at Shrewsburie, betweene the King and Lord Henry Percy, surnamed Henry Hotspur of the North. With the humorous conceits of Sir John Falstalffe. Newly corrected by W. Shake-speare. At London. 1599.

788. THE HISTORIE OF ORLANDO FVRIOSO, one of the twelve Peeres of France. As it was playd before the Queenes Maiestie. 1599.

789. THE HISTORIE OF TWO VALIANT KNIGHTS, Syr. Clyomon Knight of the Golden Sheeld, sonne to the King of Denmarke; and Clamydes the White Knight, sonne to the King of Suauia. As it hath bene sundry times acted by her Maiesties Players. 1599.

790. THE RAIGNE OF KING EDWARD THE THIRD. As it hath bene sundry times played about the citie of London. 1599.

791. THE MOST EXCELLENT HISTORIE OF THE MERCHANT OF VENICE.
Written by WILLIAM SHAKESPEARE. 1600.

792. THE FOVNTAINE OF SELF-LOVE. Or Cynthias Revels. As it hath beene sundry times priuately acted in the Black-Friers by the children of her Maiesties Chappell.
Written by BEN: JOHNSON. 1601.

793. THE SHOMAKERS HOLIDAY. Or the gentle craft. As it was acted before the Queenes most excellent Maiestie on New-yeares day at night last, by the right honourable the Earle of Notingham, Lord high Admirall of England, his seruants. 1600.

794. THE TRAGICALL HISTORIE OF HAMLET PRINCE OF DENMARKE.
By WILLIAM SHAKE-SPEARE 1603.

795. IF YOU KNOW NOT ME, YOU KNOW NO BODIE: or, The troubles of Queene Elizabeth. 1605.

796. THE WHORE OF BABYLON. Written by THOMAS DEKKER. London. 1607.
[The General scope of this Drammaticall Poem, is to set forth (in Tropicall and shadowed collours) the Greatnes, Magnanimity, Constancy, Clemency, and other the incomparable Heroicall vertues of our late Queene and (on the contrary part) the inveterate malice, Treasons, Machinations, Vnderminings, and continual blody stratagems, of that Purple whore of Roome, to the taking away of our Princes liues, and vtter extirpation of their Kingdomes.]

Books. 137

MISCELLANEOUS BOOKS.

Lent by The DUKE OF DEVONSHIRE, K.G.

797. A Discovrse of the Queenes Maiesties entertainement in Suffolk and Norfolk. Deuised by Thomas Chvrchyarde, Gent.

A Welcome Home to Master Martin Frobusher, and all those Gentlemen and Souldiers, that have bene with him this last iourney, in the Countrey called (Meta incognita).

798. An Interlude called Lusty Juventus.
Printed (London) by Wyllyam Copland. Undated.

799. The boke of Eneydos. By William Caxton. 1490.
Whiche boke I presente vnto the hye born my to comynge naturell & soucrayn lord Arthur by the grace of god Prynce of Walys . . . .

800. The Book of Fayttes of Armes & of Chyualrye.
Whiche boke beyng in frëshe was delyuered to me Willm Caxton by the most crysten Kynge & redoubted prynce my naturel and Souerayn lord Kyng henry the (vij) Kyng of englond & of fraūce in his palais of Westmestre the (xxiij) day of Janyuere the (iiij) yere of his regne & desired & wylled me to translate this said boke & reduce it in to our english and natural tonge | & to put it in enprynte . . . . .

801. Scala Perfeccōnis. Waltere Hylton. 1494.
[Wynkyn de Worde this hath sett in prynt
In Willyam Caxtons hows . . . .
The Kyngis moder of excellent bounte
Herry the Seventh that Jhū hym preserue
This myghty pryncesse hath cōmaunded me
Temprynt this boke her grace for to deserue.]

802. Here begyñeth ye lyf of Saynt Ursula after ye cronycles of Englode.
[iussi illustrissime domine dñe Margarete matris excellentissime principis Henrici Septimi. Impressa finit feliciter per me Wynandum de Worde.]

803. ΕΓΚΩΜΙΟΝ τηϛ ἀρἡνηϛ. Laudatio Pacis.
Joanne Lelando Antiquario autore. 1546.

804. Genethliacon illustrissimi Eäduerdi Principis Cambriæ, Ducis Coriniæ, et Comitis Palatini :
. . . . . Joanne Lelando Antiquario autore. 1543.
[On vellum. Presentation copy to the Prince of Wales.]

J

805. THE GOVERNAUNCE OF KYNGES AND PRYNCES. Richard Pynson, 1511.
    [Dedicated to Henry VIII.]
        Voyde of eloquence | J haue do my laboure.
        To sette in ordre | and composycion.
        My grete sympylnesse | vnder correccion.
        With ryght hole herte | in all my beste entent.
        For to accomplysshe | your hyghnesse cōmaundemet.

806. LE TOMBEAV DE MARGVERITE DE VALOIS ROYNE DE NAVARRE. Paris, 1551.
    Contains : Aux trois Sœurs, Anne, Marguerite, Jane de Seymour, Princesses Angloises, ode par Pierre de Ronsard Vandomois.]

807. ΚΥΚΝΕΙΟΝ ΑΣΜΑ Cygnea Cantio. Avtore Joanne Lelando Antiquario. 1545.
    [Dedicated to Henry VIII.]

808. THE PATHEWAIE TO KNOWLEDGE, containyng the first principles of Geometrie.
    To the most noble and pvissavnt Prince Edward the Sixte.
        By ROBERT RECORDE. I 74.

809. THE EXPEDICION INTO SCOTLĀDE of the most woorthely fortunate Prince Edward, Duke of Somerset, vncle vnto our most noble souereign lord ye Kīges Maiestie Edward the VI. Made in the first yere of his Maiesties most prosperous reign, and set out by way of diarie, by W. PATTEN LONDONER. 1548.

810. D. JOANNIS CHRYSOSTOMI HOMILIÆ SEX. 1586.
    [The first Greek book printed at Oxford.]

811. REDE ME AND BE NOTT WROTHE
    FOR I SAYE NO THYNGE BUT TROTHE.

812. D. JOANNIS CHRYSOSTOMI HOMILIÆ DUÆ, nunc primum in lucem æditæ, et ad Sereniss. Angliæ Regē latinæ factæ, à Joanne Cheko Cantabrigiensi. 1543.
    [The first Greek book printed in England.]

813. PLATONIS MENEXENVS, sive, Fvnebris Oratio. Cantebrigiæ, 1587.
    ["The first book printed in Greek at Cambridge," DAMPIER.]

814. THE CASTLE OF KNOWLEDGE. By ROBERTE RECORDE. 1556.
    [To the moste mightie and most pvissant Princesse Marye, by the grace of God Queene of England, Spain, bothe Siciles, Fraunce, Jerusalem, and Irelande : . . . .]

815. IN LAVDEM HENRICI OCTAVI, REGIS ANGLIÆ PRAESTANTISS. CARMEN PANEGYRICUM. 1579.
    [By THOMAS CHALONER.]

816. ALÆ SEV SCALÆ MATHEMATICÆ. THOMA DIGGESEO authore. 1573.
Ad honoratissimum virum Gvlielmvm Cecilivm, Baronem Burghleium.

817. GRAMMATICÆ QUADRILINGVIS PARTITIONES, autore JOANNE DROSÆO. 1544.
[With the autograph of GULIELMUS CECILIUS.]

818. A GEOMETRICAL PRACTISE, named Pantometria, . . . framed by LEONARD DIGGES Gentleman, lately finished by THOMAS DIGGES his sonne. 1571.
[To the right honorable my singular good Lorde, Sir Nicolas Bacon Knight, Lord Keper of the Great Seale of England.]

819. COMPLAINTS. Containing sundrie small Poemes of the Worlds Vanitie.
By ED.[MUND] SP.[ENSER] 1591.

820. SPACCIO DE LA BESTIA TRIONFANTE, . . . Registrato dal Nolano (Giordano Bruno). Confecrato al molto illustre et eccellente Caualliero Sig. PHILIPPO SIDNEO. 1584.

821. THE FAERIE QUEENE. Disposed into twelue books. Fashioning xii. morall vertues.
To the most mightie and magnificent Empresse Elizabeth, by the Grace of God Qveene of England, France and Ireland and Defender of the Faith &c.
Her most humble Seruant,
ED. SPENSER. 1590.

822. L'HISTOIRE NOTABLE DE LA FLORIDE . . . . . mise en lumiere par M. Basanier. 1586.
[Dedicated "a illvstre et vertveuvx seignevr Walter Ralegh."]

823. A RELATION OF THE SECOND VOYAGE TO GUIANA. Perfourmed and written in the yeare 1596. By LAWRENCE KEYMIS, Gent. 1596.
[Dedicated "To the approoved, right valorous, and woorthy knight, Sir Walter Ralegh " . . .]

824. THE DISCOVERIE OF THE LARGE, RICH, AND BEWTIFUL EMPIRE OF GVIANA, with a relation of the great and Golden Citie of Manoa (which the Spanyards call El Dorado) and the Prouinces of Emeria, Arromaia, Amapaia, and other countries, with their riuers, adioyning. Performed in the yeare 1595 . by Sir W. RALEGH Knight, ... 1596.
[Dedicated to Lord Howard and Sir Robert Cecil.]

825. THE PRINCIPAL NAVIGATIONS, Voyages, Traffiques and Discoveries of the English Nation, etc. By RICHARD HAKLUYT. Printed by George Bishop, Ralph Newberrie, and Robert Barker. A.D. 1599.

826. THE REFUTATION of the byshop of Winchesters derke declaratiō of his false articles, once before confuted by George Joye. 1546.

827. A NECESSARY DOCTRINE AND ERVDITION for any christen man, set furthe by the Kynges maiestie of Englande, &c. 1543.

828. THE ASSERTION AND DEFENCE OF THE SACRAMENTE OF THE AULTER. Compyled and made by mayster RICHARD SMYTHE doctour of diuinitie. 1546.
[Dedicated: 'To the Kynges most excellent maiestie' . . .]

829. A DECLARATION OF EDMONDE BONNERS ARTICLES, concerning the cleargye of Lōdon dyocese whereby that execrable Antychriste, is in his righte colours reueled in the yeare of our Lord a. 1554. By JOHN BALE.

830. A TRUE REPORTE OF THE DEATH & MARTYRDOME of M. Campion, Jesuite and preiste, & M. Sherwin, & M. Bryan, preistes, at Tiborne the first of December 1581. Observid and written by a Catholike preist, which was present therat.

831. A TREATISE OF TREASONS AGAINST Q. ELIZABETH, AND THE CROUNE OF ENGLAND. 1572.

832. THE EXECUTION OF JUTICE IN ENGLAND FOR MAINTENAUNCE OF PUBLIQUE AND CHRISTIAN PEACE. 1583.
[By WILLIAM CECIL, LORD BURLEIGH.]

833. A SPIRITUALL, AND MOST PRECIOUS PEARLE, teaching all men to loue and imbrace the crosse, as a most sweete and necessarie thing vnto the soule : . . . Written for thy comfort by a learned preacher OTHO WERMULIERUS. And translated into English by M. Miles Coverdale. 1593.
[With a preface: "Edwarde by the grace of God Duke of Somerset, Vncle to King Edwarde the Sixte, his excellent maiestie, and to the Christian Reader, greeting."]

834. A DECLARATION OF THE TEN HOLY CŌMAUNDEMENTES of allmygthye God | wroten Exo. 20, Deu. 5. Collectyd out of the scripture canonicall by JOANNE HOPPER [Bishop Hooper.] 1548.

835. AN APOLOGIE fvlly avnsweringe by Scriptures and aunceant Doctors | a blasphemose Book gatherid by D. Steph. Gardiner | of late Lord Chauncelar | D. Smyth of Oxford | Pighius | and other Papists . . . . against the godly mariadge of priests.
By JOHN PONET, Doctor of diuinitie and Busshop of Winchester. 1556.

836. A TREATISE OF THE COHABITACYON OF THE FAITHFULL WITH THE VNFAITHFULL. Wherunto is added, A Sermon made of the confessing of christe and his gospell | and of the denyinge of the same. 1555.
[By HENRY BULLINGER.]

837. A DISPUTACION OF PURGATORYE made by Jhoñ Frith whiche is deuided in to thre bokes.
[Directed against Sir Thomas More, and the Bishop of Rochester.]

838. THE CATHECHISME, or maner to teache children the Christian Religion. Made by the excellente doctor and pastor in Christes Churche JHON CALVIN. 1580.
A CATHECHISME, or Institution of Christian Religion. 1577.
A LITTLE CATECHISME, that is to saye, a short instruction touching Christian religion, set forth by Theodorus Beza, minister of the Churche of God in Geneva. 1579.

839. DE OBITU DOCTISSIMI ET SANCTISSIMI THEOLOGI DOCTORIS MARTINI BUCERI. 1551.

840. TOXOPHILVS, The schole, or partitions of shooting contayned in ij bookes, writtē by ROGER ASCHAM. 1544. And now newlye perused.
THE SCHOLEMASTER. 1571.
[Dedicated 'to the honorable Syr. William Cecill.']

841. A BRIEFF DISCOURS off the troubles begonne at Franckford in Germany anno Domini 1554. Abowte the Booke off Common Prayer and Ceremonies | and continued by the Englishe men theyre | to thende off Q. Maries Rɑigne | in the which discours | the gentle reader shall see the very originall and beginninge off all the contention that hathe byn | and what was the cause off the same. 1575.

842. CONTRA HIERON. OSORIUM, eiusq; odiosas insectationes pro Euangelicae veritatis necessaria Defensione, Responsio apologetica. Per clariss. virum, Gualt. Haddonum inchoata: Deindè suscepta & continuata per Joan. Foxum. 1577.
[Presentation copy to Queen Elizabeth.]

843. A TRUE REPORT of the Disputation or rather priuate conference had in the Tower of London, with Ed. Campion Jesuite, the last of August, 1581. London. 1583.

COINS AND MEDALS.

Lent by JULIUS WITTE, Esq.

HENRY VII.

Angel	II. coinage	Mint mark,	Escalop.
,,	II. ,,	,,	Pheon.
,,	II. ,,	,,	Cross crosslet.
Angelet	II. ,,	,,	Cinquefoil.
Half-groat	I. ,,		
Groat	II. ,,	,,	Cinquefoil.
,,	II. ,,	,,	Cinquefoil.
,,	II. ,,	,,	Cross crosslet.
,,	II. ,,	,,	Greyhound's head.
,,	II. ,,	,,	Escalop.
,,	II. ,,	,,	Cinquefoil.
,,	II. ,,	,,	Leopard's head.
,,	II. ,,	,,	Anchor.
,,	II. ,,	,,	Anchor.
Half-groat	II. ,, Canterbury	,,	Ton.
,,	II. ,, ,,	,,	Ton.
,,	II. ,, ,,	,,	Martlet.
Groat	III. ,,	,,	Cross crosslet.
,,	III. ,,	,,	Cross crosslet.
,,	III. ,,	,,	Pheon.
,,	III. ,,	,,	Pheon.
,,	III. ,,	,,	Pheon.
Half-groat	III. ,,	,,	Martlet.
,,	III. ,,	,,	Cross.
,,	III. ,,	,,	Martlet.
Penny	Durham	D. R. (for Bishop Ruthall).	
,,	York		

HENRY VIII.

Angel	I. coinage	Mint mark,	Portcullis
,,	I. ,,	,,	Castle.
Angelet	I. ,,	,,	Portcullis.
Half-crown	II. ,,	,,	Rose.
Half-sovereign	IV. & V. coinage	,,	Annulet, enclosing pellet.
,, ,,	IV & V. ,,	,,	O

Coins and Medals.

HENRY VIII.—*continued.*

Denomination	Coinage	Mint	Mint mark
Crown	IV. & V. coinage, Bristol	Mint mark,	W. S. (Sir W. Sharington).
Groat	I. coinage	,,	Portcullis.
Half-groat	I. ,,	,,	Martlet.
Penny	York ,,		
,,	,, ,,		
Groat	II. ,,	,,	Rose.
,,	II. ,,	,,	,,
,,	II. ,,	,,	Lis.
,,	II. ,,	,,	,,
,,	II. ,,	,,	Pheon.
,,	II. ,,	,,	,,
,,	II. ,,	,,	Lis-Rose.
Half-groat	II. ,, Canterbury		
,,	II. ,,	,,	Cross fleury.
,,	II. ,,	,,	Cross fleury.
,,	II. ,,	,,	Key.
,,	II. ,,	,,	Cross fleury.
,,	II. ,,	,,	Key.
Penny	II. ,, Durham	,,	Trefoil.
,,	II. ,,	,,	Star.
,,	II. ,,	,,	Star.
Halfpenny	II. ,,		
Shilling	Debased coinage	,,	Annulet, and annulet and pellet.
Groat		,,	Lis.
,,	,,	,,	Lis.
,,	,,	,,	Lis.
,,	,,	,,	Lis.
Penny	York		
Irish Groat	H. A. (Henry and Anne)	,,	Crown
,,	H. I. (Henry and Jane)		

EDWARD VI.

Denomination	Coinage	Mint mark
Half-sovereign	II. coinage	Mint mark, Arrow.
,,	II. ,,	,, Grappling Iron.
,,	IV. ,,	,, Ton.
Shilling	II. ,,	,, Y. (Sir John Yorke).
,,	II. ,,	,, Y. (Sir John Yorke).
,,	II. ,,	,, Countermarked "Greyhound," as worth 2½ temp. Elizabeth.
Crown	III. ,,	,, Y.
,,	III. ,,	,, Ton.
Half-crown	III. ,,	,, Y.
Shilling	III. ,,	,, Ton.
,,	III. ,,	,, Y.

EDWARD VI.—*continued.*

Sixpence	... ...	III. coinage	... ...	No Mint marks.	
Penny	...	III. ,,	... ...		
Threepence ...	...	III. ,,	... ...		

MARY.

Angel	...	I. coinage	... ...	,, ,,
Groat	...	I. ,,	... ...	,, ,,
,, ...	...	I. ,,	... ...	,, ,,
,, ...	...	I. ,,	... ...	,, ,,
,, ...	...	II. ,,	... ...	,, ,,
,, ...	...	II. ,,	... ...	,, ,,
,, ...	...	II. ,,	... ...	,, ,,
Shilling	...	II. ,,	... ...	,, ,,
,, ...	...	II. ,,	... ...	,, ,,
,, (Irish)	...	II. ,,	... ...	,, ,,
Groat ,,	...	II. ,,	... ...	,, ,,

ELIZABETH.

Sovereign ...	...	II. coinage	... ...	Mint mark, Escalop.
,, ...	...	II. ,,	... ...	,, Woolsack.
,, ...	...	II. ,,	... ...	,, Woolpack.
,, ...	...	II. ,,	... ...	,, Circle.
,, ...	...	III. ,,	... ...	,, 2 (for 1602).
Half-sovereign	...	I. ,,	... ...	,, Rose.
,,	...	II. ,,	... ...	,, Star.
,,	...	III. ,,	... ...	,, Woolpack.
Angel	...	II. ,,	... ...	,, Sword.
,, ...	...	III. ,,	... ...	,, Crescent.
Angelet	...	I. ,,	... ...	,, Cinquefoil.
Crown	...	I. ,,	... ...	,, Coronet.
Half-crown ...	...	III. ,,	... ...	,, Woolpack.
Quarter-angel	...	II. ,,	... ...	,, Plain cross.
Crown	...	I. ,,		
Half-crown ...	...	I. ,,		
Shilling	...	I. ,,	... ...	Mint mark, Martlet.
,, ...	...	I. ,,	... ...	,, Cross crosslet.
,, ...	...	I. ,,	... ...	,, Hand.
,, ...	...	I. ,,	... ...	,, Ton.
,, ...	...	I. ,,	... ...	,, 2 (for 1602).
,, (milled)	...	I. ,,	... ...	,, Star.
Sixpence ...	...	I. ,,	... ...	,, Pheon.
,, ...	...	I. ,,	... ...	,, Coronet.
,, ...	...	I. ,,	... ...	,, Cinquefoil.

Coins and Medals.

ELIZABETH—*continued.*

Coin		Coinage	Mint mark	
Sixpence	I.	coinage	Mint mark,	Cross.
,,	I.	,,	,,	Hand.
,,	I.	,,	,,	Key.
,,	I.	,,	,,	Long cross.
,, (milled)	I.	,,	,,	Star.
,, ,,	I.	,,	,,	Star.
Groat	I.	,,	,,	Martlet.
,,	I.	,,	,,	Cross crosslet.
Threepence	I.	,,	,,	Coronet.
,,	I.	,,	,,	Acorn.
,,	I.	,,	,,	Cinquefoil.
,,	I.	,,	,,	Cross.
Half-groat	I.	,,	,,	A.
,,	I.	,,	,,	Hand.
,,	I.	,,	,,	Hand.
,,	I.	,,	,,	I.
,,	I.	,,	,,	Key.
Three halfpence	I.	,,	,,	Cinquefoil.
,,	I.	,,	,,	Cross.
Penny	I.	,,	,,	Coronet.
,,	I.	,,	,,	Cross crosslet.
Irish shilling	I.	,,		
,, groat	I.	,,		
,, halfpenny	I.	,,	,,	Star.
,, ,,	I.	,,	,,	Martlet.

Lent by NATHAN HEYWOOD, ESQ.

Series of Groats.

HENRY VII. (1485-1509).
First issue. Mint mark, Rose and Sun.
,, ,, ,, Cross.
Second ,, ,, Cross crosslet.
Third ,, ,, Anchor.
,, ,, ,, ,,
,, ,, ,, Cinquefoil.
,, ,, ,, Leopard's head.
Fourth ,, ,, Arrow.

HENRY VIII. (1509-1547).
First issue, fine silver. Mint mark, Portcullis.
,, ,, ,, struck at Tournay, 1513-18. Mint mark, C crowned.

HENRY VIII.—*continued.*
Second issue, fine. Mint mark, Lis.
,, ,, ,, ,, Lis.
,, ,, ,, ,, Arrow.
,, ,, ,, ,, Rose.
,, ,, ,, ,, Cross with T.W and Cardinal's Hat (for Thos. Wolsey, York).
,, ,, ,, Mint mark, Lis.
,, ,, ,, Harp (for Ireland) with H. R.
,, ,, ,, Mint mark, Crown with Harp, and H.A.(for Henry and Anne)
,, ,, ,, Mint mark, Crown with Harp, and H. I.(for Henry and Jane)

Exhibition of the Royal House of Tudor.

HENRY VIII.—*continued.*
Second issue, fine. Mint mark, Crown with Harp, and H. K. (for Henry and Katharine).
Third ,, base silver. No Mint mark.
,, ,, ,, W. S. (for Sir W. Sharington, Master of Mint, Bristol).
,, ,, ,, No mint mark.
,, ,, ,, ,, York.
,, ,, ,, ,, Canterbury.
Third issue, base silver. Dublin.
Fourth ,, ,,
,, ,, ,, York.
,, ,, ,, Canterbury.
,, ,, ,, Dublin.
,, ,, ,,
,, ,, ,, Bristol.
Fifth ,, base. With legend of Redde Cuique quod Suum Est.
,, ,, ,,

HENRY VIII.—*continued.*
Fifth issue, base. Canterbury.
,, ,, ,, Dublin.
EDWARD VI. (1547–1553).
First issue, base silver. With large profile bust.
MARY (1553–1554).
Only issue, and of fine silver. With profile.
PHILIP AND MARY (1554–1558).
First issue, and of fine silver. With profile of Mary alone.
ELIZABETH (1558–1603).
First issue, fine silver. Mint mark, Martlet.
,, ,, ,, ,, Lis.
Second issue, fine silver. ,, Star.
In the last row are also
Sixpence of Philip and Mary, for Ireland.
,, of James I.
Groats of Charles I.
Sixpence of Commonwealth.
Groat of Charles II. (latest hammered money).

Lent by W. SHARP OGDEN, ESQ.

HENRY VII.
Angel ... ... 2nd issue. Mint mark, Pheon or Arrow.
Groat ... ... ,, London. Mint mark, Cross crosslet.
,, ... ,, ,, ,, Anchor.
,, ... ,, ,, ,, Greyhound's head.
Half-groat ... ... ,, York. ,, Martlet.
,, ... ,, Canterbury. ,, Large pellet or indistinct rose.
Groat ... ... 3rd issue. ,, Cross crosslet
Half-groat ... ... ,, York. ,, Martlet.
Penny ... ... ,, ,, ,, None.

HENRY VIII.
Half-groat ... ... 1st issue, London. Mint mark, Portcullis, with the likeness of his Father.
Penny ... ... ,, ,, Mint mark, Portcullis.
Groat ... ... 2nd issue, York. Mint mark, Cross, with T. W. (Thomas Wolsey) and Cardinal's Hat.
,, ... ,, London. Mint mark, Arrow.
Half-groat ... ... ,, Canterbury. Mint-mark, Catharine Wheel, with T. C, (Thomas Cranmer).

HENRY VIII.—*continued.*

Half-groat	2nd issue, York.	Mint mark, Key, with E. L. (for Archbishop Ed. Lee). 1531-41.
Groat	3rd issue, supposed to be at Tower.	Mint mark, Lis., annulet in forks of cross fleury.
,,	Struck for Ireland. H and A (Henry and Anne). H and I (Henry and Jane). H and K (Henry and Katharine).	

EDWARD VI.

Testoon or Shilling	1st issue.	Of base metal, weighing 78 grains for 80, dated MDCXLIX. Mint mark, Y, being struck at Southwark by Sir Jno. Yorke.
Shilling	3rd issue.	Of fine silver, with XII. upon them. Mint mark, Y, for Sir John Yorke, at Southwark.
Sixpence	,,	Like the shilling, only with VI. Mint mark, Ton, struck at Tower by Sir Jno. Throgmorton.
Penny	,,	Of base silver, for York. Mint mark, Mullet.
Crown	,,	Of fine silver, with date of 1552. Mint mark, Ton, struck at Tower by Sir Jno. Throgmorton.

MARY.

Groat	1st issue.	Of base silver. Mint mark, Pomegranate after first word on each side.

PHILIP AND MARY.

Shilling	2nd issue.	No date. Heads placed facing. No mint mark. Has XII. for value.
Sixpence	2nd issue.	Of 1554, with similar busts. No mint mark. Has VI. for value.
Groat	1st issue.	With Lis mint mark, and has the Queen's head only.
Sixpence		Date of 1556, and with the heads facing. Struck for Ireland (with the harp). Mint mark, Rose. Of very base silver.

ELIZABETH.

Half-sovereign	Mint mark, Ton.	Weighs 86 grains.
,,	,,	Cross crosslet. Weighs 78 grains.
Crown silver	,,	Figure 1, for 1601 date.
Shilling	,,	Crescent.
,,	,,	Cross crosslet.
,,	,,	Figure 2, for 1602.
Sixpence	,,	Coronet, and date 1567.
,,	,,	Hand, and date 1591.
Groat	,,	Cross crosslet.
Threepence	,,	Castle, and date 1570.

ELIZABETH—*continued.*
  Twopence ... ...   Mint mark, Martlet.
  Penny ... ...   ,,   Cross crosslet.
  Shilling ... ...   ,,   Harp (for Ireland), but of good silver.
  Penny (of copper) ...   ,,   Martlet (for Ireland), dated 1601.
  Shilling (milled) ... ...   ,,   Star.
  Sixpence   ,, ...   ,,   Star, dated 1562.
     ,,   ,, ...   ,,   ,,   ,,
     ,,   ,, ...   ,,   Lis, dated 1567.

MEDALS.
  One of Pewter, with head of Queen Mary in good relief, and of Philip, her husband, on reverse.
  Bronze of Pope Julius III., by T. O. Cavino of Padua, in celebration of reconciliation of England to the Holy See, 1554.
  Iron of Henry IV. of France, in commemoration of his victory over the League at Ivry, 1590.

GOLD COINS (2).

Lent by PH. ZIEGLER, ESQ.

EDWARD VI.
  Half-sovereign (2nd issue, 1548-1550). Southwark Mint.

ELIZABETH.
  Half-sovereign. Mint mark, Woolpack.

SILVER COINS (10).

HENRY VIII.
  Groat (2nd issue, 1526-1543). Tower Mint. Mint mark, Lis.
  Groat (3rd issue, 1543-44). Mint mark, Lis.
  Testoon (4th issue, 1544-45). Mint mark, Annulet, enclosing Pellet.

EDWARD VI.
  Sixpence (2nd issue, 1551-1553). York Mint. Mint mark, Mullet, pierced.
  Shilling (intermediate issue, 1549). London Mint. Mint mark, Y; on reverse, TIMOR DOMINI, &c.
  Shilling (intermediate issue, 1549). London Mint. Mint mark, Grappler; on reverse, TIMOR, &c.
  Shilling (2nd issue, 1551-1553). Mint mark, Y; on reverse, POSVI DEV, &c.

MARY.
  Groat. Mint mark, Pomegranate.

ELIZABETH.
   Crown. Mint mark, 1 (1601).
   Half-crown. Mint mark, 1 (1601).

Lent by MANCHESTER MUSEUM, OWENS COLLEGE.

EDWARD VI.
   Half-sovereign. Mint mark, Anchor.

ELIZABETH.
   Half-sovereign. Mint mark, Crown.
   Angel. Mint mark, Hand.

Lent by COUNCILLOR J. N. OGDEN.

Sovereign of Standard Gold of Queen Elizabeth, weighing 233 grains. Mint mark, Escalop. Struck 1584-6. Current at 30/-

---

Lent by W. S. CHURCHILL, ESQ.

MEDAL of Erasmus, of Rotterdam, born 1466, a classic and theologian, student at Oxford, and afterwards Professor at Cambridge. Lived chiefly at Basle, where he died 1536. The author of this work of art has not been discovered, although several of his works are known. They are supposed to be of German origin.

DUCATON of Philip II. as Duke of Guelderland for 1557, bearing the title of King of England, and displaying on his shield the arms of England.

DUCATON of Holland and Zeeland, as associated Countships for 1584, with the bust of William, Prince of Orange, and displaying his crest above the shield of Holland.

DUCATON of State of Zeeland, struck for the Six United Provinces in 1586, with the shield of their arms set forth. The bust on the coin is claimed to be that of the Earl of Leicester, authorised to act as Governor by Elizabeth in this year, and confirmed by the States.

MEDAL (early copy in brass), struck in the Low countries, in gold, silver, copper, after the defeat of the Armada in 1588.

SMALL BRASS MEDAL, issued at Milan, relative to the adverse fate of the Armada, with bust of Philip II., from a design by Jacopo Trici or Trezzo, with the legend : SIC ERAT IN FATIS.

JETTON in copper, issued 1597, on the victory of Turnhout, bearing the arms of France, England, and United Provinces, as associated powers against Spain.

JETTON of bronze in Piedfort, issued by State of Zeeland for 13 September, 1598, on the death of Philip II. Such jettons were usually largely dispersed on the death of Low Country notables. The legend reads: SCEPTRA LIGONIBVS ÆQVAT MORS ("Death treats in like fashion sceptres and spades").

ESCUDO of Naples of Charles V., Emperor of Germany, and father-in-law of Queen Mary. The head of the Emperor is by Ravaschiero, Director of the Mint, or under his influence.

ESCUDO of Naples of Philip as King of England, France, Naples, Prince of Spain. All the various arms duly displayed. The bust of Philip is crowned, and is by Ravaschiero. Legend: POSIMVS DEVM ADIVTOREM NOST—so often set forth on English coins.

ESCUDO of same place of Philip, without the crown, but otherwise much the same. The legend of reverse is, however, POPVLORum. SECVRITATI.

DUCADO, also of Philip, as King of England, &c., with bust, uncrowned, and issued at the same time as the two preceding pieces (1554-58), by Ravaschiero. No arms appear on reverse, but there is the legend: HILARITAS VNIVERSA. Neapolitan and Sicilian coins frequently allude to the satisfaction attendant upon the possession of their money.

INDEX OF PICTURES AND MINIATURES.

(Indexed under numbers.)

ADELMAR, Cæsare, 115
Arthur, Prince of Wales, 440
Arundel, Henry, 23rd Earl of, 63, 154, 191
Arundel, Ven. Philip, Earl of, 140

BACON, Francis, Lord, 188
Bedford, John, 1st Earl, 684
Bedford, Lucy, Countess of, 152
Bertie, R., 85
Boleyn, Anne, 32, 33, 463
Boleyn, Sir T., Earl of Wilts and Ormonde, 686
Boling, Sir John, 454
Borbonius, N., 724
Bromley, Sir H., 163
Bromley, Thomas, Lord Chancellor, 189
Buckingham, Edward Stafford, 3rd Duke of, 36, 53
Burghley, William, Lord, 100, 136, 182

CALVIN, John, 40
Case, John, 176
Cavendish, George, 92
Cavendish, Sir W., 158
Children of Henry VII., 5, 10
Christina, Duchess of Milan, 47
Clarence, Isabel, Duchess of, 3
Clements, M., 68, 71, 679
Clifford, Anne, Countess of Dorset, 153
Cobham, George, Lord, 689
Colet, John, 723
Cordell, Sir Wm., 106
Cox, Richard, Bishop of Ely, 84
Cranmer, T., Archbishop of Canterbury, 73
Cresacre, A., 68, 71, 668

DANCRY, E., 68, 71, 675
Denny, Sir A., 37
Derby, Alice, Countess of, 120
Derby, Edward, 3rd Earl of, 79, 688
Derby, Ferdinand, 5th Earl of, 116
Derby, Henry, 4th Earl of, 96
Derby, Thomas, 1st Earl of, 26
Derby, Thomas, 2nd Earl of, 25
Devonshire, Wm., 1st Earl of, 150
Dorset, Thomas Sackville, Earl of, 142
Drake, Sir F., 175, 438

EDWARD VI., 78, 88, 99, 461
Eliot, Margaret, Lady, 709
Eliot, Sir Thomas, 708
Elizabeth, 117, 131, 148, 155, 170, 177, 441, 448, 469
Elizabeth of York, 7, 9
Ellesmere, Thomas, Lord, 129
Embarkation of Henry VIII. at Dover, 58
Erasmus, 41
Essex, Lettice, Countess of, 439
Essex, Robert Devereux, Earl of, 145, 442
Essex, Thomas Cromwell, Earl of, 445, 666
Exeter, Thomas, Earl of, 187

FERIA, Jane, Duchess of, 127
Field of Cloth of Gold, 62
Fisher, Cardinal, 683
Foxe, R., Bishop of Winchester, 17

GAGE, Sir J., 703
Gardiner, Bishop of Winchester, 113, 118

Exhibition of the Royal House of Tudor.
(*Under Numbers.*)

Gargrave, Sir T., 138
George of Cornwall, 719
Godsalve, Sir J., 706
Godstone, Abbess of, 52
Gresham, Sir T., 165
Grey, Lady Jane, 102, 103
Guildford, Sir H., 681

HASTINGS, Edward, Lord, 132
Hastings, Sir Edward, 146
Henry VII., 6, 8, 11, 16, 18, 74
Henry VIII., 18, 24, 28, 33, 44, 51, 54, 58, 61, 62, 80, 82, 458, 464, 468
Heron, Cicely, 68, 71, 676
Hill, Sir Rowland, 98
Hobby, Elizabeth, Lady, 711
Hobby, Sir P., 710
Hungerford, Mary, Baroness, 130
Huntingdon, Catherine, Countess of, 56
Huntingdon, Henry, 3rd Earl of, 178, 183

JEWELL, J., Bishop of Salisbury, 43

KATHERINE of Aragon, 24, 31, 65

LEICESTER, Robert, Earl of, 137, 147, 171
Lister, Jane, Lady, 698
Lygon, Sir W., and Family, 95

MALTRAVERS, Henry, Lord, 87
Margaret, Countess of Salisbury, 42
Mary I., 82, 110, 111, 122, 467
Mary Tudor, dau. of Henry VII., 19
Mildmay, Lady, 121
Mildmay, Sir W., 124
More Family, 68, 71
More, Sir Antonio, 126
More, John, jun., 68, 71, 677
More, Sir J., 68, 71, 674
More, Sir Thomas, 45, 59, 64, 68, 70, 71, 673

NORFOLK, Thomas, 2nd Duke of, 14, 690, 691
Norfolk, Thomas, 3rd Duke of, 49
Norfolk, Thomas, 4th Duke of, 139, 184
Northampton, William P., Marquess of, 685
Northumberland, Thomas, Earl of, 125
Nottingham, Charles, 1st Earl of, 149

OLDHAM, H., Bishop of Exeter, 4
Oliver, Isaac, 443
Oxford, Edward, 17th Earl of, 456

PADDY, Sir W., 144
Paget, Charles, 151
Palmer, Sir A., 101
Palmer, Eleanor, 185
Parker, Elizabeth, Lady, 697
Parker, M., Archbishop of Canterbury, 192
Parr, Katherine, 35, 459
Parry, Sir T., 716
Pembroke, Mary, Countess of, 141
Philip II., 109, 112
Poins, J., 717
Pole, Cardinal, 108, 128
Poyntz, Sir N., 48, 707
Price, H., 39

RALEIGH, Elizabeth, Lady, 119
Raleigh, Sir W., 179, 465
Ratcliffe, Lady, 699
Reskeymer, J., 718
Richmond, Margaret Beaufort, Countess of, 1, 2
Roper, Margaret, 68, 71

SALISBURY, Robert, 1st Earl of, 180
Seymour, Jane, 34, 57, 67, 462
Shakespeare, William, 163*
Seymour of Sudeley, Thomas, Lord, 66, 83, 460
Shrewsbury, Elizabeth, Countess of, 159
Shrewsbury, George, 6th Earl of, 160
Shrewsbury, Gilbert, 7th Earl of, 162
Shrewsbury, Mary, Countess of, 167
Sidney, Frances, Lady, 181

Index of Pictures and Miniatures.

(*Under Numbers.*)

Sidney, Sir P., 172, 174, 447
Somerset, Edward Seymour, Duke of, 89, 466
Southampton, Thomas, 1st Earl of, 30
Southampton, William, Earl of, 687
Southwell, Sir R., 704
Spencer, Sir John, 143
St. Loe, Sir Wm., 156
Stokes, A., 105
Strange, George, Lord, 27
Suffolk, Charles Brandon, Duke of, 12, 13
Suffolk, Frances, Duchess of, 105
Suffolk, Henry Grey, Duke of, 93
Suffolk, Katherine, Duchess of, 696
Surrey, Frances, Countess of, 692
Surrey, Henry Howard, Earl of, 81, 455
Sussex, Thomas, 3rd Earl of, 133*

Talbot, Lady Grace, 164
Throckmorton, Sir Nicholas, 97
Trafford, Sir Ed., 104
Trafford, Elizabeth, Lady, 133

Unton, Sir H., 169

Vaux, Elizabeth, Lady, 694
Vaux, Thomas, Lord, 693, 701

Walsingham, Sir F., 173, 186
Wards and Liveries, Court of, 136
Warham, W., Archbishop of Canterbury, 46, 682,
Wentworth, Thomas, 1st Baron, 94
Willoughby, Catherine, Lady, 91
Willoughby de Eresby, Peregrine, Lord, 168
Winchcombe, John, 86
Winchester, William, 1st Marquess of, 134, 135
Wingfield, C., 705
Wolsey, Cardinal, 29, 60, 72
Worcester, Wm., 3rd Earl of, 90
Wyat, Sir T., 702

Yelverton, Sir Christopher, 166

Zouch, Joan, 700

INDEX OF EXHIBITORS.

(Indexed under pages.)

HER MAJESTY, THE QUEEN, 11, 21, 23

ALDENHAM, Lord, 84, 85.
Ames, Lieut.-Colonel, 88
Ancaster, Earl of, 9, 20, 30, 32, 56
Antiquaries, Society of, 7, 13, 38, 45, 97, 119-124, 128
Arundell of Wardour, Lord, 65
Ashley, Right Hon. Evelyn, 19

BAKER, G. E. Lloyd, 91
Bedingfeld, Sir Hy., Bart., 5, 14, 15, 102, 103
Bevan, Ven. Canon, 91
Bingham, Rev. F., 91
Birmingham Museum and Art Gallery, 78, 79
Blair, A. C., 98
Brewers' Company, 63
Bridewell Royal Hospital, 20, 31
Butler, Charles, 16

CAMBRIDGE, St. John's College, 2
    Ditto   Emmanuel College 40, 41
    Ditto   Jesus College, 25
    Ditto   Trinity Hall, 30, 39, 118
Canterbury, Archbishop of, 18, 62, 85, 86, 87
Chester, Corporation of, 116
Chetham College, 10, 88, 134
Churchill, W. S., 91, 134, 149, 150
Clare, A., 62
Colnaghi, Martin, 20, 22, 24
Copeland, Colonel, 114
Cullum, G. Milner-Gibson-, 46, 47, 100, 101, 105

DAY, Robert, 91, 93, 94, 95
De Rothschild, Alfred, 115
De Trafford, Sir Humphrey, Bart., 36, 44

Denbigh, Earl of, 34, 88, 92, 94
Dent, Mrs., 4, 5, 8, 9, 24, 28, 30, 32, 52, 57, 58, 88, 89, 90, 98, 99, 113, 114
Derby, Earl of, 2, 9, 10, 27, 34, 39, 40, 97
Devonshire, K.G., Duke of, 4, 5, 8, 11, 12, 15, 27, 33, 37, 38, 46, 50, 51, 52, 53, 54, 55, 59, 60, 62, 91, 97, 125, 128, 129, 134-141
Dilke, Right Hon. Sir Chas., Bart., M.P., 33, 87, 97
Dillon, Viscount, 38, 57
Donington, Lord (Trustees of the Late) 2, 6, 16, 20, 37, 43, 44, 49, 55, 56, 58, 60
Dormer, Captain Cottrell, 39, 42
Durham, Dean and Chapter of, 40

EGERTON of Tatton, Lord, 34, 42, 62
Evans, Sir John, K.C.B., F.R.S., 26, 85, 93
Eyston, John, Esq., 24, 25

FERGUSSON, Right Hon. Sir Jas., Bart, M.P., 97
Frere, Mrs. Temple, 115

GIBBS, Hon. and Rev. Kenneth, 82, 85, 86
Greene, T. Whitcombe, 92, 93
Griffiths, Mrs., 94
Griffiths, W., 94

HANFSTAENGL, F., 125-128
Harley, John, M.D., 26, 33, 63, 88, 98
Herries, Lord, 96
Hertford, Marquess of, 14, 24, 29, 128
Heywood, N., 94, 105, 145, 146
Holt, Robert D., 114, 115
Hopkinson, the Rev. Francis, 93
Huth, Alfred, 91, 92, 100-105

Index of Exhibitors.

(*Under Pages.*)

Jackson, C. J., 113, 117, 118
Jackson, John, 36

Kenyon, Lord, 39, 61
Kilbourn, G. G., 67, 71, 72, 73, 76-78

Leveson-Gower, Chas., 129
Lloyd, Miss M., 92

Malet, Col. Harold, 93
Manchester, Corporation of, 88
Martin, G. E., 33, 43, 53, 54, 61
Molyneux, W. More, 129-134
Montagu, Sir Samuel, Bart., M.P., 115

Newton, Lord, 81
Norfolk, Duke of, K.G., 6, 19, 23, 29, 47, 51, 52, 56, 60, 98, 114
Norwich, Corporation of, 116

Ogden, James N., 149
Ogden, W. S., 37, 62, 87, 95, 96, 146-148
Oscott College, 63, 82, 83, 85, 86, 87
Owen's College, 149
Oxford. All Souls, 114
 Ditto Christ Church, 4
 Ditto Corpus Christi College, 3, 7
 Ditto Jesus College, 15, 94
 Ditto Merton College, 17, 24
 Ditto St. John's College, 20, 37, 49, 58

Pembroke, Earl of, 5, 48, 125
Plymouth, Mayor and Corporation of, 58
Ponsonby-Fane, Hon. Sir Spencer, K.C.B., 25, 26, 62
Pritchard, George, 100-104

Radcliffe, C. J., 24, 44
Richmond and Gordon, Duke of, K.G., 46
Robinson, Sir J. C., 9, 93

Sackville, Lord, 21, 39, 40, 48
Science and Art Department, 9, 26, 62, 106-112, 129
Slingsby, Captain, 41
Sotheby, Major-General, F.E., 12, 13, 24
Speaker, Right Hon. the, 17
Spencer, Earl, K.G., 20, 29, 35, 41, 42, 48, 49, 98
Spiller, W. H., 66, 67, 71-73, 75, 76
Stonyhurst College, 81, 82, 83
Stuart, Mrs., 92
Sumner, Miss, 17, 21, 22, 55, 129

Throckmorton, Sir W., Bart., 34
Trollope, Hon. Mrs., 34

Vaughan, Cardinal, 96

Watts, W. H., 87, 94
Westminster, Duke of, K.G., 114, 115
Whawell, S. J., 66, 68-70, 72-75, 78
Willson, T. J., 64, 65
Witte, Julius, 142-145
Wynne-Finch, Lt.-Col. Chas., 36, 52

York, Corporation of, 117

Ziegler, P., 148, 149
Zouche, Lord, 12, 31, 32, 50, 51, 56, 57, 59, 60, 61, 67, 78

www.ingramcontent.com/pod-product-compliance
Lightning Source LLC
Chambersburg PA
CBHW030300170426
43202CB00009B/825